The *Seceders*

Religious Conviction &
the Abolitionist Movement
in the
Town of Manlius,
New York,
1834 – 1844

by

Alethea A. Connolly

Copyright © 2013 by Alethea Ann Connolly

All rights reserved. No part of this book may be used or reproduced in any manner whatsoever including electronic, mechanical, information storage and retrieval systems without written permission, except in the case of brief quotes embodied in critical articles and reviews. Send requests to 1400 Kinne St., East Syracuse, New York 13057.

Cover image from an engraving in John Warner Barber and Henry Howe's *Historical Collections of the State of New York; Containing a General Collection of the Most Interesting Facts, Traditions, Biographical Sketches, Anecdotes, &c Relating to its History and Antiquities, with Geographical Descriptions of Every Township in the State,* published in 1842.

Cover design by Sarah Argus
Printed by United Imaging & Printing, Syracuse NY 13206

ISBN: 978-0-9844884-5-2

LCCN 2013951402

The sole role of Oh, How Upstate Enterprises with respect to *The Seceders* has been to provide Bowker registration of the book. Responsibility for the content in all respects is that of the author.

To my mother, Elizabeth Duquette Connolly, who enjoyed a good book as much as finding an unexpected treasure at a garage sale.

CONTENTS

Acknowledgments — iii

Introduction — vi

Prologue — 1

1. The Seceders from Vermont — 3
2. The Revivals — 7
3. The Evil of Slavery — 16
4. A Grand Revolution — 22
5. The Presbyterians — 28
6. Taking Sides in Fayetteville — 36
7. And I Will Be Heard — 41
8. The Center Cannot Hold — 46
9. The Cotton Connection — 50
10. An Uncommon Marriage — 57
11. Conflict in Fayetteville — 62
12. A Clash of Titans — 70
13. Silencing Debate — 75
14. Equality, Politics & Fraternity — 83
15. Don't Panic! — 92
16. Cider & The Liberty Party — 99
17. The Colored American — 108
18. Crusading Uphill — 115
19. The Woman Question — 121

20.	The Baptists	131
21.	What Happened on High Bridge Hill ?	141
22.	Confrontation & The Cost of Zeal	148
23.	The Lone Seceder	157
24.	Westward Ho!	163
25.	An AfterWord – They Had Names	169
	Endnotes	189
	Other Bibliograhical Sources	245
	About The Author	249

ACKNOWLEDGMENTS

"How do I thank thee, let me count the ways..."

My apologies to Elizabeth Barrett Browning, for tampering with one of her memorable poems. I wanted bells and whistles, perhaps a little parade, to tell readers about the many people who helped me find my way through the shape-shifting maze of research, writing, and publication details, but her words are clearly more elegant.

First let me say that it has been my good fortune to have had the generous, knowledgeable counsel of Barbara S. Rivette, Town of Manlius Historian. She has encouraged me every step along the way, and provided context and details of local history that would have taken me many years to find and understand. When she came across information pertinent to my subject, I often received a gracious correspondence with clippings and articles enclosed in my mailbox.

I have tried to apply some of the diligent hunting and gathering research skills of independent scholar Kathy Crowell. Kathy assisted me in many ways. One of my treasured memories is of the two of us defying wind and traffic, as we walked up the old High Bridge hill with a ball of string, measuring and calculating where the old Reformed Methodist meeting house once stood.

These dedicated historians, shared time, resources, insight, and even proofing skills, with ample doses of humor that helped me keep my eyes on the end zone.

Much research into primary documents was done at the

Onondaga Historical Association Research Center in Syracuse, New York. During my years of sifting through old historical newspapers, records, and registers, I have always been graciously assisted by research staff Karen Cooney and Sarah Kozma, and by archivist, Pam Priest.

Holly Sammons, and the Local History and Archives Department staff at the Onondaga County Central Library in Syracuse, accommodated my many requests for searchable local history records, including archival microfilm documents and newspapers vital to my research.

Old historic American newspapers of the 1830s and 1840s were a primary resource, and staff members at various repositories, including those already named, aided my efforts to locate originals, photocopies, transcripts, microfilm, and online access. For several years Linda Ryan at the Fayetteville Free Library Local History Room directed my wanderings into files, microfilm, and other gems in the well-organized local history room. Manlius Historical Society staff ferreted out church records, diaries, logs, reports, photographs, and postcards that greatly expanded my research. Many times I tracked back to their files to gain a wider view on what I had first perceived as an isolated event.

I was able to examine many local and abolition newspapers at the Onondaga Historical Association, the Special Collections at the Syracuse University Library Research Center, and the Utica Library Genealogy Room. Digitized online access to historic newspapers has been a tremendous aid to researching at home, and thanks to Cornell University, Tom Tryzinski's fultonhistory.com site, and services such as NewsBank and GenealogyBank, these resources were accessible to me at all hours of the day and night.

I spent many hours at the Onondaga County Court House looking into property and incorporation records. Downstairs in the catacombs of archival records, Margaret Kopp and her diligent staff retrieved the older deeds, common plea cases, judgment dockets, maps, microfilms, etc. The Onondaga County Surrogate Office staff were always gracious when I appeared with another request for copies of estate records.

It has been an informative and enjoyable experience to tap into the experience and knowledge of the town and village historians both in Onondaga County and Cayuga County. In addition to Barbara Rivette, I was graciously assisted by Town of Scipio Historian, Sandra Gilliland, and Judy Furness, Historian for the Town of Ledyard. Staff members at the Cayuga County Historian's office, were generous with their time, and suggestions. The resources of Cayuga County on the Underground Railroad, and Freedom Seekers of the 19th century cited in my endnotes, opened up valuable avenues of research to me, and I am grateful.

Donna Burdick, Smithfield Town Historian in Madison County, introduced me to the town's local heritage. Author Norm Dann, a resident of Peterboro, enlivened my knowledge and appreciation of abolitionist Gerrit Smith when I visited the Smith estate in Peterboro.

Early in my research, when I sought to discover more information about the High Bridge Methodist Episcopal meeting house, Ray Leonard, Archivist for the North Central New York Commission Archives & History, gallantly helped me sift through shelves and boxes of old Methodist Episcopal Church records.

Ed Reichert, Civil Engineer at the Onondaga County Department of Transportation, spent time gathering old

v

county road maps of the High Bridge Road, County Road 8, now Route 92, and helped me confirm the location of the High Bridge Union Church. Thomas B. Lutz, Sr., Engineering Technician, and Michael P. Arsite, Land Surveyor, at the Region 3 office of the New York State Department of Transportation in Syracuse, were also instrumental in identifying the two church properties on the High Bridge Road hill. I enjoyed these conversations immensely, and am most grateful for the generous time these professionals extended to me.

I want to thank Patty Mason at Noreen Reale Falcone Library at Lemoyne College for helping me access several important journal articles, and Lemoyne College for extending me a guest library card.

To early draft reader, Helen Landfear, cheerleader, Eileen Altieri (who passed into eternity this year), and steadfast friend and supporter, Ann O' Brien, and yes, family and other friends who put up with my disappearance from society, ah well, what can I say, bring on the bells and whistles, and the roll of the drum...

Thank You!

INTRODUCTION

As you drive from Lyndon Corners to the village of Manlius just past the light at Woodchuck Hill Road, you may still see the old district school off to the left, covered by a defiant blue tarp. The solidly built stone schoolhouse built in 1849, now in private hands, has witnessed countless bursts of inventive enterprise and controversy just beyond its door.

The schoolhouse fronted the old High Bridge hill road on the westside of Limestone Creek. Wagons, stage coaches, and foot travelers made their way across footpaths and roads into neighboring Fayetteville and to Manlius Village, a thriving crossroads in the early 1820s and 1830s.

From the intersecting turnpikes one could travel east through Cazenovia and Utica all the way to Albany, or west to the salt marshes, or Canandaigua. Manlius was a busy commercial junction with its comings and goings of freight-hauling teamsters, drovers, and stage lines bringing the mail and latest news by word of mouth and newspapers from the east. Such news often provoked lively discussion in the taverns. One story was that Manlius Four Corners, as the neighboring village of Fayetteville was called in those early days, had gained recognition as the village "with four taverns but no meeting house."[1]

That reputation didn't last long. A religious impulse aroused an enthusiasm in some residents for personal salvation, here, as it did in many villages and hamlets of the region. Revival events sometimes rivaled the intensity and excitement of local party campaigns and election days. The town of Manlius experienced a peculiarly vibrant surge of both religion and politics during these years.

By 1836, there were three churches in the village of Manlius, and within five years, prospering Fayetteville two miles north, had four denominations with places to worship. Churches, chapels and meeting houses were being built in hamlets and villages throughout the town, offering a great diversity of worship, moral opinion, sanctions and roads to salvation. After one grand revival, residents in the small cluster of households on High Bridge built themselves a meeting house in 1839.

Some historians called this early western frontier the "burned-over district," because these revival enthusiasms stoked such fervor and excitement. Revivals came and went, but in some residents the spirit ignited an indelible energy and sense of mission. Personal salvation required action, they believed, to rid society of its selfish and unjust practices and institutions. Numerous reforms engaged activist citizens in the 1830s and 1840s, but the anti-slavery crusade proved to be the most volatile.

While slavery seemed to be a remote issue of little concern to most residents in this Central New York town in Onondaga County, a small number of slaves had been brought here during the early westward migration. They had lived and worked there, some for close to twenty years. New York State lawmakers had set the wheels of a gradual emancipation in motion back in 1799, but it wasn't until 1827 that slavery was outlawed throughout the state.

Still, slavery continued and expanded in many states, especially in the cotton, rice and tobacco states, and many Americans gained benefits from this involuntary servitude. For some religiously motivated reformers, the continuation of chattel slavery in the nation was dishonorable, immoral, and flagrantly unjust.

In 1835, eight years after state emancipation, a number of citizens in the town of Manlius were no longer willing to remain silent about the evils of slavery. They joined with others throughout the state and became an integral part of one of the greatest reform campaigns in American history. It was a contentious issue. Public buildings and churches often closed their doors against abolitionist lectures, but undeterred, speakers took their cause outside into a grove, or apple orchard.

It was a time when some citizens, angered by abolitionist "agitation," as opponents called it, denied the rights of free speech, assembly, and the press to other citizens. The age of the common man gave eligible voters a private bullhorn to voice opinions on local and national policy decisions, and with great gusto they argued and registered their views. Religion and politics contended for authority, and the last word.

The anti-slavery movement was a slow dogged effort, renewed and sustained against waves of opposition, apathy, and inertia locally, and throughout the nation, but leaders stepped forward, convinced that their religious faith meant nothing without good works, benevolence, and freeing the oppressed.

Some anti-slavery supporters believed they could persuade other members of their congregations to actively raise their voices as friends of the oppressed slave. Others felt they could not remain members of a church that tolerated slave owning, and left. These seceders urged others to join them. A few left as a single act of moral integrity. There were such seceders in hamlets and towns throughout the county, but a surprising number of them were located here.

All this happened years before an anti-slavery crowd in Syracuse "made history" when they rescued an alleged fugitive slave named William Henry from a city jail in 1851. The event was called the "Jerry Rescue." It was before Harriet Beecher Stowe's book *Uncle Tom's Cabin* awakened the consciences of many people in the nation to the cruel nature of slavery.

There were some men and women in Manlius who were ahead of their times.

Along the west bank of Limestone Creek and up the hillside road, people of High Bridge confronted the ebb and flow of economic good times with financial misfortune, debts, and setbacks. They mulled over and argued the same local and national conflicts of principle and self-interest as their neighbors. At times their meeting house opened its doors to controversial anti-slavery messengers when others refused to do so, though not without dissension.

Records are few and scattered, but it seemed to me a worthy effort to descend amidst the ruins to examine what these men and women confronted in themselves, and in their society, in the very early days of the anti-slavery movement in the town of Manlius.

Good Country Preaching

...there was a large hollow buttonwood tree. Elder Smith of Moscheto Point said it was so big that he once preached a sermon inside to thirty-five persons. When some doubt was expressed, he added in a firm tone:

"Had they chosen to come, it could have held fifteen more." [2]

Carl Carmer,
Dark Trees to the Wind
A Cycle of York State Years

PROLOGUE

HIGH BRIDGE GETS A CHURCH
August, 1839

Rev. Elijah Bailey was sixty-one when he returned to High Bridge on August 25, 1839 to deliver the installation sermon in the newly built Reformed Methodist Society meeting house. Zebina Baker, a local preacher, had enthusiastically reported the church being built that spring. A week-long revival, or "protracted meeting," as it was called, had so excited local residents that they started putting up their meeting house while the Spirit was still upon them.[1]

The official church installation was announced in the *Fayetteville Luminary,* a Methodist newspaper published by Wesley Bailey. Wesley Bailey, the evangelist's youngest son, also an ordained Reformed Methodist minister, read the Scripture at the ceremony. Elder Bailey's colleagues, Rev. William Lake of Granby, and Rev. Jeremiah Fry of Connecticut, and preachers from churches in Central New York were all there. [2]

It was no doubt a triumphal moment for Elijah Bailey. He was then serving as pastor of a Reformed Methodist Church in Brewster and Dennis, Massachusetts, since 1836. Twenty-five years ago, he, and a few dozen men and women, mechanics, farmers, preachers and exhorters, seceded from the Methodist Episcopal Church in Readsboro, Vermont. He was a tradesman, not a seminary-trained clergyman, but like several other zealous members he believed the church had veered off the simple path of Bible religion into pride and folly amidst an artificial, corrupting hierarchy.

He still had strong family ties in the Manlius area where he had settled fifteen years earlier. A son Alfred, and two daughters, Evaline and Phylina, lived in prospering Fayetteville. Wesley, Eunice, and their children, were nearby, having moved from South Cortland to Fayetteville that year, bringing the church newspaper business with them.

Lydia Smith Bailey, Elijah's wife, mother of eleven children, had died, and was buried at High Bridge in 1831. His brother, Rev. James Bailey, was a church leader in Cardiff, in the town of Lafayette, ten miles southwest.

Like many westward-bound families after the War of 1812, the Baileys migrated in stages. They left southern Vermont and set down roots in Central and Western New York. Many attended the celebration at High Bridge in August of 1839, almost twenty-five years after their secession. It was more than the fulfillment of one man's dream. It was a beacon of hope and faith for many. It gave visible testimony that this small congregation, and the neighborhood that had welcomed it, had its own identity, had come of age, and with God's blessing, would continue to thrive.

CHAPTER ONE

THE SECEDERS FROM VERMONT

> The awareness of professional privilege became a focus as more and more democratic energies arose among laymen... [1]
>
> Whitney R. Cross,
> *The Burned-Over District*

Elijah Bailey was born in Douglas, Massachusetts to James and Susan Bailey in 1768. At age 23, he married Lydia Smith, and within a year they left Douglas and moved to Readsboro, Vermont, a small mountainous hamlet where ten of their eleven children were born.

He was an industrious, energetic man, respected by his fellow townsmen. By trade a cooper, he also ran a grocery store. John Fairbanks, the town clerk, and Elijah's brother-in-law, kept the town records at the store, as was the custom. From 1794 to 1811, Bailey had been elected to most of the town's offices, everything from sealer of weights and road tax collector to state assemblyman. [2]

While steeped in his family's Congregationalist views, Elijah Bailey was swept up in the enthusiasm of early Methodist preachers. He took up evangelizing, though unlettered and unschooled in theology. As the War of 1812 drew to a close, discontent in the Methodist Episcopal Church in Readsboro and neighboring Whitingham turned to outright criticism.

Elijah and several other laymen denounced clerical authorities who they believed were taking away rights and privileges granted to itinerant lay preachers. They argued against an aristocracy of appointment and policy-making, claiming founder John Wesley never ordained clergy, and had relied on lay preachers. Their objections were ignored. So Elijah and a dozen other members, including Pliny Brett, an ordained minister from Massachusetts, seceded from the Methodist Episcopal Church.

They were not the first ones disturbed by a seeming return to British aristocracy. Irish itinerant preacher, James O'Kelly, was an unquiet rebel and dissenter, and also a pain in the neck to Bishop Francis Asbury in the 1780s.[3] He seceded after years of denouncing the managerial control bishops wielded over lay preachers. O'Kelly gained quite a following.

Several years earlier, Elias Smith led a breakaway faction from the Methodist Episcopal Church not far from Woodstock, Vermont where he was raised. The Vermont hills seemed to nurture independent thinkers and self-proclaimed evangelists. As the harassed Frederick Plummer found out, they were not always welcomed.[4]

It would be easy to write off these critics as just rebellious malcontents, but for those shaped by a revolutionary mindset, signs and practices of aristocracy were reminders of unwanted monarchy and its privileges.

So, the Readsboro secession of 1814 was not the first – nor the last rupture. Their "back to basics" biblical faith included respect for lay preachers and itinerants. They accused the Methodist Episcopal Church of abandoning "the true spirit of methodism," which they said, was "to raise a holy people."[5] Some called them prophets; others labeled them fanatics.

By February, the Readsboro seceders were joined by representatives of other Methodist dissenters. They then adopted "Articles for Faith and Practice," pledging themselves to avoid "evil of every kind, taking the name of God in vain, profaning the day of the lord by working or drinking, the buying or selling of men, women and children with the intention of enslaving them...fighting, quarreling, brawling...singing that is not for the glory of God...needless self-indulgence, and the spirit of war." [6]

An Experiment in Community

In 1815, the group decided to create a collective association. They jointly purchased 100 acres of farm land between Hoosac, New York and Bennington, Vermont. The farm community experiment was short-lived, however. Their start-up timing couldn't have been any worse. The miserable weather of 1816 tested their endurance. The "summer without sun" with frosts that ruined crops, was remembered as the bleak, infamous "winter we froze to death." With families and livestock to feed, finances were drained. They were not the only New Englanders that packed it up and decided to go west to find greener pastures. The collective broke up after two years.

The experiment brought several benefits, despite unfulfilled expectations. They had created strong associational bonds and organizational structures, deepened their knowledge of Scripture, honed leadership skills, and toughened their resolve. When they dissolved, they scattered. Most went west, bonded by kinship, familiarity, respect and commitment. They were, they believed, sent forth to spread the word. Still, they had families and needed to make a living, so they first looked for good farmland and opportunities to thrive.

James Bailey, Elijah's brother, and his sister Hannah Bailey Stearns, and husband George Stearns, were the first to settle in Onondaga County, according to one descendant. They brought their families to Cardiff, in the town of Lafayette, during the winter of 1816-1817.[7] Caleb Whiting also preceded Elijah Bailey into New York. Whiting settled first in Springfield, 50 miles east. Friend, and brother-in-law, Ezra Amadon, sister Elizabeth, Captain John Fairbanks, and sister Experience, went further west to Cattaraugus County.

Not everyone encouraged Elijah Bailey's mid-life decision to leave home, kin, and stability to preach along barely trodden byways.

He was forty-eight, when he and his family left the Hoosac community.[8] His daughter Philena, the youngest, was only an infant. Wesley was eight, Evalina eleven, Susannah thirteen, Alfred fifteen, and Lydia seventeen. It is not clear whether the entire family trekked with Bailey and William Lake to Canada, before they rooted themselves in Manlius. Elijah Jr., the eldest son, remained in Vermont.

Elijah moved first to Rhode Island, then to Canada, and finally to Manlius, Onondaga County in Central New York by the early 1820s, perhaps encouraged by his brother James, or the fact that supporting a family was getting harder as an itinerant preacher of a small unknown sect.

It is clear the four youngest children, including Wesley, experienced much of their formal schooling intermittently before they settled in Manlius.

Elijah and Lydia may have been forging a spiritual vision of God's golden kingdom, but they were also trudging on foot, by wagon, and by ox cart on hardscrabble road.

In the early 1820s, they finally settled in the town of Manlius, where youngest son Wesley Bailey later reported the family remained for eighteen years. It seemed, however, that Elijah spent most of his time preaching elsewhere. [9]

In October 1842, when neighbor Andrew Balsley died, Bailey wrote a tribute in the *Methodist Reformer* memorializing his gratitude.

> For surely we were homeless, and he took
> us in and in repeated instances administered
> to the necessities of our family while the father
> of the writer was engaged preaching the word
> of life. [10]

CHAPTER TWO

THE REVIVALS

There is no caution in the word of God against feeling too much, or giving too much, or doing too much. [1]

> Elder Jacob Knapp,
> *Autobiography*

But many of them were destitute of classical and theological furniture; of feeble natural abilities: erroneous in sentiments; boisterous, vulgar, and abusive in their manner of preaching.... [2]

> Rev. James H. Hotchins,
> 1848

In the heydays of religious enthusiasms of the 1830s, local clergy were wary of revivals. [3] The excitements they stirred threatened to upset the stability, decorum and leadership in local churches, though Methodist, Baptists, and some Presbyterian churches found them a vibrant source of recruitment.

The small farmer, artisan, mechanic, mill worker, and their families in rural communities throughout Central and Western New York, however, flocked to these occasions to experience spiritual conversion, refreshment, and community. These were lively social events often drawing hundreds from miles around.

Until the middle class experienced a tamer version of these gatherings, they generally perceived them as vulgar, lower class religious events. In times of personal distress, financial depressions, and other national crises, however, attendance swelled.

When Elijah Bailey arrived in Manlius about 1821, he was a Reformed Methodist elder, a man of independent mind, who believed he and his associates were being true to John Wesley's vision by seceding. They were plain speaking men, not schooled in grand academic oratory. It is true that some, like William Lake, were quite exuberant in their preaching, and had a reputation for kicking up a bit of excitement. Still, there were many who felt moaning and shouting one's repentance was far better than drifting asleep on a hard, cold bench.

The Second Great Awakening

Revivals, camp meetings, and church-raisings had long been part of the religious culture of New England. Men like Bailey, Brett, Lake, Whiting, Amadon, Fairbanks and Fry, carried their religious culture westward from the mountains of Vermont and Massachusetts into the valleys of New York, Ohio and Canada. Central and Western New York came to be known as "the Burned-Over District" because so many evangelists had fired up towns with revivals sparking thousands of conversions, new energies and hope, and at times, controversy.

Charles Grandison Finney, considered by some religious historians the greatest evangelist of the 19th century, is credited with igniting a "second" wave of religious enthusiasm throughout Northern and Western New York. Ordained in 1827 as a Presbyterian minister by the St. Lawrence Conference, despite lacking the formal seminary training usually required, Finney was a powerful and skilled preacher. He rejected strict Calvinist notions that individual sinners were predestined to damnation, that they were naturally depraved. He sought to jolt a person into awareness of sin, and instill a desire for repentance. This usually required a personal conversion.

Conversion, for Finney, was one's ticket out of gloom, doom, and powerlessness. He believed anyone could be saved from the horrors of condemnation. One had only to turn from selfishness to God, and extend love and goodwill toward your neighbor. This social aspect included responding to the evils of one's society. Sabbath-breaking and drunkenness were then serious concerns, and as time went on, slavery became identified by evangelists as a serious moral failure and estrangement from God. To participate in reform efforts was in itself an outward sign of true sanctification. [4] When converted, and individuals lived a benevolent life, then justice would flow into laws and institutions.

Most New England seminary-trained clergymen were uncomfortable and disconcerted by Finney's theology and practices. He allowed people to pray out loud (sometimes simultaneously) and to come forward and ask those gathered to support them as they prayed for repentance. Women were allowed to pray in his public gatherings. All these "new measures," they complained, were improper.

However, Finney was convinced these "new measures" were beneficial, and got people's attention. He did not back down when criticized for his methods and language. According to revival historian, William McLoughlin, Finney defended his "undignified" style, and "challenged critics to show the fruitfulness of their means." [5]

Yet, disapproving clergymen were aware that if they did not compete for new members by participating in these gatherings, rival churches and other sects would likely reap the influx of new converts. In the 1830s, church leaders tried to control the enthusiasms of such events as popular evangelists continued to crisscross Western New York and inspire followers, and attract crowds.

Disturbers of the Peace

While conservative New England clergy stigmatized Finney and his followers as fanatics, many common folks believed emotional expression was a manifestation of the Holy Spirit.[6] They preferred plain and simple language that was relevant to their daily lives and active participation, rather than being preached at. No doubt there were risks when hundreds of strangers from miles around assembled, and were encouraged to humble themselves by exposing their sinfulness.

Pastors in the towns were anxious for new converts, but this did not mean they opened their arms to a wide spectrum of beliefs and practices. They did not. They were guardians of their denominational creed.

On one occasion, Marsena Stone sought advice from his classmate, Nathan R. Chapman, during a revival at the Presbyterian Church in Jamesville, just west of Manlius. The revival was led by Rev. Luther Myrick and Augustus Littlejohn.

Stone experienced a deeply-moving personal conversion, but when some people at the church expressed "contempt" for immersion, a practice he and several others found acceptable, they turned around and "went to Manlius and were baptized into fellowship at the Baptist Church by Rev. Charles Morton." [7]

If one place proved intolerant, there seemed to be a spectrum of new opportunities opening up where one felt more comfortable. Internal church conflicts flared in Jamesville, as it did in many early settlements, as unfamiliar theology, worship styles, views on authority, slavery, and temperance were introduced by newcomers and itinerant preachers. These often clashed with earlier established practices.

Manlius Fourth Church, on the Erie Canal, was the scene of much confusion in the early 1830s. According to Presbyterian historian Rev. James H. Hotchkins, this church "was torn to pieces" by Rev. Luther Myrick and other "errorists." [8]

The same trouble, he said, afflicted the Matthews Mills church in North Manlius, whose members also came from the nearby town of Sullivan in Madison County. Myrick was accused of fomenting "unionism," that is, trying to unite denominations into one Christian church. Other preachers were blamed for spreading the error of "perfectionism," and inciting members to secede from the church.[9] Turmoil in local churches continued throughout 1834, and no more dramatically than in Manlius.

The Condemnation of Rev. Luther Myrick

At all levels of authority, from local church sessions and regional presbyteries, to synods and General Assembly meetings, the Presbyterian leaders scrutinized those preaching in their congregations for evidence of heresy. From their institutional viewpoint, trouble started when fanatics and zealots came to town. In the 1830s, particularly, all manner of evils were associated with "perfectionism," as espoused by preachers such as Myrick and Littlejohn.[10] There was confusion about exactly what teachings were condemned, but an anxiety about methods and style disturbed many clergy elders. What inspired some seemed dangerous to others, and many citizens, churchgoers or not, went to see and hear for themselves.

One talented revivalist, who got mixed reviews, was Rev. Luther Myrick. Myrick preached in Manlius, Fayetteville, Jamesville, Oswego, Verona and Cayuga during the 1830s. In 1833, he preached at the Congregational Church in Jamesville. Soon after, the once united church fragmented. Myrick, and other revivalists, were blamed for the "wars and contentions" which disrupted church harmony in Jamesville.[11] This accusation, however, ignored the fact that there were denominational factions within the Congregational congregation already trying to assert control before their arrival. One faction tried to organize under the Dutch Reformed jurisdiction. Another argued over whether to align with Presbyterian or Congregational structure and authority. Methodist-oriented worshippers, who were comfortable with revivals and camp meeting style preaching, decided to build their own church.

In August 1833, the Oneida Presbytery, however, had exhausted its patience with Rev. Myrick's unorthodox preaching and practices. With complaints and testimony from various local presbyteries, they brought him to trial on charges of heresy. He was prosecuted and convicted before a presbytery session in Utica on October 22, 1834. An eye witness account named clergy, lay men, and women, who spoke for and against Myrick.[12] It was a most unpleasant proceeding.

Two years after he ceased being a Presbyterian minister, Myrick found another pulpit to share his views. One might say, the Oneida Presbytery accidentally opened a Pandora's box. Denied the preaching desk, he took up the printing press, and started editing the *Union Herald,* an anti-slavery, unionist newspaper published in Cazenovia, thereby expanding his outreach, and aligning himself with other non-denominational spokesmen, such as Gerrit Smith and William Goodell. Together, they urged members to leave their sinful church structures and join union congregations.

Down, But Not Out!

This anti-denominational crusade never gained wide support. Only a few left their church affiliations and joined union congregations. However, clerical authority was not popular among many Yankee emigrants. Most people in the towns were not formally members of any church. Post-Revolutionary men, as Nathan Hatch observed, were less docile and less deferential to authority. [13] They wanted basic simple truths, not florid speech-making, and they didn't want distant councils and bishops to lord it over their local congregation.

When it came to these, and other evangelical beliefs and practices, the Reformed Methodists had a lot in common with the Reverend's Charles Finney and Luther Myrick, though the Baileys did not seem to have any formal connection with the Finney revivals, or Luther Myrick.

Elijah Bailey left Manlius not long after his wife Lydia died in 1831. His children were adults then. He accepted a ministry position in Massachusetts where he later remarried. His son, Wesley Bailey, who taught in a district school, may have observed some of the local upheaval concerning Myrick's heresy trial, but his life course was also shifting to Western New York. He, wife Eunice, and two month old son Elijah, moved to Erie County in the fall of 1834, where Wesley began preaching as a newly ordained Reformed Methodist minister.

If the Myrick trial was the talk of Manlius Village, events in northern Manlius encouraged titillating gossip, and with these perfectionists, the Reformed Methodists had no common fellowship.

The Spiritual Wives Scandal

During the 1830s, evangelizers from Delphi, DeRuyter, Salina, and Verona found welcoming households in rural northern Manlius in which to hold prayer meetings.[14] A desire to live a more perfect holy life was a natural outcome of deep personal conversion, and numerous revivals had introduced seekers to such experiences. Yet, some evangelists lacked wisdom and guidance. They underestimated the benefits of structure and authority, and failed to realize unlimited freedom had its own dangers.

A few overconfident preachers veered onto unorthodox paths. They began to question whether man-made laws were binding as one advanced into the higher states of holiness. Rev. Erasmus Stone, one local evangelist, was reported to have shared a vision of men and women in the heavens gazing with longing at each other. He interpreted this to mean that married men and women in the present state were not partnered with their real soul mate, and the heavenly-bound were searching for their true spiritual partners.[15] Well, that notion got a lot of attention.

John Humphrey Noyes, who was developing his own unorthodox interpretations of religious and marital matters, was aware of these happenings in New York. He accused these "foggy-thinking" New York Perfectionist of being "completely given over to anarchy and imbecility." [16] Noyes, however, was also a perfectionist evangelizer, and was ambitious for spiritual leadership.

Holiness movements seemed to thrive in rural communities of Central and Western New York, where rapid social and economic changes in the 1830s threatened family values, structures, and stability. Some sought answers and support in living a simple, disciplined, biblical faith. In later years, several northern Manlius perfectionists subscribed to Noyes' religious newspaper, *The Witness*. [17] When Noyes created his own perfectionist experiment years later, he came under harsh scrutiny for some of the same accusations evoked ten years earlier by Erasmus Stone's vision. [18]

Such stories alarmed ministers who feared the gates of hell had opened and unleashed breakdowns of morality. To what extent these stories were true is unclear, though it appears a few households were disrupted by consequences of such "fuzzy" thinking.[S] Still, the stories gave pastors an opportunity to sternly warn their members away from such fanatics.

The High Bridge Reformed Methodists

Whatever eccentricities these mid-1830s religious movements sparked in a few Manlius hinterland households, such extremes did not characterize the Reformed Methodist Society at High Bridge. Reformed Methodists had some beliefs and practices in common with other perfectionists, but their views and practices were distinctly rooted in a strict, primitive Methodism.

They were, it seems, criticized by some people because of their belief in the power of prayer to heal spiritual and temporal diseases. When Wesley Bailey mentioned this in his history of Reformed Methodists, he refrained from offering his own opinion, saying instead: "we leave others to judge." [19]

The Reformed Methodists may have discomforted some townspeople by aspects of their witness, but it was not likely due to their frugal, simple, Bible life-style, or their opposition to taking the name of God in vain, working or drinking on the Sabbath, or denouncing fighting, quarreling, or brawling. These were uniformly condemned by most churches. Their insistence on vesting authority in local churches, and upholding the equal rights of laity, may have been criticized by some, but in many ways they were similar to the Congregationalists. What distinguished them from many of their denominational and unchurched neighbors, was their strong condemnation of slavery, their strict policies against intoxicating drink, and their rejection of war. These were principled positions they held for twenty-five years.

CHAPTER THREE

THE EVIL OF SLAVERY

Believe me, I shall honor the Quakers for their noble efforts to abolish slavery...[1]

Patrick Henry,
Quoted in *Republican Monitor,* 1835

It is a maxim long ago imbibed, that we never stand still in religion – We either raise higher, or sink lower. [2]

Rev. Elijah Bailey,
South Cortland Luminary, 1837

Many holiness seekers, including the Reformed Methodists, rejected slavery as a moral evil. While mainstream denominations accused perfectionist sects of all manner of deviations, they avoided confronting their own slackened commitments.

Methodists had written language against slavery in their discipline in the late 18th century, but within twenty years they succumbed to pressure and regressed, eliminating this discomforting condemnation so as not to affront southern members. It was the Quakers who mounted early, strong and persistent efforts to end slavery in New York State. A manumission society founded in the late 1780s worked for years to get New York state legislators to begin a process for ending slavery, but slave-holding New Yorkers refused to consider any option that would not guarantee them compensation for their property.

Through the dedication of both Manumission Society founder John Jay, and Governor Daniel Tompkins, a gradual abolition law passed in 1799, officially ended slavery in New York State in 1827, though non-residents were allowed to bring their slaves into New York for some years. Free blacks, however, were not allowed all civil rights.

On slavery, Reformed Methodists believed they were true to founder John Wesley's discipline. In 1837, Rev. Wesley Bailey, editor of the newly-launched denominational newspaper, *South Cortland Luminary*, published John Wesley's sentiments which appeared in his letter to William Wilberforce. Wilberforce was a convert of John Wesley and served in England's Parliament. John Wesley's letter urged Wilberforce to work untiringly to outlaw the slave trade:

> ...O be not weary of well doing! Go on, in the name of God and in the power of his might, till even American slavery (the vilest that ever saw the sun) shall vanish away before it....Your affectionate servant... [3]
>
> John Wesley, 1791

The Reformed Methodists must have been optimistic about their continued evangelizing successes. In 1837, their small chapels and meeting houses stretched from Vermont and Massachusetts, to New York. It seemed an opportune moment to inaugurate a weekly denominational newspaper. Steam powered printing presses were faster, paper and postal deliveries cheaper, and an increasingly literate public widened opportunities for a reading market.

Newspapers became vital informational channels unifying and keeping church members informed, reporting conference decisions, ordinations, and major events, educating, inspiring, and warning their members away from tempting oratory of other evangelists.

When Wesley Bailey became editor of the *South Cortland Luminary,* the Boston abolitionist newspaper *Liberator* was in its sixth year, and *Friend of Man*, an anti-slavery weekly published in Utica, had completed its first year. Though *Freedom's Journal*, the first black-owned and operated weekly, published in New York City shut down in 1829 after a two year run, it was replaced in 1837 by *The Colored American.* Newspaper editors exchanged papers, clipped and reprinted stories from each other. In his first issue, July 18, 1837, Bailey thanked Horace Greeley for generously sending him a batch of publications. [4]

If the *South Cortland Luminary* publishing committee wanted to steer clear of politics, they faced a challenge in doing so when they brought their publishing operation into South Cortland, as Homer and Cortlandville, just a few miles north, were quickly becoming a hub of the county's anti-slavery movement. The controversy had festered in the Homer Congregational Church for several years, resulting in at least one pastor's resignation. The national assembly had a similar eruption. Southern slaveholders and their conservative allies conspired to end the antagonism by ejecting northern abolition-friendly synods out of the national union. The schism was widely discussed and argued in many localities close to Auburn's Theological

Seminary where the ejected churches and synods were planning to unite their resources and protest. The controversy was a focal point of argument in churches, and in the United States Congress.

So, by 1838, it is not surprising that editor Bailey was increasingly adding reports about slavery in his columns, especially as the subject erupted in the United States Congress.

On March 8, 1838, Bailey told readers "65 petitions signed by about 6,500 persons," seeking to end the slave trade in the District of Columbia were "laid on the table."[5] Such efforts to stop the flood of citizen petitions did not thwart ex-President John Q. Adam. He continued to bring them to the floor of the House of Representatives. "Mr. Adams," wrote Bailey, said he "had about three hundred and fifty petitions" that he felt duty-bound to present, "signed by about thirty-five thousand persons..."[6]

Southern slave-holding congressmen, with sympathizing northern allies, were enraged at organized northern abolitionists and decided to circumvent the right of reading slavery petitions by using procedural rules. It was a mistake. Once the right of petition was attacked and denied to citizens, anti-slavery spokesmen had a new weapon to use against slavery's powerful defenders.

Editor Bailey did not have to rely on reprinting articles about anti-slavery from other exchange newspapers. There was a great deal of local anti-slavery activity in Cortlandville and Homer, where many members of the Presbyterian and Congregational churches had united to form a county-wide anti-slavery society in May 1837. County leaders joined the state society and became vigorous organizers and spokesmen. On

April 19, 1838, the *South Cortland Luminary* reported their anniversary meeting listing all the resolutions passed by its members.[7] While anti-slavery concerns edged into its columns, the most prominent subject continued to be "Equal Rights" and "Conference Rights." Despite having seceded from the Methodist Episcopal Church twenty four years earlier, Reformed Methodist leaders continued to criticize its structures, policies, and conference decisions.

> By equal rights, we understand that all men are born equally free; none has preeminence over his brother and in the formulation of the rules and regulations of the Church, the various members possess equal rights; ...[8]

Dissent within the Methodist Episcopal Church increased in 1838. The May Annual Conference, warned ministers against "agitating" the subject of slavery by attending anti-slavery conventions, preaching abolition lectures, or forming anti-slavery societies as these would "disturb the peace and harmony of the Church."[9] Bailey rallied behind dissenting Methodist Episcopal ministers who complained bishops were abusing their authority, quoting a letter John Wesley had written to Bishop Asbury in 1788, saying he would rather be called "a knave, or a fool, a rascal (or) a scoundrel" than be called "a bishop."[10]

The dispute over power exercised by bishops and laity rights within the Methodist Episcopal Conference once again arose with a fury.

When Wesley Bailey moved his young family back to Fayetteville in 1839, he brought the printing press with him. It had been a challenging beginning for the young family. Two years in Erie County, two years in South Cortland. Certainly not easy for Eunice Kinne Bailey, who was caring for her second son, Ansel Kinne Bailey, along with five year-old, Elijah, trying to make do on her husband's newspaper and printing job income. Now back in Fayetteville, they were at least closer to family again – the Kinnes of DeWitt and Baileys of Fayetteville and High Bridge. [11]

Fayetteville opened up new opportunities for reporting and advertising, as well as, Bailey hoped, subscriptions and expanding influence for the publication. As there was no local newspaper to compete with at the time, he was optimistic about the future of the business.

When he had left the village in 1834 in the midst of local religious controversies, a formal anti-slavery organization had not yet been formed. He returned a practiced Reformed Methodist minister, an editor of a newspaper, and would soon become an important leader in "agitating" the anti-slavery movement. No small contribution to be sure, but the anti-slavery controversy he found in Fayetteville and Manlius, was at full throttle when he arrived. It had been sparked by others. It all started in October, 1835.

CHAPTER FOUR

1835: A GRAND REVOLUTION

...and if we do not die, we mean to see that revolution accomplished, and our land free from the tread and fetter of the slave. [1]

James C. Jackson

It was but one day; it was in a little place; it was an extraordinary occasion. [2]

William Thomas

Wesley Bailey was not the only local man skilled with words who believed ending slavery was a worthy religious cause. James Caleb Jackson, three years younger than Bailey, was a talented, persuasive writer. He was born in Manlius in 1811. By the time he was in his mid-twenties, he became so convinced that slavery was a sin that he devoted over fifteen years of his life to speaking and writing about it, before his health broke down, and even that did not stop him.

Jackson was the son of Dr. James Jackson, an army surgeon in the War of 1812, and Mary Ann Elderkin. His parents were early co-founders and supporters of the Presbyterian Church in Manlius. The elder Jackson returned to farming when his health began to fail. He died in 1829. Like many sons with a widowed mother and siblings, James left school and worked the farm.

Jackson was sixteen in 1827 when New York State's emancipation law declared slaves free within its boundaries. It is hard to imagine Jackson being blind to his neighbor's slaves for long. In 1820 the United States census counted 15 slaves in the town of Manlius. Most had been brought into the state when their owners had relocated from Dutchess, Ulster, Cayuga counties, and from Maryland and Virginia.

The Jackson household that year was in close proximity to Philip Lenison and Thomas Denison, two free colored households. Three neighbors owned slaves. [3]

Whatever local disapproval there was regarding human bondage, it seemed, no one interfered in anyone else's private business. Even though slaves were emancipated in the state in 1827, slave labor ran a thriving global economy. That economy, and its benefits, extended directly north and west. There were no organized anti-slavery societies then. That changed after 1834, and Jackson played a significant role in stirring up local efforts to push emancipation onto the national stage.

Young Jackson married Lucretia Edgerton Brewster, and they bought 145 acres of land in Mexico, New York. The harsh farm life wasn't easy for him. His interests leaned toward medical training, like his father, and also toward the religious ministry, favored by his mother. While considering what professional avenues he should pursue, he became involved in local civic and religious issues in the county.

In the mid-1830s, anti-slavery speakers traveled through towns all along the Erie Canal route to explain southern slavery's cruel realities and to urge good church people, biblically-rooted people, to support emancipation. Most did not see any connection to their local personal lives, or to their faith, and while itinerant evangelists were a common feature of village and country life, this particular subject stirred heated debates.

James Jackson chose to side with the oppressed slaves. He believed slavery was a grievous sin, and therefore, all slaves should be freed. Inspired by this religious conviction, he joined Algernon Savage and Ransom Goss Williams, two friends, and together they went into nearby villages and towns to speak about slavery. [4] When his two zealous friends moved on, Jackson found support for his lectures among the Gilbert family of Mexico.

Only a few encouraged him to pursue this unsettling, financially insecure career. He failed to win over some of his in-laws. Uncomfortable as this was, Jackson persisted, and then a life-changing moment thrust him into the spotlight.

The Extraordinary Occasion

It was October 21, 1835, and opponents of slavery had arrived to take part in a convention in Utica to create a statewide organization. Hundreds of delegates converged on the city. Jackson came on a packet boat from Fulton with a contingent from Oswego County that included John Clark and Rev. Luther Myrick. It is said Jackson was introduced to Gerrit Smith on this ride to the meeting. [5]

The atmosphere in the city was tense. Efforts to stop the meeting had been encouraged by leading officials for weeks. The October 7th issue of the *Onondaga Standard* told readers many citizens vehemently objected to Northern agitation for "immediate emancipation" of slaves in the South. [6]

Some Utica Common Council members believed they were obligated to honor the right of assembly and free speech of their fellow citizens. They voted 7 to 4 to allow use of the court house, but this decision was soon overruled by other "men of property and standing." [7] The convention delegates quickly redirected themselves to the Bleecker Street Presbyterian Church, which was made available to them. However, they were soon followed by a determined contingent, who marched into the church and demanded the assembly stop its proceedings.

The intruders appeared to achieve their goal, though the constitution had already been approved by delegates. The *Onondaga Standard* reported all this happened in a civil deliberative fashion, that is, "good and respectable citizens" calmly persuaded the convention to adjourn." [8] No big to-do, according to official reports.

Well, That Was One View

There must have been more to it than this serene portrayal, because the Cazenovia *Republican Monitor* called the intruding delegation "a mob," a bunch of "depraved and ignorant vagabonds." [9] *The Cortland Republican* protested the whole lawless episode as "shameless conduct." [10]

The Cazenovia and Cortland newspapers, however, were in the minority. Most newspapers justified the defensive intervention against the "impropriety" and reckless plan of abolitionists to hold such a meeting in their city. They assumed their opinions and objections trumped the constitutional right of other citizens to peacefully assemble. Perhaps they thought it their civic duty to warn delegates in advance, as they did, saying "evil consequences" would result. But their warnings did not stop delegates from ultimately accomplishing their goal. [11]

After William Thomas had interviewed many eye witnesses, he published an impassioned account. He wanted this outrage to be remembered. Instead of cowering and abandoning their goals under fire, he said, many attendees defied intimidations. "*It was,*" he said, "*but one day; it was in a little place; it was an extraordinary occasion.*" [12]

James Jackson certainly believed it was an extraordinary occasion, and later recalled that "not less than perhaps a thousand men" had gathered outside as delegates completed their business. Jackson reported that they finished forming the state society and constitution and elected officers amidst "the howling of the mob." [13] Some of the rabble harassed delegates as they left. A shocked Gerrit Smith invited those who had regrouped to continue the meeting at his home in Peterboro the next morning. It was twenty-seven miles from Utica. Over a hundred took the canal boat as far as Canastota. James C. Jackson was among them. So was William M. Clark of Pompey. Jackson and Clark walked the uphill road from Canastota in the pre-dawn hours, Jackson cheering on bedraggled and muddied pilgrims. As people came out of their homes, he shouted, "Come put on a clean shirt and come along with us. We have begun the grandest revolution the world has ever seen...." [14]

On that same day, William Lloyd Garrison was seized by a mob in Boston.

If vigilante mobs, whether of propertied or landless citizens, seemed to rule Utica and Boston on October 21, 1835, they misinterpreted a short-term victory as a success. Their abrasive denial of constitutional rights of peaceable assembly and speech to other Americans gained the abolitionists sympathizers. Their invasive opposition, in fact, created abolitionist heroes.

When resolutions were ratified the next day in Peterboro, and local county leadership was selected for the New York State Anti-Slavery Society, Jackson walked forty-three miles home to Mexico refreshed and on fire.

From that point on, Gerrit Smith became a formidable and incessant voice in the crusade against slavery. He was not alone. Others, inspired by the solidarity of this noble cause, headed back to Manlius, Fayetteville and Pompey.

CHAPTER FIVE

THE PRESBYTERIANS

> Identification with an unpopular social movement such as abolitionism would almost certainly penalize a church in terms of both membership and financial contributions. [1]
>
> John R. McKivigan,
> *The War Against Proslavery Religion*

The Smith Brothers & Sisters

Gerrit Smith and Luther Myrick were Presbyterians. Jackson's parents were pillars of the Manlius Trinity Presbyterian Church. Presbyterian clergymen from across the state attended the first New York State Anti-Slavery convention in Utica in 1835 in large numbers. They were a conspicuous presence there. If Smith, Myrick, and Jackson were buoyed by this show of witness, and anticipated their church would become a strong vocal advocate for oppressed slaves, they were too optimistic.

The October 1835 event was a high water mark of witness by local Presbyterian clergymen against slavery. The dilemma for Presbyterian churches, north and south, was clear:

how to handle increasingly antagonistic views on this moral and economic issue "within the family" was a disturbing quandary. This was especially true for Presbyterian and Methodist Episcopal congregations since both had large memberships in the South.

Yet it seemed to some northern "family" members, who despised slavery, that conservative trustees, clergy, men of property and standing, had bent over backwards to placate southern slave-holding members, despite the fact their denominations had long ago pronounced against slavery as an evil.

Rev. Carlos Smith was minister for Trinity Presbyterian Church in 1835. His services had been renewed since 1832. He was a very orthodox man on theological matters, and probably admired by many in the presbytery for such conservative views. Clearly he showed his by-the-book principles when he pressed a heresy case against the perfectionist revivalist, Rev. Luther Myrick. Some members of the church attended Myrick's protracted meetings, much to Smith's disapproval.

Rev. Smith went to the Utica anti-slavery convention, apparently believing the 1818 General Assembly declaration that slavery was "utterly inconsistent with the law of God." [2] His brother, Rev. Stephen Smith, pastor of Fayetteville's Presbyterian Church two miles away, who registered his attendance at the convention, must have concluded the same.[3] Both brothers were certainly aware that there was no unanimity among Presbyterians on the subject, despite the General Assembly's earlier condemnation of slavery. What the statement meant, or required, was contested many times during the seventeen years that followed. In Central New York, however, an increasing number of Presbyterian ministers, no longer believed there was evidence to support a gradual harmonious approach. The colonization plan supported by many, they believed, neither worthy, nor workable.

When the mob dispersed the Utica meeting, and some attendees retreated directly home, Rev. Carlos Smith joined the reassembled delegates in Peterboro. They met in the Presbyterian Church and completed organization of their new state anti-slavery society. Smith served on a committee to draft resolutions and recommend local leadership. He was named Onondaga County officer for the state anti-slavery society. [4]

Trinity Presbyterian Church records show that on August 15, 1835, the trustees voted to employ Rev. Carlos Smith as their clergyman for another year. The Utica-Peterboro convention was held October 21-22. The next entry in the trustee meeting minutes is for August 8, 1836, when they voted a three person committee "to assess a tax for hiring a clergyman and other expenses..." [5]

On April 10, 1837, some eight months later, the following decision is recorded: "*It is not expedient to employ the Rev. Mr Toby as our minister.*" [6] So, what happened to Rev. Carlos Smith, and why is there no entry in the trustee minutes about his departure? Did his departure have anything to do with his being named Onondaga County representative to the New York State Anti-Slavery Society? Had the Presbyterian national governing Assembly clamped down on abolitionist clergymen? Yes, it did.

Annual supply contracts for ministers were essentially one way lay people, usually, through the office of trustee, retained control over their local churches. They selected competent preachers they could afford, whose views were comfortable with their own, and they did not veer far from orthodoxy. A surprising number of clergymen lived hand to mouth, shuttling through a revolving door of annual contracts as controversial issues on revivals, intoxicating drink, and slavery became contentious among members in a congregation. A decision to renew, or not to renew, a clergyman's contract, gave laymen leverage, but left many ministers, and their families, in precarious financial situations.

It happened to ministers in all denominations. The pulpits of Unitarian Theodore Parker's brother clergymen in Massachusetts were closed to him, he reported, because of his anti-slavery views. "My life seems to me a complete failure socially; here I am as much an outcast from society as though I were a convicted pirate." [7]

The benevolent-minded might feel slavery in the South was wrong, but most Americans, North and South, did not believe organized societies, paid lecturers, and a deluge of publications aimed at ridding the nation of this entrenched southern institution, was the right way to go. Besides, it was a matter for the South to decide, not the North.

Rev. Stephen S. Smith, Carlos' brother, then supply preacher at Fayetteville Presbyterian Church, also attended the Utica meeting. An anonymous letter writer was granted ample space in the local Syracuse newspaper to protest clergy endorsement of the Utica convention. The signer called himself VERITAS, apparently choosing to conceal his identity, as he publicly chastised Smith and other clergy for getting involved in politics. [8]

By 1837 Rev. Stephen Smith was also no longer at Fayetteville Presbyterian Church. Rev. Ethan Smith, father of Carlos and Stephen, had during these two years, ministered at Pompey Hill, less than twelve miles away. A graduate of Dartmouth, who had ministered in New Hampshire, Massachusetts, and Vermont, he was a scholarly man who saw to it that his daughters, as well as his sons, received a broad academic education. In 1823 he authored "A View of the Hebrews," where he explored a theory that Native American tribes were descended from the lost tribes of Israel. [9]

It was a difficult time for the entire family. Bathsheba Sandford Smith, Ethan's wife, died at Pompey Hill in the spring of 1835 and was buried there. The Smith men, including elder Ethan Smith, after a year of dealing with loss, controversy, and unrenewed contracts, were faced with seeking ministry positions elsewhere.

The Smith brothers left clear evidence of their anti-slavery sentiments and activities, but so too did their sisters. Grace Fletcher Smith married Rev. Job R. Martyn in 1827. He attended the founding New York Anti-Slavery Society meeting in Utica in October 1835. Grace, "Mrs. Reverend Martyn," as she was called, became the first director of the new Ladies' New York City Anti-Slavery Society. [10] As author Amy Swerdlow points out, the goal of this group was to recruit one antislavery woman from every Protestant congregation to sit on its board of managers." Grace was also a manager of the New York Female Reform Society. [11]

Her sister Sarah Towne Smith, a temperance advocate who also lived in New York, took on the role of editor of the *Moral Reform Advocate* in 1835. Sarah, had musical talent, but her father saw to it that her advanced education included both Greek and Hebrew, and other "masculine" subjects, so she ably turned her skills to literary and reform projects.

Ellen Chase Smith, the youngest of the ten Smith children, while living in Pompey Hill with her family, met and later married, Charles B. Sedgwick in 1837. [12] He was a promising lawyer with increasingly strong anti-slavery sentiments, which the Smith family clearly embraced.

Charles B. Sedgwick was one of those young men, who, aspiring to make a difference on life's broader stage, forged a career in the midst of social upheaval. To what extent his moral and social conscience was influenced by Presbyterian and Congregational clergymen, such as the Smiths, and Rev. John Gridley, who succeeded Ethan Smith at Pompey Hill in 1836, is arguable, but that his personal experience and professional education were reinforced by such visible witness and relationships, is strongly suggested. [13]

These clergymen actively stood on the side of the oppressed slaves. During the 1830s, there were several instances where strong witness and mentorship inspired and advanced a commitment to human rights in men seeking legal, political, and religious careers.

Rev. John Keep was a mentor to several young men. Keep was a very active pastor at Homer's Congregational Church for over ten years. He was President of Cortland Academy's Board of Trustees, and on Hamilton College's board. He nourished a generation of young reformers that included Nathan R. Chapman, another up-and-coming lawyer, who in 1836 became principal of Fayetteville Academy, before setting up his law practice. Keep became a staunch revivalist. He suffered the consequences for frequently condemning slavery and the liquor business in Homer, and bringing in revivalist speakers who did the same. In 1833 a cadre of financial supporters objected, and when Keep notified the presbytery of their withdrawal of support, and offered his resignation, the presbytery chose not to contest Keep's decision. [14]

Perhaps the most significant local example of how preaching a moral message and giving witness influenced the career of a young man, was Theodore Weld. Weld came under the mentorship of revivalist Rev. Charles G. Finney, and Charles Stuart. As a result of their inspiration and support, Weld trained a 'holy band' of seventy anti-slavery agents. One of those he influenced was Rev. John Keep, who by 1834 was at Oberlin College. There, Rev. Keep cast the deciding yes vote, as President of the Board of Trustees, to admit Negroes to enter the college. [15]

Rev. Carlos Smith began his services at First Church Congregational, Painesville, Ohio, on October 1, 1836, where he remained until 1843. [16] The anti-slavery movement there was just as controversial as in Manlius, but Smith seems to have maintained his anti-slavery sentiments. Theodore Weld had preached and lectured his way through the state, so the ground was well stirred up. From 1840 to 1843 Smith served on the Board of Trustees of Oberlin College. [17]

Though these Smiths resided in Manlius, Fayetteville, and Pompey Hill for less than a decade, and are not well-known or acclaimed, the family left visible footprints in the local and state anti-slavery movement. [18] They were Congregational and Presbyterian ministers and educated women, who took the unpopular road less traveled by, "when to take a stand against slavery in the early 1830s," as author Milton Sernett declared, "was to invite trouble." [19]

So, they moved on, to another town, to another church- Rev. Stephen S. Smith to Buffalo, Rev. Ethan Smith to Salina, Rev. Carlos Smith to Painesville, Ohio.

CHAPTER SIX

TAKING SIDES IN FAYETTEVILLE

> The friends of immediate emancipation... owe it to the cause of truth and justice, to adopt such measures as shall vindicate the doctrines of American liberty, and prevent our valued republican institutions from becoming a cloak to the most odious and irresponsible despotism. [1]
>
> *The Liberator,*
> October 3, 1835

Rev. Stephen S. Smith, as a clergyman serving at the Fayetteville Presbyterian Church, was the most conspicuous resident who was denounced in October 1835 for publicly supporting a state organization to seek immediate emancipation of slaves, but he was not the only one. There were 362 signers to the call for the organizing meeting published in a Utica newspaper three weeks before the convention date, and reprinted in *The Liberator,* the abolitionist newspaper, on October 3.

Twelve were from Onondaga County, all of them from the village of Manlius and Fayetteville. The signers called themselves "the friends of human rights." [2] They saw their decision as righteous, as obeying the law of God, as well as a defense of the true meaning of "American liberty." Those who opposed them, called the signers agitators, disturbers of the peace, and took steps to stop them.

Opposition meetings were called well in advance. These opponents were respectable New Yorkers who sympathized with southern slaveholders and resented the abolitionist campaign of newspapers and tracts being sent to their states. *The Richmond Enquirer* appealed to northern editors to stop these reckless agitators. Many did just that by approving of forceful opposition in their newspaper columns.

Southern sympathizers met and denounced abolitionists as "incendiaries" in Utica that September. *The Onondaga Chief* cheered citizens and grand jury actions against abolitionist meetings in Boston, Albany, Utica and Western New York. For weeks, the Syracuse newspaper encouraged an anti-abolitionist campaign. [3] Their articles and columns assailed immediate emancipation of slaves as a danger to the Union, adding that it was a matter of states' rights. The North had no business interfering in domestic affairs and institutions of another state of the Union. Some of these arguments were complex, and deserved reasoned consideration. Some were fear-based.

Syracuse newspapers agreed that anti-slavery literature might cause "alarm among those who live in the midst of a slave population," and consequently, could "beget a spirit of rebellion among the black population of the south..." [4]

Onondaga County Opposition Mounts

On September 30, the *Onondaga Standard* published an announcement of a public meeting in the city aimed at responding to the current northern agitation of the immediate emancipation of "the Slave population of the South." [5] The letter was signed by sixty residents of the county. Among the signers were Elijah Phillips and John Fleming, Jr. John Watson of Manlius, First Judge of Common Pleas, and attorney Hicks Worden of Fayetteville, attended the meeting. Spokesmen in the crowd charged emancipators as being reckless and dangerous, as intruding into "the domestic relations of the southern state," and endangering the Union. [6]

The *Onondaga Standard* published the VERITAS letter on October 7, which named the following twelve men of Fayetteville who endorsed the call for a statewide anti-slavery convention: "Rev. S. S. Smith, Rev. Oren Hyde, Rev. W Hutchinson, B. Hibbard, James Stewart, Philip Flint, John McViccar, D. Thompson, James Francis, Randal Palmer, Elijah Payne, Samuel Edwards." [7]

It is evident that Manlius townsmen were passionately divided over this issue, as they were elsewhere. While the majority of the population in hamlets, villages, and cities across Central New York in 1835, were undisturbed by such conflicts, the publicly exposed controversy in Fayetteville and Syracuse over emancipation raised many issues and fears long ignored. Here, however, the overwhelming majority did not silence the committed minority.

Differences of Opinion with Deep Roots

In his study of northern opposition to the anti-slavery movement, Lorman Ratner observed, "Quite unintentionally," abolitionists "had raised and aggravated a whole series of basic and complex issues." [8] Some southern slaveholders were still on hyperalert after the Nat Turner slave rebellion of 1831, in which over sixty white people were killed by rebelling slaves in Virginia. Sympathizers in Onondaga County felt compelled to reassure their southern brethren that these "mad abolitionists" did not represent widespread northern opinion. [9]

These conflicting views didn't start in 1835, nor were they caused by these few fervent, yet increasingly well-organized abolitionists of Boston, New York City, Utica, Peterboro, and Fayetteville, New York.

The states' rights argument was as old at the United States. Whether the individual sovereign states had agreed to form a union under a national flag or not, the binding nature of that federal cooperation was often challenged. It was a vortex of clashing personal and sectional interests, and tough figuring out how to keep it all in balance.

It wasn't just a "southern issue." Some New Yorkers cheered when Governor Martin Van Buren invoked states' rights reasoning to denounce the national bank as intruding into the duties and affairs of states. Other New Yorkers were only too happy to share in the benefits and rewards of canal and road improvements funded by state taxes, while many of their town neighbors resented their taxes being used to benefit a geographically advantaged few. [11]

The issue of slavery went back to the nation's beginnings. Donald G. Mathews traced its roots to a pragmatic compromise forged in the early Constitutional debates. Tolerance may have kept the nation from splitting apart, but it was a bad bargain that glossed over real sectional differences between northerners and southerners, condemning one enslaved race to be beasts of burden for another's comfort. [12] Expediency, it seemed, required all to turn a blind eye to an institution detested by many. The "sensitive scar tissue" that resulted, the author observed, never healed. [13]

The architects of the U. S. Constitution cannot solely be blamed for the cultivated prejudices and self-interests of generations that followed. In both North and South, there were many who feared the results of emancipation. Even a majority of those who believed slavery an unjust moral evil, did not believe the Negro should be entitled to the same civil rights and privileges granted to white citizens. [14] It was easier to blame abolitionists for exposing the injustice, than to face realities that fueled opposition.

It was easier for a resident in New York to believe that the issue had little to do with them, to blame slavery solely on the South. [15] What had the North to do with this southern problem? "A lot," abolitionists were saying. It was unpleasant to hear that even without ever intending to profit or benefit from this cruel institution, an employee in a cotton mill, or a customer of cotton, coffee or sugar products, might be complicit in it. Tragically, slave labor was the bedrock of economic and commercial profits throughout the nation.

All these complex issues, prejudices, and fears were now being exposed, and something had to be done.

CHAPTER SEVEN

....AND I WILL BE HEARD

> If we would preserve our liberties, we must check the first approaches of tyranny, whether clothed in the robes of office, or masked under the form of popular feelings. [1]
>
> *The Liberator*, 1835

What happened in Fayetteville and Utica was in part due to reformist impulses stimulated by revivalist experiences during the 1830s. It was also the fruit of the organizing abilities and relentless moral courage of William Lloyd Garrison. The efforts of the Quakers and the Manumission Society who focused on the issue for over two generations, preceded him, but Garrison was the right man at the right time - a professional agitator armed with a printing press. He founded the abolitionist newspaper *Liberator* in Boston in 1831, and in his first issue of January 1, 1831, he announced with eloquence and daring:

> I am in earnest – I will not equivocate-
> I will not excuse – I will not retreat a single inch.
> AND I WILL BE HEARD. [2]

And he was. Within a year he gathered a core group of citizens committed to anti-slavery goals into the New England

Anti-Slavery Society, and began to slowly mobilize a movement.

In one publication he exposed the "benevolent" American Colonization Society as deceptive, and racist. The colonization program, he said, was based on persuading slave-holders to voluntarily send their freed slaves back to Africa, a remedy made attractive because willing slave owners would be promised a reimbursement for their property loss. At the same time, it was a program that would decrease the number of free blacks as well.

This analysis awakened many conscientious Presbyterian, Methodist and Baptists in Central New York to rethink their gradualist anti-slavery sentiments and motivations.

Garrison's anti-colonization crusade "kindled a fire" and became a textbook campaign for abolitionists." [3] In December 1833, he launched the American Anti-Slavery Society, and within two years local anti-slavery societies were springing up in New Hampshire, Maine, Vermont, Rhodes Island, and all over Massachusetts. He reported success and resistance. His newspaper, supported more often by free blacks than sympathizing whites, exposed the nature and extent of slavery.

Utica soon became an abolitionist training outpost with reformers like Beriah Green at the helm of the Oneida Institute in Whitesboro. The Presbyterian-sponsored Oneida Institute was a manual labor school that mixed physical work with classical studies, and also as Green required, accepted black students. During 1834, anti-slavery organizing was gaining momentum in New York towns, colleges, seminaries and churches.

Lecturers and organizing agents were dispatched into Western New York setting in motion one of the greatest public education efforts ever unleashed. This propelling dynamic spun off of Garrison's early efforts ignited attentive hearts and minds in districts well-evangelized by Rev. Charles G. Finney and his admirers.

Slaveholders and their allies struck back in October 1835. In Utica, hundreds listened to resolutions and speeches at the Presbyterian Church. In Boston, a mob marched to breakup an assembly of women where William Lloyd Garrison was scheduled to deliver a speech.

The occasion was the first anniversary of the Boston Female Anti-Slavery Society meeting at Faneuil Hall. When a shouting crowd pressed closer toward the hall, Mary S. Parker, assembly president, urged Garrison to withdraw. Shortly after, the Mayor burst into the hall and warned the women he could guarantee them safety, only if they departed immediately. Agreeing to leave, the women, black and white, left together.

> Hisses, sarcastic cheers, and racial epithets assailed the procession...to Mrs. Chapman's house...seven blocks south. [4]

Garrison was captured, barely rescued from the mob, placed in jail and warned out of the city.

Onondaga County Begins to Organize

All this happened the same day the mob besieged the Bleecker Street Presbyterian Church in Utica where hundreds gathered to organize a New York State Anti-Slavery Society. But the anti-slavery campaigns continued. According to Myers' study of early New York anti-slavery agents and societies, New York State had 103 anti-slavery auxiliary societies by May of 1836. The following year it had 161 additional societies. [5]

The first year anniversary of New York's anti-slavery society was celebrated in October, 1836. Once again, of the Onondaga County delegates attending, the majority were from Fayetteville and Manlius. County delegates included, John McViccar, Horace Robins, Samuel Edwards, Philip Flint, Darlin Thompson, Stephen. S. Smith, Charles Clark, Seth Conklin, and W. W. Porter. The minutes, published in *Friend of Man*, show that McViccar was voted a county officer (Vice President) for the following year. [6] Rev. Amos Tuttle, the new pastor at Fayetteville Presbyterian Church where McViccar and Philip Flint were trustees, was sympathetic to the movement so the church doors continued to be open to anti-slavery lectures and meetings.

On March 15, 1837, Samuel L. Gould, an American Anti-Slavery Society agent, and Charles Stuart, came to Fayetteville and organized the Onondaga County Anti-Slavery Society.[7] Gould was fresh from surviving a mob attack launched at a meeting sponsored by the Poughkeepsie Anti-Slavery Society at Second Presbyterian Church. Attackers "swarmed the pulpit, ripped his clothes, and hit him with rocks as he sought shelter in the residence of his host, Dr. Thomas Hammond." [8] The mob then roamed the streets breaking windows.

Charles Stuart, an English-born citizen, was reared a Presbyterian. He came to Utica in 1822 where he taught, and later became principal at Utica Academy. A Finney revivalist, he mentored Theodore Weld, who organized "the holy band" of anti-slavery speakers. When Stuart accompanied Gould to Fayetteville, Theodore Weld's family had just moved from Apulia to Manlius.

In the first two years, despite organized resistance in Utica and Syracuse, a nucleus of Fayetteville, Manlius, and Pompey anti-slavery society members, had succeeded in expanding the membership within Onondaga County.

CHAPTER EIGHT

THE CENTER CANNOT HOLD

>...a convention is to be held at Auburn on the first of the month, of the twenty five presbyteries that were rescinded by the late general Assembly of the Presbyterian Church. Such divisions are generally unpleasant, but not always unprofitable...[1]
>
> *South Cortland Luminary*,
> August 3, 1837

The agitation against slavery, along with increasing theological differences that were considered by some as major deviations from orthodox theology, finally reached a boiling point in the Presbyterian General Assembly. Efforts by northern abolitionists to get the church to condemn slavery as an evil, and a sin, continued to alienate southern church members.

In the Manlius and Fayetteville Presbyterian churches, conflicts had surfaced regarding revivalist excesses and strategies to emancipate slaves. The Smith brothers exemplified one northern perspective in the conflict. Not only had they participated in the 1835 Utica convention that established the New York State Anti-Slavery Society, but eight months later, as independent members, they attended the Third Year Anniversary of the American Anti-Slavery Society in New York City.[2] John McViccar was listed in the 1837 national American Anti-

Slavery Report, as secretary of the local anti-slavery organization in the town of Manlius, where membership rose from 60 to 112. [3]

William Lloyd Garrison, however, was not making it easy on church-going abolitionists with his increasingly severe criticism of the clergy.

When the Presbyterian General Assembly met in Pittsburgh that June, the opposition barely succeeded in stifling the slavery debate by various manipulations. Finally, a majority decided to exclude the topic, declaring any further "consideration of slavery would tend to distract and divide our churches." On the question of whether the subject of slavery should be "indefinitely postponed," 154 delegates voted yes; 87 said no. [4] Among those who objected to this maneuver was Onondaga Presbytery delegate, John H. Lathrop. The Onondaga Presbytery, despite opposition, had managed to send one of its more liberal representatives to voice concern over the church's retreat from public witness. Such protests continued but the majority ruled the day. [5]

Theodore Weld was discouraged. Garrison was disgusted that Lyman Beecher, the foremost Presbyterian theologian, and President of Lane College, was speaking out against immediate emancipation. [6]

Defenders of orthodoxy, states' rights and gradualist emancipation, fearing the momentum would eventually swing against them, rallied their troops. They found allies prior to the General Assembly, who were willing to tolerate slavery for the sake of a greater good, which they called "harmony and union." They had devised means of silencing once and for all those heretical agitators and disturbers of the peace, most of whom came from the churches in New England, Western New York, and Ohio.

Southern backed conservatives simply muscled out synods and presbyteries where the loudest and insistent agitations and liberalisms were allowed to carry on their activities. Each side blamed the other. Lyman Beecher believed Southerners "got scared about abolition." He blamed Senator John C. Calhoun for conniving and stirring up resentments." [7] Southern Presbyterian theologian James Henly Thornwell, however, said the real issue was national unity. If the church divided over slavery, then civil bonds unifying states under one national allegiance would fall away. He blamed abolitionists and their "continued agitation of slavery" for such a fearful outcome. [8]

Robert H. Nichols, in writing a history of Presbyterianism in New York State, took the view that the Assembly found another reason to eject these churches. The Assembly justified its actions by pointing to "gross disorders" of these errant synods, even though some northern presbyteries and synods were as conservative as southerners in terms of theology. [9]

Nonetheless, it was a premeditated scheme. The conservative "Old School" delegates met in convention before the Assembly opened and perfected their legislation and tactic to eject four synods (Western Reserve, Utica, Geneva and Genesee). In doing so, as Paul Conkin pointed out, they rid themselves "of the four synods with the strongest abolitionist movements, the reform-oriented", and those "most tied to New England Congregationalism and the New Haven theology." [10]

Manlius and Fayetteville churches in the Onondaga Presbytery and the Geneva Synod, were thus thrown out of the General Assembly, along with Chenango, Cayuga, Tioga, Cortland,

Bath, Delaware and Chemung. These included 28 presbyteries, 599 churches, 509 ministers, and an estimated 50, 489 communicants. The Onondaga Presbytery had 18 ministers, 22 churches, and an estimated 2,559 communicants. [11]

Henceforth, these presbyteries were called "New School." Now that they were separated from their "Old School," and southern association, did these presbyteries give strong anti-slavery witness? Not necessarily, though many of the strongest, most persistent voices, clerical and laity, came from New School churches. Struggles continued within individual churches and presbyteries.

CHAPTER NINE

THE COTTON CONNECTION

> In 1845 the canal [Erie] carried east in quantities worthy of record, not only such materials as iron, lead, wool, leather, and potash, but also ironware, woolen and cotton cloth, furniture, brooms, glass, soap, candles and starch. [1]
>
> Victor S. Clark,
History of Manufacturers in the
United States, 1607-1860

A most striking feature of the 1840 Manlius Village horizon, according to Barber and Howe's state gazetteer, were the "cupolas" of three "cotton mills."[2] They were, in fact, the only cotton factories built in Onondaga County. While there were no cotton fields stretching along the rolling hills and valleys of

50   ALETHEA A. CONNOLLY

Central New York, textile manufacturing had rapidly expanded beyond New England's mill towns during the War of 1812. The fledgling American government stopped imports of manufactured goods from Britain, thus guaranteeing a favorable advantage for American-made products.

The waterways of the Mohawk Valley and Central New York offered an enticing opportunity to enterprising New Englanders, men from Massachusetts and Rhode Island with textile factory experience, who migrated westward. If textile manufacturing proved successful in New England, Onondaga County entrepreneurs might, as some speculated, capitalize on Limestone Creek water power and other assets to produce thread and cloth for a rapidly expanding population. Why not?

The Manlius Manufacturing Company was up and running on the southeast corner of what is now Seneca and Mills Streets by 1816. [3] In 1832, there were two cotton mills using 2,160 spindles that made 460, 000 yards of cloth annually. [4]

Manlius farmer, Orson Smith, reminisced how fascinated he and his sister Abigail were when they examined cotton bought at Azariah Smith's store, paying one dollar for four pounds.

> We never had seen a pound before
> and asked mother if it grew on sheep,
> was told no, on stalks like milk weeds.
> This was the best cotton we ever see...[5]

Making a profit, however, was a challenge, and at times a great disappointment. Cotton prices rose and fell. Competition in a national and global market increased. As early as 1815, the Manlius Manufacturing Company had petitioned the U. S.

House of Representatives to pass protective legislation against imported cotton products.[6] Britain imported 75% of her cotton from the South. Southern cotton producers cried foul, saying this forced them to buy high priced British products, and discouraged British purchase of raw cotton from them. While some mutually beneficial alliances were promoted, the market goals of New England, Middle Atlantic, Southern, and West were often at odds with each other, and the South blamed their shrinking cotton profits on northern political alliances.

In 1845, there were two factories in operation in Manlius and production had increased to 635, 931 yards of cloth.[7] In 1850, the Manlius Factory used 135,000 pounds of raw cotton. The Limestone mill used 138,600 pounds.[8] That year there were 15 men and 28 women employed at the Manlius Factory, and 43 females and 28 males at the Limestone Manufacturing Co.[9]

Factory work was long and tedious, but for some poor women it was an opportunity. Nancy Woloch's study of factory workers, noted that the mills saved some women "from a hopeless poverty," and taught many young women "regularity" and "industry," and other habits of good order.[10] Some large companies, including the Manlius Factory, ran company boarding houses, which she maintained, offered "an unusual combination of opportunities: income, independence, and community."[11]

Still, whenever prices for a company's cotton goods dropped, proprietors sometimes staved off a shutdown by lowering the wages of their workers. This happened in 1843, when one of the Manlius cotton factories lowered wages for its women workers, promising to raise them when profits returned. A year later, when their wages still remained low, despite increasing profits, the women protested they could not continue to work without the return to their former wage level. One operative reported, they were "driven from the boarding house," but responded quickly in a public protest, marching through the village "carrying banners inscribed "Equal Rights." [12]

Increasingly, children were employed for many of the tedious jobs requiring skills to maneuver in and around the looms. Factory rooms, often poorly ventilated, with lint drifting through the rooms were not healthy environments.

The viewpoint of one boy who worked in a Manlius cotton mill was published in Barber & Howe's historical overview of New York, and later repeated in Henry C. Van Schaack's history of Manlius Village. Young James O. Rockwell's memory of the drudgery is not a cheery one. While "employed in tending a picking machine," he made drawings and wrote rhymes. One image depicted "an overseer" who was "dragging a boy towards the door" with the following verse under it.

> The factory life
> Is full of strife;
> I own I hate it dearly;
> And every boy
> That they employ
> Will own the same, or nearly. [13]

While the factory worker experienced strife, cotton manufacturing partners discovered the business was very competitive and precarious as global markets of raw cotton, and cotton products expanded. Some partners went into debt and sold out to others.

Smith recalled that even Azariah Smith, a smart businessman with extensive investment in Manlius cotton operations, had his ups and downs. Azariah, he said, "made more blunders and on a larger scale" than others. According to Smith, Deacon Sherman confessed to him one day when he was buying apples, that he had "bought eighteen shares of this factory stock at $50 a share." It was not a wise investment, as the Deacon confessed that when he sold his shares, "he got only $50 for his total stock." [14] If women mill workers felt cheated a few years earlier, some of the investors weren't happy with their unexpected losses either. In 1850, Manlius Factory agent Franklin May claimed in his testimony that the factory hadn't made "any profits or income" for some time. [15]

While the Manlius cotton mill operations suffered serious setbacks, those in New York Mills near Utica, and those in Lowell, Massachusetts, and Rhode Island, thrived and expanded. So too did all their interrelated enterprises. In fact, Noble Prize-winning economist, Douglass C. North put it bluntly, "cotton" is what "helped tie the country together." But, the other side of this economic growth, he said," exacted a severe and tragic human price through slavery and the prejudicial treatment of free blacks." [16]

When abolitionists came through Western and Central New York towns and spoke about the emancipation of slaves, they were at times refused a church or meeting place in which to speak. There were many reasons for opposition, but it is reasonable to suggest that such righteous denunciation of slave ownership and labor touched a sensitive nerve in a village with cotton mills.

Most town consumers, businessmen, sellers and buyers, mill owners and mill workers, did not make any connection between King Cotton and slave labor in the South, and themselves. This was not unusual. Certainly, few wanted to be associated with such a miserable implication, but even the few, who at this time made such connections also didn't want to step into their neighbor's private business. Better the blind eye, some believed.

For Isaac, Esther, Philip, Robert, Jenny, Jane, Ebenezer, Prince, Whitington, David, and Peggy, and other ex-slaves that had lived and worked in Manlius, and for those who remained in the town after 1827, the blind eye was a familiar practice. [17]

In May 1835, Rev. Samuel J. May, a Unitarian minister, attended the Anti-Slavery Society Meeting in New York City, when a prominent merchant approached him outside. The merchant agreed slavery was an unfortunate situation, but economies of the South and North had "adjusted to it." Any rupture would be disastrous. In other words, "business necessity" compelled them to intervene.

> ....we do not mean to allow you to succeed. We mean, sir,...to put you Abolitionists down,—by fair means if we can, by foul means it [if] we must.[18]

Anti-abolitionists, North and South, mobilized. Still, by the third anniversary meeting of the American Anti-Slavery Society, members in local anti-slavery societies in Manlius had doubled.

The *Seceders* 55

"The Riot in Philadelphia"

May 17th 1838

Dear Bro. Myrick:

I hasten to inform you, that the Pennsylvania Hall, lately erected on this city, and consecrated to free discussion and the cause of humanity, is now wrapped in flames as the effect of mob violence, and probably not less than twenty thousand people out in the streets, attempting to witness the scene...

Last evening, the meeting was addressed by Angelina E. Grimke Weld, in a peculiarly eloquent and impressive manner.

Previous notice had been given, that she would speak; and so great was the excitement that the house was filled at an early hour; even every nook and corner. The congregation would number 3,500, while multitudes went away who could not get in.

The meeting was repeatedly disturbed during the evening by savage yells without and the dashing of windows with stones and brick-bats...the street on which the Hall stood had been lined with mobocrats.

The work of destruction commenced about 8 o'clock this evening...by 9 o'clock, they had the Hall of Free Discussion in flames...

I had the pleasure of attending the wedding of Brother Weld and Sister Angelina E. Grimke last Monday evening; - about 40 distinguished abolitionists of both sexes were present....

Yours, for the perishing,
J. Cross [1]

(Union Herald, May 25, 1838)

CHAPTER TEN

AN UNCOMMON MARRIAGE

...for the teacher of the Seventy was
Weld; their method was the evangelism
of the Great Revival... [2]

Gilbert Hobbs Barnes
The Antislavery Impulse, 1830-1844

When Ludovicus Weld retired from his pastorate at Apulia in July 1837, he moved with his wife Elizabeth and daughter Cornelia, to Manlius, where they joined Trinity Presbyterian Church. What details the parents knew of Theodore's dangerous anti-slavery preaching during the mid-1830s is not clear. Some reports published in anti-slavery weekly newspapers noted their son was many times stoned "even while he spoke from the pulpit." [3] Perhaps a good thing not to know. Both the Manlius and Fayetteville Presbyterian churches then still had strong anti-slavery supporters among their members, despite the departure of the Smith clergymen.

Theodore Weld was considered by Wendell Phillips as "the genius of Abolition revival." He was Rev. Ludovicus Weld's eldest son. [4] As a young man, Theodore had traveled in the south and became appalled at slavery. Not long after his return, at his aunt Sophia Clark's urging, he attended a revival in Utica directed by Rev. Charles Finney. [5] His conversion and internship with Finney expanded his zealous preaching. He had great success in many places in Ohio and Pennsylvania. He brought his lecture tour to Utica four months after the mob had broken up the state organizing meeting. He met success in some towns, but hostility in others.

Weld became an inspirational instructor of a "holy band" of reformers who he trained revival-style in a stirring set of sixteen lectures. The task, and intense use of his voice in these lectures, ended his speaking career. "Shortly after the close of the convention, he collapsed, burnt out." [6]

Many of his friends were shocked when he announced in 1838 he planned to marry Angelina Grimke of Philadelphia, a most outspoken and unorthodox Quaker woman. Angelina defied social standards, speaking in public to both women's and mixed gender audiences, about slavery and women's rights, though initially the latter had not been her intent. When taken to task by Catherine Beecher, Rev. Lyman Beecher's daughter for so doing, she wrote back to Miss Beecher, "investigation of the rights of the slave has led me to a better understanding of my own..." [7]

Years before Theodore met the Grimke sisters, Angelina and Sarah, had lived on the family plantation in South Carolina. Sister Sarah, the eldest, accompanied her father to Philadelphia, and when he died there, she remained. Angelina came several years later. There, they joined the Hicksite Quaker community and began association with the small, but fervent women's anti-slavery group. Angelina gradually gained confidence in her speaking skills. At Weld's invitation, the sisters were the only two women present when he gave his revivalist instructions to his "seventy" anti-slavery society agents. [8]

Boston abolitionist Ann Weston questioned, "what man would wish to have such a wife?" [9]

Angelina was surprised by the reactions of colleagues to their announcement. She told Theodore some of her friends were "almost *offended* that I should do such a thing as to get married," believing we are both "public property." [10]

Theodore and Angelina celebrated their wedding in Philadelphia on May 14, 1838 attended by friends Gerrit Smith, William Lloyd Garrison, Alvan Stewart, the poet James Whittier, and other well-known abolitionists, and two ex-slaves of her father that her sister Anna had freed. Shortly after, Angelina spoke at the women's anti-slavery convention meeting in the city. The unruly crowd gathering in the streets outside was as huge as those listening intently inside the building. Mob intimidation was alive and well in Philadelphia. The next day the liberty bell atop the Pennsylvania State House tolled the alarm, but to no avail. "By midnight," as author Henry Mayer described the scene, "only the blackened granite walls remained." [11]

This uncommon couple then traveled to Manlius to visit Theodore's parents.[12] If Theodore's father wondered about his new daughter-in-law's dangerous ventures and opinions on equality of rights, public speaking, and the promotion of immediate emancipation of slaves, he seemed to have expanded his mind or graciousness and accepted her, according to Theodore. It is likely, Elizabeth Clark Weld, Theodore's mother, and a wide circle of Clark cousins, gave the couple, and sister Sarah, a warm welcome. Anti-slavery commitment was supported in many Clark family households.

On the women's side, Sophia Clark, who married Elizabeth's brother Erastus, was an active member of a woman's moral reform association in Utica.[13] Both she, and her nephew Theodore, were inspired to activism by the religious revivals of Charles G. Finney. Theodore's first cousin, William M. Clark, who met his wife when living in Manlius in 1837, began aiding fugitive slaves to escape to Canada with his cousin Edwin in Oswego, two years later. Like Theodore, William spent some of his youth in the South, witnessing slavery first hand there.[14]

When Theodore announced his engagement to his parents, he wrote with delight to Angelina, that their "forebodings" were for naught as the Welds accepted their daughter-in-law "with exceeding tenderness and warmest welcome."[15]

The marriage of Quaker Angelina to Presbyterian Theodore had consequences, however, and sister Sarah writing from Manlius to friend Elizabeth Pease about the wedding, told her both Angelina and she "will be disowned." She seemed not disturbed by exclusion from the Hicksite Quaker community, and simply noted that "We feel no regret at this circumstance..."[16]

Weld's colleagues worried his family life might diminish his prominent role in the abolitionist cause, because he no longer lectured. He did not drop out of the movement, however, but turned his talent and energies toward writing and publishing. He had done so in 1837, when he published *The Bible Against Slavery*, but his joint literary effort in 1839 with Angelina and Sarah, proved to be a blockbuster. *American Slavery As I See It: Testimony of a Thousand Witnesses*, a collection of personal narratives, eye-witness accounts, and items clipped directly from southern newspapers, exposed and contradicted any perception of slavery being a benign institution. Many editors feared to publish it. Although it was an extraordinary educational tool, it was also a powerful propaganda tool.

In 1841, Angelina wrote to Lewis Tappan, a powerful New York City merchant also committed to ending slavery, explaining the complicity of northern manufacturers and all those who "deal in the products of slave labor." The slaveholder, she explained, " is only one partner in a large firm," but the company is tied "to all those who reap the comforts and conveniences from such chattel bondage." [17]

"American slavery," was, as Alvan Stewart succinctly described," a pyramid of crime." [18]

CHAPTER ELEVEN

CONFLICT IN FAYETTEVILLE, NEW YORK

> I am well-satisfied with the constitution as it is, ...and certainly do not wish it amended for the purpose of placing persons of color upon an equality as to voting, with our white citizens. [1]
>
> Governor Marcy, Albany, N. Y.
> October 13, 1838

Ever since the New York State Anti-Slavery Society was launched in 1835, energetic, talented individuals turned evangelical enthusiasm into devising strategies to achieve their goals. Abolitionists in Peterboro, Cazenovia, Fayetteville, Manlius and Pompey kept in touch with each other through meetings, letters, and since 1836, abolitionist newspapers.

Leaders emerged locally and statewide, but disagreements, as might be expected, also arose among them. After four years, some abolitionist leaders, frustrated that their church leaders refused to publicly reject slave ownership, sought other means to advance immediate emancipation. Gerrit Smith of Peterboro and Rev. Luther Myrick of Cazenovia, publisher of the *Union Herald,* had lost patience with their Presbyterian leaders. Rather than be complicit in what they believed a moral evil, Smith and Myrick formally withdrew from "pro-slavery" church affiliations. With a small group of followers, they started forming Union congregations that rejected tolerance of slave selling and slave ownership. They were convinced sincere Christian abolitionists should "come out" of churches where tolerance of slaveholding made them complicit in the sin of slavery. William Goodell, editor of *Friend of Man*, an abolitionist newspaper, also believed an association of non-denominational Christians was essential.

However, their efforts did not convince a majority of churchgoers to abandon their church denominations.

Furthermore, a core group within the New York State organization came to believe that moral persuasion and educational efforts were failing to effect results. They decided that the ballot box was the best way to get emancipation and legal rights for freed slaves. Goodell, Smith, Alvan Stewart, James Birney, and L. P. Noble began to shift to this strategy. Myrick was not convinced electoral politics was a wise strategy. Neither was William Lloyd Garrison. Nor Theodore Weld who chose not to bind himself to any political organization.

The first ballot box strategy was to promote questioning prospective candidates in the major parties as to their anti-slavery positions. Questionnaires were lengthy and demanded unequivocal pledges. Some candidates refused to comply, and the effort proved disappointing, ineffective, and hopeless.

Gerrit Smith sharply criticized Whig and Democrat candidates, calling them captives of pro-slavery powers. Unless candidates answered satisfactorily all questions, he maintained, such candidates should not be supported by "true" abolitionists. Smith was then presiding leader of the New York State Anti-Slavery Society. This criteria was questioned by some who did not agree with this standard for judging who were authentic abolitionists.

Such a definition seemed to mandate that immediate emancipation be the single priority issue a "true" abolitionist must use in his voting decision. It required men to abandon their party affiliations whenever their party's candidate position was in doubt, and to disregard all other issues that might be current subjects of concern and interest.

When some anti-slavery society members chose to act on their own, and exercise freedom of conscience to choose the best candidate within the Whig or Democratic party, they were publicly rebuked by state central coordinating leaders. This conflict erupted at an anti-slavery meeting presided over by John McViccar in the village of Manlius, on January 8, 1839. [2]

John McViccar, a Fayetteville merchant, was one of the founding members of Fayetteville's Presbyterian Church in 1830. He was a successful businessman, investing in local grist mills, saw mills, a tannery and shoe store, and with Sardis Ward, "opened one of several warehouses built on the Erie Canal." [3] He was active in the local anti-slavery movement before it crystallized into a state organization in October 1835.

At the New York State Anti-Slavery Society meeting in Utica, October 20, 1836, McViccar was named a Vice President representative for Onondaga County, the same day Gerrit Smith was chosen President by the over 400 attending delegates. The event marked the first anniversary of the Utica anti-slavery convention. [4]

When English abolitionist Charles Stuart helped Samuel Gould inaugurate a county-wide organization in March 1837, delegates met at Brother McViccar's house where agents expressed their thanks for the generous collection of "nearly 80 dollars" being donated to the American Anti-Slavery Society.[5] It was a substantial donation for these times. The group asked that Brother George Storrs, a Methodist minister from the New Hampshire Anti-Slavery Society, attend their next meeting. Storrs was one of two ministers censured in May 1836 by the Methodist Episcopal Conference in Cincinnati for his lecturing on immediate emancipation in the town just prior to the assembly.[6]

Now four years after the state organization was founded, some leaders wanted to change the focus of abolitionist strategies, and urged others to abandon their traditional church and party affiliations. Such recommendations became more demanding and objectionable to other members. On January 8, 1839, McViccar refused to follow the more radical path being taken by abolitionist colleagues. He had no intention of leaving the Fayetteville Presbyterian Church, nor did he choose to abandon his Whig political allegiance to candidates he believed worthy of election. This brought him into conflict with Gerrit Smith and the central committee, who were urging the state organization agenda toward a more explicit political abolitionist position.

Among those reported as attending the meeting were Rev. Amos C. Tuttle, pastor of the Fayetteville Presbyterian Church, James C. Fuller, a Quaker from Skaneateles, Charles Sedgwick of Pompey, Darlin Thompson, William Eager, Esq., Baptist Elder Jacob Blaine, Baptist preacher J. N. T. Tucker, Rev. Ludovicus Weld, and Rev. A. C. Lathrop.

The one day meeting got off to a smooth start. The organization's constitution was accepted. Then Rev. Tucker requested to read a letter written to him by Gerrit Smith telling reasons why he chose not to attend this meeting. Despite some objection, Tucker read Smith's letter, which called this county group a "Pro-Slavery Party." Several members were deeply offended. Rev. Tuttle called for a censure of Smith, but this motion failed. Arguments ensued. McViccar rejected an accusation that he improperly promoted the election of party men who were not abolitionists.

The dispute escalated. McViccar defended Victory Birdseye, the former congressman and the Whig candidate seeking re-election to New York State Assembly, as an abolitionist, regardless of whether or not Mr. Birdseye had answered questions posed to candidates about their abolitionist views. In addition, he defended his own "right to vote for such men as he saw proper."

J. N. T. Tucker disputed McViccar's actions based, he said, on the fact that the State Convention had mandated that members vote at the polls only for men who they as voters would have the "full assurance" of their abolitionist positions. How could this be, if such candidates did not respond to questions submitted, he challenged.

Charles Sedgwick rose to his feet. "I cannot sit still," he declared, "and hear Mr. Birdseye so slandered and vilified..." Sedgwick said Birdseye was "a member of the Pompey Anti-Slavery Society," a man who had already advanced the cause of "the colored man," and helped "secure the rights he now enjoys." [7] Sedgwick announced he was "not willing to be controlled by the ultraism of the leading men of the society." Soon after, president McViccar resigned his seat, and Rev. Amos C. Tuttle withdrew from the society.

J. N. T. Tucker, then taking on duties of meeting secretary, arranged and sent the minutes to the *Union Herald*, and they were published in the February 9, 1839 issue. Tucker was considered a talented journalist and preacher, a fervent abolitionist, and known to be particularly antagonistic to the Whig Party. He endorsed Gerrit Smith's leadership and, whether from unrestrained zeal, or poor judgment, his actions aggravated serious differences of opinion within the membership.[8] The wound was deeper than some chose to admit.

Donald Mathews, in his introduction to *Agitation For Freedom*, observed that members often got carried away with rhetoric, oratory, and personal opinions. They overstated their case, preferring at times to "confront their opponents and polarize," opinions, rather than "conciliate" their differences.[9] Perhaps among unfriendly audiences, this tactic worked, but among colleagues, public humiliation had dubious benefits.

William M. Clark, who coordinated anti-slavery supporters at Manlius Presbyterian Church early in the movement, was not happy about this flare-up. He mentioned the incident in a letter to Gerrit Smith. Smith acknowledged the incident and estrangement, but reminded Clark, that he had not brought the letter to the public meeting, nor did he report the meeting to the newspaper. These, he said, "were published by Elder Tucker - not by myself. I believe they acted with good intent," he wrote, "but acted wrongly."[10]

This explanation, and Tucker's later comments, did not immediately mend the breach opened within the local county movement. McViccar, Tuttle, and Clark do not appear as attending the next meeting. Tucker's February report confessed there was some fear the episode was a sharp setback to organizing a county-wide anti-slavery society, but he minimized the harm done, and reported Gerrit Smith regretted his language was misunderstood as labeling county officers as "lovers of slavery" because they cast "pro-slavery votes." Patching up hurt feelings was one thing, but backing away from a newly charted strategy was another. Moving forward, Tucker wrote some men "recanted their support" of Birdseye and Seward in the recent election, and denounced their old political party loyalties, and he hoped that Mr. Clark would do likewise. [11]

Such public divisiveness was troubling. Personal ambitions and egos sometimes ruptured the thin membrane binding members together in the local, state and national anti-slavery movement. How to bring together, and sustain, a working army of fiercely independent men, was no small task. Business meetings hosting society speakers were often crammed with prepared resolutions leaving little time for adequate discussion. There were many strong-minded, talented local individuals, as well as state committee leaders, all convinced their voices must be heard, their opinions acknowledged. It is no wonder consensus was hard to build and sustain.

Such conflicts were grist for partisan newspapers. The *Republican Monitor* of Cazenovia, a Whig publication, charged Gerrit Smith in its November 27, 1838 issue with accusing supporters of William H. Seward and Victory Birdseye, Whig Party candidates, of being "pro-slavery men" and "sheep stealers." [12] Smith's remarks, they said, were made at an anti-slavery meeting held in Cazenovia on October 31.

John Fairchild, editor of the Whig newspaper, to support his accusations, accompanied his report with an article reprinted on the same page from *Colored American*. *Colored Amer-*

ican was published between 1836 and 1842 in New York City by, and for, colored readers. Its primary goal was the advancement of free colored people and peaceful emancipation of slaves.

The excerpt reprinted in the *Monitor* expressed disapproval of the infighting it saw going on among abolitionists. It found dogmatic and dictatorial claims of one faction over another distasteful and harmful. While agreeing that abolitionists are bound to "vote for the best men," this did not require a man, the paper counseled, to sacrifice his judgment to some "powers that be" because all the candidates do not come up to his standard. [13]

While the motive of the *Monitor's* editor for publishing this viewpoint may have been primarily partisan, the public display of abrasive divisions within the anti-slavery organization had far-reaching effects among black and white supporters.

CHAPTER TWELVE

A CLASH OF TITANS

THE AMERICAN ANTI-SLAVERY SOCIETY

1840 -1841

> We fully believe that the third party movement will be a failure; but, time alone must determine... we have acted in perfect harmony. But the cord is broken – the bonds are sundered, and God alone foresees the result...They have, doubtless, acted in good faith. We pass no censure. [1]
>
> Rev. Luther Myrick,
> Quoted in *National Anti-Slavery Standard*

While local Onondaga County abolitionists weighed the pros and cons of shifting ideologies, strategies, and allegiances, cracks widened within the parent organization. William Lloyd Garrison catapulted the slavery issue into national prominence when he launched the Boston-based publication, *The Liberator,* in 1831, a publishing venture he first tested with members of the city's black community. He hoped, as biographer Henry Mayer expressed Garrison's vision, to "redeem the nation's patriotic creed by making 'every statue leap from its pedestal' and rouse the apathetic with a trumpet call that would 'hasten the resurrection of the dead.'" [2]

Garrison initiated the founding meeting of the American Anti-Slavery Society in Philadelphia in 1833. Between 1834 - 1836, an energetic recruitment campaign fanned out from New England into New York and westward, which inspired the creation of hundreds of auxiliary societies. The New York State Anti-Slavery Society was one of its powerful foundlings. After several years of intense engagement, Garrison's analysis and views of reform needs changed. He began incorporating elements of a non-resistant philosophy into his abolitionist newspaper, and this disturbed some members.

Garrison believed a systemic corruption flawed the nation's constitutional government, leading him to reject political parties, elections, and voting as means to achieve reform. Many agreed that human institutions were often corrupted by self-perpetuating inequalities, but his attacks on such fundamental institutions unnerved some of his supporters, especially those seeking pragmatic means to advance emancipation goals through legislatures and the courts.

In addition, his attacks on clergy seemed vengeful. Some conservatives disliked his fraternizing with blacks in public and social gatherings. Many were offended by his inclusion of women participants in reform organizations. A few wanted to open the focus of the abolitionist newspaper, *The Liberator*, toward political strategies. This growing discontent within the membership finally led to confrontation.

A scheme to redirect control of the movement, and newspaper, surfaced early in 1839. It came during the Massachusetts Anti-Slavery Society annual meeting on January 23, 1839. Henry B. Stanton, a new agent employed by the society, led the charge challenging Garrison. The precipitous maneuver failed, but Garrison was stung when he saw grave disloyalties within his executive committee, and by Stanton.

Months later, at the July 31- August 2, 1839 national anti-slavery convention in Albany, several New York political abolitionists again pushed the agenda for a separate abolitionist political party. They failed to get a full endorsement. Garrison led the opposition, viewing party politics as a deviation and distraction from the movement's original strategy. A majority of members agreed with Garrison.

Editor William Goodell reported in *Friend of Man* that "much diversity" existed at the Albany convention. That was an understatement. Goodell and New York colleagues eagerly promoted the third party movement. Garrison argued vigorously against it, saying moral suasion efforts should be continued. He protested any resolutions asserting abolitionists now had "a duty" to go to the polls to validate their anti-slavery beliefs. He had no faith in electoral politics. He also objected to the exclusion of women from the convention, saying "all persons" should have been invited to attend. [3]

Those eager to organize a third party at the Albany convention backed off for the moment. With so much diversity, tension, and ambition, the center could not hold. The showdown occurred at the May 12-15, 1840 meeting in New York City.

The straw placed on the already laden camel's back was Abby Kelley. Kelley was an energetic member of the New England Anti-Slavery Society, and a Quaker. Early in the meeting, she was appointed to the business committee, an act which ignored traditional gender spheres of activity for men and women in public. Lewis Tappan, a wealthy supporter, and other key members, refused to serve on the committee. As the meeting proceeded with resolutions read and voted upon, Tappan with a substantial number of supporters retreated downstairs and founded a rival anti-slavery group. [4]

While Quaker poet James Whittier wrote to his sister reporting, "Our friend Abby...was the bombshell that *exploded* the society," she was only the last, dramatic straw that gave dissenting members the opportunity to break away and forge their own course of action. [5]

The schism that resulted also caused black members, especially clergy members, to redefine loyalties, as some did not want a total break with their congregations. Some chose to affiliate with the new AFASS created by Lewis Tappan, but many did not want to sever relations with Garrison. [6]

Author McKivigan believes the accomplishments of the American and Foreign Anti-Slavery Society, a more moderate church-friendly organization that arose when Lewis Tappan seceded from the parent AASS, is vastly under-acclaimed by historians of the early anti-slavery movement.[7] He notes, in its first year of operation in 1840, the primary leadership of the AFASS was conducted by men affiliated with Congregational, New School Presbyterian, Baptist, and Methodist Episcopal Churches. [8]

It was evident that ministers in the Manlius and Pompey Congregational and Presbyterian Churches had provided strong leadership in the mid-1830s, but after 1836, despite courageous efforts by AFASS members to promote anti-slavery reform through their churches, conferences, presbyteries, and assemblies, the results were by the mid- 1840s, terribly disappointing, and disillusioning. The resistance was too strong.

Meanwhile, those seeking to devote time and energy to the ballot box strategy (Alvan Stewart, Gerrit Smith, William Goodell, and James Birney) intensified their efforts to attract support and establish a new political party dedicated to abolitionist goals.

These factions within the anti-slavery movement were forced to compete for membership and financial support. Still, there may have been some positive outcomes to this fragmentation. Since it was now clear that this monumental task confronted formidable resistance, different approaches might prove beneficial. Multiple strategies and approaches might add new members, if only faction spokesmen would tone down their antagonisms and stop sniping at each other. That generous disposition was hard to maintain.

CHAPTER THIRTEEN

SILENCING DEBATE IN THE CHURCHES

> There as in all the country, the Churches and political parties were adapted to slavery as it was, and were unwilling to be disturbed by it. Indeed, it was the judgment of these bodies that the prosperity of both Church and State demanded that the old state of things be undisturbed. [1]
>
> Rev. Jermain Loguen,
> A.M.E. Zion, Syracuse, New York

For those trying to advance anti-slavery sentiments within their mainstream denominations, the task seemed like rolling a jagged boulder uphill each day. John McViccar had some early success in Fayetteville's Presbyterian Church before the denomination split into New School and Old School divisions in 1837. Each year since, anti-slavery supporters and sympathizers struggled with conservative colleagues in the local church and Onondaga Presbytery to select a representative who would bring a strong voice on the issue to the annual New School Assembly. While the schism two years earlier had divided the conservative, Old School (most slave-holding southern synods being members in Old School), from the more liberal northern and western New School, positions were not that clearly defined.

"New School" presbyteries, including those of Central New York, were generally more repulsed by slavery, but were not unified in what to do about it. Many did not support radical abolitionist goals and tactics. The Synods had suffered a shocking blow when ejected by the General Assembly in 1837. Many clergymen wanted the issue to just disappear off the agenda, but several individual presbyteries persisted in sending resolutions on the subject. No matter how conservative members tried to avoid dealing with the issue, some action had to be taken.

On May 16, 1839, John McViccar, neither a Garrisonian radical nor a third party enthusiast, was commissioned with Rev. Alvah Day from Lenox in Madison County, to represent the Onondaga Presbytery at the national General Assembly in Philadelphia.

Delegates were quick to coalition with like-minded members to advance their positions and increase their voting strength. Not surprisingly, one faction joined forces to silence discussion on the disruptive slavery question, this time by seeking a vote to rescind an earlier decision. The General Assembly had, at a prior annual meeting, allowed lower presbyteries and synods the authority to decide their own position on slavery. At the time, the General Assembly thought it the best way to avoid future arguments on the subject during the national meeting. Since then, however, a wide spectrum of conflicting resolutions had been passed in presbyteries across the country. This year, a vote was proposed to eliminate the local option, which would then hamper future efforts by abolitionists to push resolutions on to the agenda.

McViccar and Day, with forty-one other members, sought to ward off this maneuver. They failed, but protests kept the dispute alive. Dissatisfaction must have been high, as two "interlocutory meetings" (private informal sessions) were held, and finally the Assembly agreed to continue to let lower agencies decide what would be the best way "to remove the evil." [2]

When C. C. Goen studied New School and Old School Presbyterian experiences after the schism in 1837, he concluded that New School, while having many conservative clergy and members, "harbored - and heeded many voices of anti-slavery while the Old School refused to discuss it." [3] McViccar and Day's efforts exemplified that claim, since despite great resistance, anti-slavery supporters tenaciously preserved the right, ensuring local channels would be available to speak out on slavery, if only those chosen to attend would do so.

When abolitionists pushed harder than a local church or presbytery was willing to go, they ended up like Luther Myrick, out of the church. Rev. Abishai Scofield, a graduate of Auburn Theological Seminary, pursued his staunch abolitionist views, which was easier during the early 1840s when he ministered at the Presbyterian Church in Peterboro. However, in the mid-1840s, he publicly denounced the Presbyterian Church for giving fellowship to slaveholders, and not long after, was tried and convicted by the Onondaga Presbytery. After leaving the Presbyterian Church, he created a Free Church in Hamilton, New York. [4]

Sometimes a group of members from a local congregation took steps to voluntarily leave their church affiliation, if they felt the church failed to stand strongly against slavery and slave-holding. On May 25, 1838, Syracuse was the scene of such rebellion. On that day Charles A. Wheaton, Seth Mann, Ezra Stiles, Dr. John W. Hanchett, and George Smith defied Presbyterian leaders who demanded abolitionist sentiments be excluded from the pulpit, and left the Presbyterian church and organized the First Congregational Church of Syracuse. [5]

John H. Lathrop, who represented the Onondaga Presbytery at the contentious General Assembly meeting in Pittsburgh in 1837, joined them and was elected a deacon. Wheaton, Mann, and Smith were elected Elders. In a show of solidarity with this new anti-slavery congregation, Rev. Albert D. Peck, a local Methodist Episcopal minister, appalled by his own church leaders maneuvers to silence abolitionist voices, took part in the ceremony. [6]

The Mighty, Mighty Pen

When Wesley Bailey and his family arrived in Fayetteville in August 1839 with the *Luminary* printing press, the local option victory in the Presbyterian Church had recently been won in Philadelphia, and the anti-slavery movement, nationally and locally, was embroiled in its own factional arguments. He had witnessed similar conflicts in church communities in Cortlandville and Homer, but his primary focus now was the Methodist Episcopal Church, and similar internal conflicts broke out at their Annual and General Conferences.

Anti-slavery tensions erupted in the Oneida and Black River Conferences in the mid-1830s. While numerous Methodist Episcopal anti-slavery clergymen continued to urge the church to recommit to its early strong condemnations, presiding bishops took steps between 1836-1840 to stifle public discussion within annual conferences. [7] Bishop Elijah Hedding, formerly of the New England Conference, had moved to New York, and during 1837 visited northern and western conferences in the state. He believed anti-slavery arguments only aggravated existing disharmony. [8]

When the Oneida Conference met at Cortlandville in August, 1837, many attendees wanted an open discussion of slavery resolutions sent from New York Mills and Auburn. Hedding lectured the assembly that debate on the subject would be unwise. He urged members to "abstain from all abolition movements and associations." [9] Those wanting open discussion at Cortlandville lost the vote 30 to 43, but the tally showed positions of the ordained members were by no means unanimous. [10]

The following year, the Annual Conference met in Ithaca. The New England Conference sent a request to the New York Conference asking the assembly to approve their statement excluding slavery from the Methodist Episcopal Church. The resolution was read, then laid on the table, the same tactical procedure used in Congress to bury it by inaction.

Rev. Albert D. Peck, whose family resided in DeWitt, was disgusted with these high-handed manipulations. A member of the Black River Conference, he was assigned to Syracuse in 1838. He wrote his wife, exasperated by what was going on, saying he wasn't sure he would be a Methodist preacher much longer, as "'head-quarters was laying "a heavy hand upon abolitionism wherever it can be done." [11] Though only ordained a few years, Rev. Peck pledged not to yield "an iota of what I deem essential to anti-slavery principles." [12]

Manlius and Fayetteville Methodist Episcopal congregations were in the Oneida Conference's Cazenovia District. The Manlius Methodist Episcopal church reported a steady membership of between 130-155 during these years, while the Fayetteville congregation grew much slower during the 1830s when they were troubled by financial problems and dissension.

In 1840, Rev. Elias Bowen was presiding elder of churches in the Cazenovia District. Rev. Horace Tremaine supplied preaching in Fayetteville, and Rev. Benajah Mason was assigned to Manlius.[13] That year the Methodist Episcopal Annual Conference was in Baltimore. When representatives of New England's Conference continued to pressure the chairman to bring anti-slavery petitions to the floor, their requests were blocked.

Rev. Lewis Curts examined the history of Methodist Episcopal General Conferences, and concluded that when bishops assumed powers never committed to them to stifle anti-slavery agitation they "only added fuel to the fire, until it set the whole Church ablaze."[14]

Bailey watched and published. He applauded dissenting Methodist Episcopal clergy, especially their decision to form an anti-slavery society. The Reformed Methodists had long ago charged bishops with overstepping their powers and denying their own members a right to speak through the channels provided to them. Here bishops were, Reformed Methodists believed, doing that again, when they avoided restating their earlier condemnation of slaveholding so as to not offend their southern and conservative membership.

The Reformed Methodists Speak Out

Reformed Methodists closely watched the dissent in the Methodist Episcopal Church expand. In a series of three articles on "Conference Rights," Bailey argued recent conferences demonstrated bishops maneuvered to silence clergy raising anti-slavery resolutions, going beyond their role as "presiders." Instead of chairing meetings, he said, they were usurping powers to deny others rights to speak that were guaranteed to them. [15] It was an issue that touched the scar tissue of the Reformed Methodist experience. They had proclaimed these principles since their secession in 1814.

In the April 19, 1838 issue of *South Cortland Luminary* Bailey wrote the "cause" Reformed Methodists embraced was no partisan, modern abolitionist position, and they would continue to speak out on the "moral" issue of American slavery, " believing it to be one of the foulest blots on our national character." [16]

Whether in sympathy, or anger, at what they saw happening within the Methodist Episcopal Church, or the desire to dissociate from any perceived passivity on the slavery issue, the Massachusetts Reformed Methodist Conference meeting in October affirmed a more active position about slavery saying that members "will take all proper measures for its abolition." [17] Elijah Bailey attended that meeting as representative of both the New York and Western New York Conferences.

Once in his new Fayetteville publishing office, Wesley Bailey settled into an expanded printing operation, and provided ministry services as needed to the newly celebrated Reformed Methodist meeting house built in the High Bridge hamlet, just two miles south of the village.

His printer's tongue seemed to have sharpened a bit, whether defending or exposing. He chastised those passive conservatives who hurled abuse at so-called "agitators," and who felt virtuous while they "tamely submit to things as they are." He found the shallow, lack of critical thinking of those comfortable in the "mainstream of public opinion," unworthy. [18]

In the Town of Manlius...

January 8, 1839: John McViccar chairs Onondaga County Anti-Slavery meeting in Manlius Square.

Union Herald, February 9, 1839

February 14, 1839: Legislature of New York – In Senate PETITIONS presented ....By Mr. Edwards, of inhabitants of Manlius, for a repeal of the excise law; of ladies of the same town, on the same subject....

Albany Argus, 2-19-1839

March 9, 1839. Legislature – In Senate. PETITIONS...By Mr. A. Smith, on the subject of slavery; (also) for the punishment of seduction by imprisonment, from ladies of Manlius, Onondaga County...

Albany Argus, 3-12-1839

March 20, 1839: Cotton Factory & Flouring Mill for Sale. Manlius...also 2 stores, 7 Dwelling Houses, a joiners' and Cooper's Shop, Barns, ... & 63 acres of land...1392 spindles, 31 looms...Situated near center of village. There is in the village two other cotton factories.

Commercial Advertiser, March 22, 1839

April 2, 1839: Onondaga County, Fayetteville (Manlius) "We have just finished our canvas of the vote of the day, and the real democracy of Manlius have triumphed over the combined forces of whiggery. Dr. Taylor, our worthy ex-member of congress, is elected supervisor by a majority of 134...."

Albany Argus, 4-9-1839

CHAPTER FOURTEEN

POLITICS, EQUALITY & FRATERNITY

> To your Tents, O Israel
> People of Manlius.- Republicans,
> who feel an emotion of virtuous liberty,
> to the polls, and secure the inestimable
> privilege of freemen...[1]
>
> *Manlius Republican*
> November 2, 1830

What to do about slavery became an increasingly divisive political issue, in and out of the churches. People differed in perception, knowledge, attitude, and of course, self-interest. Politics had become entertaining, and quarrelsome, a mixture of revival preaching and street theater. This spirited process was not unique to the town of Manlius, but it was competitive, and sometimes bitter. Anti-slavery activities and politics in Manlius can be better understood by looking back at changes, conflicts, and events in the late 1820s that took on, and fostered, unusual local intensities.

An increased participation of "the common man" in politics was one of these developments. The years of Andrew Jackson's presidency (1828-1836) has sometimes been labeled "the era of the common man," marking a great historic period when humble American tillers of soil, hewers of wood, mechanics, coopers, boatmen, and mill workers, gained a measure of equality with more wealthy and prominent men of the nation.

The fact that more white male citizens became eligible to vote when property qualifications were eliminated in the 1820s, suggests such an assumption is grounded in fact. [2] Theoretically then, even the poorest white male, age 21 and over, walking to the polls, was equal to the man driven to the ballot box in a fine carriage.

While thousands more voters drove their wagons, or walked to town, stopping at the taverns to argue the issues, on election day in 1828, they had little power to select candidates to run for county, state and national offices. That privilege was managed by an inner party elite, who quickly seized control through organized campaigns, sponsoring newspapers and pamphlets, parades and rallies complete with singing and marching bands.

Edward Pessen claimed little real power came into the hands of "common folk" then. Power was held tightly, he said, by "the shrewd, ambitious, wealthy, and able politicians who knew best how to flatter them." [3] And although farming was the occupation of two-thirds of the population then, those who voted on laws in state legislatures were primarily "merchants, lawyers, men of affairs and eminence." Even in Western New York, where religious piety was prominent, the author said, "a small elite – much more mercantile than evangelical in outlook," provided leadership in community endeavors. [4]

Still, party leaders knew they had to attract the new voters to their position. Much local political talk was about how to get one's products to market, who should pay for roads and canal feeders, how much protection manufacturers should get from tariffs, who should regulate banks. There were differing views about state and federal powers, of personal economic benefits and disadvantages.

Still, even if one's feet were on a lower rung of the American dream ladder, most Yankee Americans and their descendants, shared the same enterprising goals of money-making and climbing higher. When they had the right to vote for local, state, and national offices they believed they had leverage to access and protect some of these rewards and benefits.

The Rise of the Anti-Masonic Party

Throughout the mid-1820s and 1830s, Manlius voters gave majorities to the Democrat-Republican ticket. Andrew Jackson was a campaign manager's dream.

The hero of the Battle of New Orleans, a man of humble roots, "Old Hickory" was shaped into a popular folk hero.

Though Jackson lost the presidential election of 1824 in a four-way race, he won it in 1828. Voter participation in the election was over 80%. He championed states' rights, lashed out at the National Bank, and condemned greedy trading of charter privileges for power and patronage.

The Democrat Party, however, looking toward keeping Jackson in the presidency a second term, was jolted by a seemingly inconsequential event that occurred in a little town 125 miles west of Manlius, New York. It is strange that the disappearance of a single man in September 1826 caused such an uproar. It was a kidnapping, a murder, revelations of a secret society, and a conspiracy that agitated the public mind for several years.

It all started in Batavia in Genesee County, New York, when William Morgan was presumed kidnapped and murdered, many believed by members of the Fraternity of Freemasons. Morgan, an ex-Mason, had threatened to publish secret knowledge used by the fraternity. Soon after, he disappeared. Some said he was weighted down with stones in the Niagara River.

Citizen protests might have been short-lived had local and state officials acted to investigate the kidnapping and charges of murder. It appeared, however, that officials ignored the public outcry, and in some instances, obstructed inquiries, leading some to suspect there was indeed conspiracy and collusion in the mysterious disappearance.

As time went by, anti-Masons took their suspicions to the ballot box. They pointed out, sometimes with shrill bombast, that titles, oaths, secrecy, and mysterious rituals used by the Masonic order were contrary to a patriotic republican government, and the equal rights of American citizens. While "secret societies, devoted to worthy ends, were in great vogue," Hal T. Avery explained years later, they were "bitterly attacked by equally large groups," who believed that secrecy employed by these societies "covered sinister and political purposes." [5]

Many, especially Jacksonian Democrats, were shocked when this new Anti-Masonic Party won fifteen seats in the New York Assembly that November. Andrew Jackson was a Mason. So was presidential hopeful Henry Clay. At a February convention in LeRoy (near Batavia) the following year, seceding Masons gave testimony and published their proceedings in newspapers across the state. Author Charles McCarthy asserts these publications provided a "powerful stimulus to the new cause and made many converts." [6]

In the Town of Manlius

The intensity of this controversy was keenly felt in Manlius. Thurlow Weed, an astute Anti-Mason politician, wrote in his autobiography years later, that the conflict became "more embittered and relentless" than any he had joined. [7] In the midst of town meetings and heated debates, clergy, elders and deacons of the Presbyterian, Methodist, and Baptist Church did their own soul searching. What position should they take?

Manlius had the oldest Masonic lodge in Onondaga County. Military Lodge 93, Free & Accepted Masons, was chartered in 1802, and started out with seventeen members.[8] Many were enterprising and successful men in the town. Manlius citizens were conflicted and slow to mobilize, but were soon swept up in the political crusade as anti-Mason newspapers sprang up like mushrooms.

Leaders of the newly built First Baptist Church in Fayetteville felt compelled to respond to this anti-Masonic fever, and on Nov. 11, 1829, the Church and Society called on Freemason members "to dissolve all connection" with the fraternity and "its obligations, laws, usages or customs." [9]

McCarthy believed many Freemasons were "innocent of any wrong" and tried to "remain neutral" but when they were denounced, they were "drawn into the conflict." On the other hand, as opponents saw it, the abduction and murder of Morgan, whether a rare instance or not, involved "the obligations and teachings of the order." [10]

Opponents of Masonry in Pompey organized themselves in April 1830. In Manlius, Henry Van Schaack, a young lawyer, took an interest in the controversy and attended the Anti-Masonic State Convention in Utica that August. Convention delegates focused their opposition to "secret societies" and depicted Freemasons as "anti-republican and at war with the spirit of our government."[11] The convention was chaired by William M. Clark of Pompey. Francis Granger and Samuel Stevens, were nominated as candidates for Governor and Lieutenant Governor. The movement had now become a third party in New York State.

The following month, Manlius resident, Elnathan Cobb, was one of four delegates chosen to represent Onondaga County at the Seventh Senatorial District Convention. The district at that time encompassed six counties. Auburn's William H. Seward, was selected at the convention to run for this Senate seat.[12]

In October a county-wide Anti-Masonic convention was held in Syracuse. Leaders called for reform against the corruption, mismanagement, and control of a clique of "designing and selfish individuals" (putting blame on the Albany Regency led by Martin Van Buren) whose measures were "anti-republican" and "sinister." Delegates chose Congressional nominees and four Assembly seats in the New York State Legislature.[13] Azariah Smith, a well-known, respected businessman of Manlius, was nominated for the Assembly.

The momentum accelerated during pre-election weeks. On October 23rd, a "Great Anti-Masonic Meeting" was hosted by John Smith in Fayetteville.[14] Darlin Thompson chaired the meeting, and Elijah Rhoades was appointed secretary. In all, nine resolutions were adopted. Freemasonry was declared "a dangerous institution" and a "serious obstacle to detection and punishment of crime." It was suspected of corrupting "the integrity of Grand Juries, and the impartiality of petit juries," and also undermined the independent exercise of the "elective franchise." [15]

Manlius citizens who attended the meeting urged Fraternity members to leave the society and avoid censure. [16] Each side fueled by political opportunism and old loyalties, lashed out at opposition candidates in their partisan newspapers. The attacks, at times, resembled a street brawl. Van Schaack's letters published in the *Onondaga Republican,* pummeled Dr. William Taylor, a Democrat and high-ranking Mason, as "the Royal Arch Doctor." [17] Azariah Smith, running with Anti-Masonic support for the New York Assembly, received a share of such partisan abuse. Rumors were spread that he was in favor of an unpopular proposal to divide off part of the town to create a new town to be named DeWitt. And on, and on, it went.

Though the Anti-Masonic Party had a short life span, it helped shape New York State politics, and some of that was evident in Manlius. It exploited latent class tensions, fears, and tenacious beliefs. It made visible the fluidity of shifting factions and schisms, and intense personal loyalties. Formerly a duel between mostly land-owning interests and those loyal to De-Witt Clinton, the great canal builder, now the Anti-Masonic movement, having roiled the waters, strode boisterously into election politics as the uninvited guest.

Out of such dissonance and jostlings came new combinations of interests and goals. One step child was the Whig Party. The local organized reaction against Masonry, provided leadership opportunities for men like Charles A. Wheaton of Pompey and Darlin Thompson of Manlius. Some, like Elijah Rhoades, Azariah Smith and John McViccar emerged from the movement as Whig Party men. When they aligned with the new Whig Party, some brought along their human rights and equality concerns. They supported William Seward for the Senate, and later for Governor of New York State.

On the other side of the electoral battle were Manlius Democrats, who had held power in town for the last twenty years. Dr. William Taylor was their standard-bearer, and a Lodge brother. As a Freemason, Taylor was also a political target of their campaign, though he was popular with many of his townsmen, and weathered the storm.

Since Democrats had a large southern membership, Dr. Taylor tried to avoid any head-on confrontation when the slavery question was pushed on to the legislative agenda. He maintained New Yorkers had no business interfering in the conduct of commerce in other states. For a time, in the town, a backlash against the anti-Masons gave victory at the polls to Dr. Taylor and the Democrats.

David Volkin assessed that early political support in Manlius was so solidly Democrat, sometimes called "Bucktail," and later "Jacksonian," that new parties had an uphill battle in gaining leverage.[18] He believed, however, 10-20% of voters in town "were swayed by current issues such as suffrage, slavery, internal improvements, and Freemasonry."[19] In several instances, that 10 to 20% might be enough to determine an election. And it was.

The Freemason controversy in Manlius was, in some ways, a foundational experience that served as instruction to anti-slavery supporters six years later. It demonstrated that a compelling belief, a religious principle, can energize participants, and draw to itself skills, resources, and talent to its purpose. It was a prelude and guide to grassroots organizing. It also showed how powerful a newspaper could be in the service of one's goal. From then on, every movement, party, and reform sought to persuade, or pay editors, to be on their side. Many started their own newspapers.

The movement may have put a few fanatics and zealots on the platform, but it was also a training ground for talented, energetic men who wanted to contribute to the common good. Some men who started their political activism in the Anti-Masonic Movement, later became elected officials, and gained prominence trying to end slavery in this nation, a complex and protracted reform goal. These movers and shakers also created their newspapers and political parties.

In some places in the state, organized Anti-Masonry had little durable influence on local history. In Manlius and Fayetteville, it stimulated public debates on the meaning of privilege, equality, and human rights, topics that reappeared five years later, in the early days of the anti-slavery movement.

CHAPTER FIFTEEN

DON'T PANIC!

> After years of thinking that they were uniquely virtuous and that God had smiled on the American republic...Americans had some real problems on their hands. [1]
>
> Ted Widmer,
> *Martin Van Buren*

As the summer of 1837 approached, banks began to fall like a row of dominoes. A financial collapse was spreading from the banking and commercial center of New York City across the nation. Though President Martin Van Buren inherited much of this disaster from the Jackson years, many thought he was doing little to alleviate the misery.

Jackson was cheered by the agrarians and common folk in 1832, when he denounced the Second Bank of the United States, whose charter required renewal to continue. The Tennessee native believed the bank was a monstrous tool used by privileged, powerful business interests to the disadvantage of salt-of-the-earth farmers and laborers, especially those in the West. In 1833 he removed federal deposits from the National Bank, and placed deposits in numerous state "pet" banks, thereby decentralizing the control of currency.

From Revere Thompson's point of view, writing in 1909, this was a disaster. It resulted, he said, in "a descent into chaos." Everybody who chose to, leapt "into the banking field." Private banks and state chartered banks ventured into business, all issuing a currency whose value should have been questioned. There was no national standard or regulation. "That crushing failure should follow, was natural," concluded Thompson. [2]

During the first weeks of May 1837 all banks in New York City suspended payments and over 300 firms failed. Seven months later, in January, a total of 618 banks had collapsed, and during the prolonged crisis, 33,000 insolvencies were recorded. [3]

Still, in addition to Jackson's aggressive dismantling of the National Bank, other stresses contributed to the economic decline. Waves of hopeful immigrants, land speculation, rapid railroad and canal building, loose credit, much government debt, Congressional stalemates, partisan infighting, and clashing personal political ambitions all exacerbated financial suffering across the nation.

In his memoirs, Orson Smith, a successful farmer in Manlius, recalled one of those precarious times when there had been a mad rush to Michigan "to buy corner lots at 1.25 c per acre." The result was, he said, "the red dog money came from Michigan, against our safety fund, and the crash of 1837, came to five or six companies." [4]

In the midst of a widening depression, blamed mostly on Jackson and Van Buren Democrats, Whig Party leaders saw their chance. Though they shared some goals with their opponents, they emphasized economic growth, optimistic nationalism, and an active government. They believed the national government must do something in the face of such misery to intervene and promote prosperity for the state and nation.

Partisan clashes were ideological, each claiming high ground. These Jacksonian Democrats espoused "government is best which governs least" which meant government neither stepped in to advance, nor to relieve, consequences of the mysterious wheels of the economy. They also mistrusted commerce, paper money, banks, and believed the true virtuous citizens were farmers. Most of all they feared a loss of state power. Those aligned to commerce and manufacturing tended to reject such lofty agrarian rhetoric, and enthusiastically sought government support for internal improvements, roads and canals to drive the engines of progress and prosperity.

Nowhere was this tension more evident than in Central and Western New York. Carol Sheriff called the Erie Canal venture "the paradox of progress." Many New Yorkers actively campaigned to make the Erie Canal bigger, and, of course, beneficial to them personally. [5]

Manlius Village was a good example. Businessmen there who had missed out on reaping the early commercial advantages that their Fayetteville neighbors enjoyed with the canal, wanted to get their slice of the pie. Fayetteville's entrepreneurs had moved quickly, dug and built their way into the Erie Canal highway, giving them access to the markets and products moving along the waterway.

Now, Manlius men turned their attention to getting government support for building canal feeders and railroads to obtain their share. [6] Some believed Whig leaders in elected office would offer them their best chance. They worked hard to elect sympathetic candidates.

They were hopeful. The Whig Party swept to victory in the New York State Assembly during the November 1837 elections. During 1838-1839, Azariah Smith, Victory Birdseye, Phares Gould, and James R. Lawrence lead the Whig Party from Onondaga County. Whig Party candidate, William H. Seward of Auburn, edged out Democrat William Marcy in the county to take the governorship. [7]

Financial security and opportunity were, no doubt, the priority concerns of most citizens in town, but a small group of highly committed abolitionists took this favorable moment to press their goals.

The Great Petition Campaign

Slavery petitions were presented to the New York State Legislature during early 1839, from Albany, Clinton, Chautauqua, Westchester, Genesee, Monroe, Essex, Wayne, Genesee, Yates, Ontario, Livingston, and St. Lawrence counties. [8]

The *Albany Argus* reported one of these anti-slavery petitions was submitted by Azariah Smith of Manlius.[9] The two year petition campaign orchestrated by national and state anti-slavery societies engaged thousands of men and women, who carried petitions from door to door to enroll sympathetic neighbors and church members.

Elizabeth Weld was a lead female signature on one petition against admission of Texas to the union as a slave state. Most signers were members of the Presbyterian Church in Manlius Village. Rev. John Gridley, the Congregational minister at Pompey, and his wife Arabella, got signers on a similar petition. [10]

In February 1839, James Bailey, Wesley Bailey's uncle, a Reformed Methodist elder, had taken the lead in Lafayette, and succeeded in getting 63 males and 17 females to sign a call for "abolition of slavery in the District of Columbia" and "in the territory of Florida." A second petition was submitted seeking to "prohibit the traffic in human beings between the several States." [11]

Former President John Q. Adams, now in Congress, provided a safe haven for such petitions, at least for a while. He seemed to enjoy frustrating his southern colleagues by figuring out ways to present heaping stacks of petitions. The previous year, he introduced 350 anti-slavery petitions in one day. [12] The sheer scale of citizen involvement amazed Congress, though southerners were particularly distressed at this display against them.

Southern Congressmen, and their conservative northern allies, resented this orchestrated rebuke, and began using the procedure of "laying on the table" to block introduction of anti-slavery petitions. The "gag" order, introduced by New Hampshire Democrat, Charles G. Atherton, halted reading of petitions, but it also ignited a firestorm. This bloc of representatives had denied citizens of New York a constitutional right to petition their representative assembly with their grievances. New York State legislators, bombarded with protests from Whigs and abolitionists, felt the heat of this controversy. Now what? Would New York leaders ignore the affront?

Wesley Bailey reported in the *Luminary* with disgust: "Thus the right of petition has been denied to the free citizens of the United States." [13] Yet abolitionists turned the political insult to their advantage. They succeeded in awakening many northern citizens to the power southern slaveholders and their northern friends wielded, which served to rally more listeners and sympathizers to their cause.

Manlius was in the 23rd Congressional District, which then included Onondaga and Madison counties. It was represented by Democrat, Nehemiah Earll. When the gag resolution was proposed, 108 of the New York delegation voted against it. However, Earll was one of six New Yorkers who sided with the bloc of southerners to impose the gag rule, and Bailey reported that fact. [14]

The reaction in New York legislative chambers in Albany was partisan and bitter. Whigs baited their colleagues asking if New York State representatives were going to tolerate an abuse of our citizens. Not wanting to get caught in the swamp of public slavery arguments, some Democrat legislators headed for the doors. The debate hinged primarily on the denial of a constitutional right of citizens to petition.

The Albany *Evening Journal* denounced Van Buren Democrats in the Assembly. When a resolution was proposed in the Assembly protesting Atherton's gag maneuver and those New York congressmen in Washington, D. C. who supported it, several legislators seemed to disappear. The Albany editor accused them of "hiding and skulking" to avoid a public vote on it. [15]

The Assembly debate of February 12 was particularly heated. Various maneuvers to derail, or soften, the resolution failed. Assemblyman Victory Birdseye of Pompey voted to censure Atherton, and in April when William Seward proposed to extend New York's right of trial by jury to persons here, who others claimed were fugitive slaves, Birdseye agreed. [16] It was a controversial move, and it caused some concern among Seward's Whig colleagues.

Yet as 1839 ended, the economic depression was still *the* dominant issue in New York State. It had been, for one Cicero man, a rough few years. Asa Eastwood wrote in his diary that neither his store, nor his farm, prospered during these years. He was troubled "by various payment on debts and loans." When "he sold cattle and grains in 1840, the price had fallen." "These five years," he said, added more hard struggle to his life "with but little gain." [17]

Francis Baylies, a former Massachusetts Congressman wrote to his New York brother-in-law in Troy, venting his frustration at President Van Buren. His reluctance to intervene, Baylies argued, has resulted in "mere anarchy" with this currency problem unsettled, and prices "sinking rapidly" on what Americans were putting on the market. [18]

Clearly many agreed with Baylies, it seems, because Van Buren lost a second term. Seward won a second term as Governor by a narrow margin, and Manlius residents, Azariah Smith and Elijah Rhodes, won their election to the New York State Legislature.

CHAPTER SIXTEEN

FRUSTRATION, CIDER & THE LIBERTY PARTY

> It was 1840, and men had gathered from the country for miles around for the parade, the campaign speeches and the cider. William Henry Harrison, hero of Tippecanoe, was candidate for president against Martin Van Buren. ... How they drank hard cider and how they sang about Tippecanoe and Tyler, too, was long remembered...[1]
>
> Fred E. Dutcher
> *Once Upon a Time* (1930)

The anti-slavery societies across the nation worked hard to get men and women involved in the petition campaigns, but there were many motivations that brought eligible male voters to the polls in the 1840 national election. There were plenty of concerns and issues, most being economic, which brought voters off the farms, out of warehouses, shops, banks, and mills to the villages to do battle over party principles, self-interest, and moral convictions.

When Seward ran for re-election as Governor in 1840, he was applauded by abolitionists. In 1839, he refused to extradite three black sailors claimed by Virginia's Governor to be men under that state's jurisdiction. Encouraged by this defiance, some abolitionists supported Whig Party candidates, though

Whig Party bosses warned Seward against getting too close to radical political abolitionists. Meanwhile they portrayed Democrats as being "controlled by southern principles," responsible for causing the downfall of many "northern yeoman and tradesmen." [2]

Van Buren, who was blamed for the long painful depression, had benefited from good working relationships with southern leaders in Virginia and Georgia. He tried to straddle the unpopular slavery controversy, so as not to offend these southern allies, but such artful dodges became transparent. Ted Widmer, who authored a biography of Van Buren, claimed such maneuvers were not unique. Van Buren, he said, did what most politicians did who faced volatile controversies: "He dances around it, trying to placate the people, and offering various concessions to maintain his support." [3] But this time, it didn't work.

The power balance in Washington, D. C. was at stake. New western territories opened up, and settlers rushed in on the heels of speculators with dreams of cheap land and new opportunities. Then, the answer to the question of whether these new "states" would allow slavery within their boundaries, was critical. A "union" of states they might call it, but there was an almost tribal loyalty to one's region, to economic, commercial and political interests of ones own section, which often transcended what was good for the nation as a whole. With all this additional territory and population, who would benefit the most?

Consequently, the 1840 campaign was one of passion and prejudice. Many voters anxious for relief, opportunity, and stability never saw the storm brewing along the fault lines of sectional competition. Whether "the untutored voter" knew he was being seduced by hard cider, dramatic displays, processions, and flamboyant oratory, may not have mattered in the rip-roaring campaign days leading up to the election. [4]

While the Whig Party was drawing under its broad political umbrella commercial interests and anti-masons, some opponents of slavery worried about a southern conspiracy to advance the "slave power" westward. Many abolitionists did not trust the traditional parties to advance their agenda, because of these competing sectional interests within the Whig Party and Democrat Party.

The Rise of the Liberty Party

After four years of non-stop anti-slavery suasion efforts, some New York abolitionists became disenchanted with their seemingly unproductive strategy. They had experienced hostility, threats, assault, destruction of printing presses, so by now they understood they confronted an intense southern resistance. Naive or not, they had courage and determination. So, they decided to seek voting power where it counted-in legislatures and executive seats, where men made and executed policy. They needed to go beyond questionnaires and interviews of main party candidates to assess their commitment to prioritize ending slavery.

A core group of politically convinced New York abolitionists met in Albany in April 1840, and nominated James Birney for president. It was the launching of an abolitionist political organization called the Liberty Party. The Whigs were dismayed and infuriated, as was William Lloyd Garrison. They feared this effort would draw off anti-slavery supporters from their own party, and weaken their ability to defeat Democrat candidates.

Several local men, including Darlin Thompson, Nathan R. Chapman, and L. P. Noble, agreed with Alvan Stewart, James Birney, and Gerrit Smith that the Democrat and Whig parties were too burdened with sectional issues and other priorities. With southern slaveholders in both major parties, the slavery issue conflict was always avoided in order to pass other legislation. Some abolitionists agreed and switched loyalties to the Liberty Party. Rev. Luther Myrick disagreed. He had no faith in party politics. Neither did Garrison who denounced this new tactic.

Soon after, James C. Jackson joined the New York political faction. He became convinced that moral principles could be sustained even at the ballot box. One choice didn't have to exclude the other. Thus, in Central and Western New York, much of the state anti-slavery membership followed the lead of Gerrit Smith, Alvan Stewart, William Goodell, and James Birney in a politically, ambitious direction.

Their nominee, James Birney, a converted slave owner from Kentucky, was the perfect choice to showcase their revivalist abolitionist beliefs. Still, the Liberty Party hardly seemed a numerical threat entering on the electoral battlefield.

It was the rambunctious 1840 campaign of "Tippecanoe and Tyler Too!" The year the "old war hero" William Henry Harrison defeated New York's not-so-favorite son, Democrat, and former Governor, Martin Van Buren. Onondaga County racked up a fragile Democrat majority with the help of Manlius, while Whig victories rolled through neighboring Oswego, Cayuga, Madison, Chenango, Cortland counties. [5] Syracuse newspapers hardly noticed James Birney was a candidate for president. Birney tallied 7000 votes in the first national election under the Liberty Party banner.

The Seceding Methodists

Wesley Bailey was intently engaged in unifying Methodist dissenters, so he didn't jump on the Liberty Party bandwagon the first time it went through town. He still believed the influence of a righteous Christian congregation gave a powerful moral witness. At the same time, it was to his benefit that a wider newspaper readership be gained. The *Fayetteville Luminary* was solely supported by the Reformed Methodists, subscribers, and advertisers. Financing any small town weekly was risky business, let alone one sponsored by a small denomination whose members were scattered over a few New England and Mid-Atlantic states.

Bailey's primary attention to developing a larger denominational constituency, an alliance of seceding Methodists, also offered him an opportunity to expand the outreach of the paper, and consequently, a subscription and advertising base.

In June 1841, he, his uncle James Bailey, and father Elijah, then a pastor in Brewster, Massachusetts; Rev. Marcellus Barnum, and Charles Clark, attended a convention of seceding Methodists and other Christians at the Wesleyan Methodist Chapel in Utica. Though the number attending was small, and disagreements arose, delegates from New York, Massachusetts, Ohio, New Jersey, and Michigan focused on common themes of consensus including church government, slavery, temperance and the rights and privileges of colored members. [6]

Elder Elijah Bailey, then in his early 70s, was given the honor of chairing the convention. In his memoirs, Rev. George Pegler characterized Elijah Bailey as "a man of deep piety" who possessed "a clear head and sound judgment," whose part in Methodist reform was long and deep. [7]

When the assembly decided to hold a convention that summer, they invited lay members and clergy who had, or were, contemplating leaving the Methodist Episcopal Church, members of small independent Methodist congregations, and other interested Christians. The invitation made it clear that membership in the new association excluded not only slaveholders, but "their apologists", as well as those engaged in "the manufacture, use, or sale of spirituous liquors except for medicinal, chemical, or mechanical purposes." They also stated that there would be no distinctions or privileges among members, and no inequality based on "either condition or color." [8]

The convention started on August 31 at the High Bridge meeting house with fifty representatives of the Wesleyan Methodist Church, Reformed Methodists, and Methodist Society who discussed, refined, and agreed upon articles of belief and "measures of cooperation." [9] At the conclusion of the two day meeting, David Plumb, on behalf of Wesleyan Methodist seceders, announced that from henceforth Wesley Bailey's newspaper, the *Methodist Reformer*, would represent and expand coverage to include, their mutual interests and goals. The October 7 edition announced that Manlius resident, Heman Ward, would be traveling agent for the *Methodist Reformer*, and would soon start his travels though Onondaga, Cortland, and Broome counties. [10]

The Baileys, and other dissenting Readsboro colleagues, must have been encouraged by this expanding approval of clear and faithful Methodist principles. It had been thirty years since their complaints were ignored by the Methodist Episcopal Church Conference; since a dozen laymen and their families had sought to reclaim the original intent of John Wesley. They were a small fraction of Christians, but they were not alone.

The Liberty Party Seeks Recruits

While overwhelmed by "log cabin" hoopla, and a resounding Whig victory of William Henry Harrison in 1840, Liberty men began to rally for the state election in 1842. They were not short on vitality, but they had to convince anti-slavery allies that the state agenda was a worthy way to advance the cause.

On December 30, 1841, they pleaded their case at the anti-slavery meeting in Fayetteville's Presbyterian Church. Darlin Thompson chaired the meeting. Nathan R. Chapman, who opened his law practice that year, recorded the minutes. James Jackson preached about the third party movement with patriotic and evangelical vigor.

The argument for political action was solid. The law, he said, "is made by the lawmaker," and citizens vote for the lawmaker, so, the "people of the North" are just as "responsible for the continuance of Slavery in the District of Columbia, the territory of Florida, and for the international Slave Trade," as voters elsewhere. It was obvious, Liberty men said, the two great parties offered little help in changing the status and suffering of the slaves. [11]

Another resolution put forth by party leaders, charged Christian churches with being "delinquent of duty" for not actively seeking the end of slavery, aroused more debate. [12.] While their arguments made converts, the report of the meeting shows that a number of anti-slavery supporters felt it was enough to work hard to adopt a new strategy, but not necessary to spend time in hurling abuse at each other, and discrediting traditional parties and churches.

Since the very origins of the Manlius-Fayetteville anti-slavery effort, local members showed a distinct reluctance to follow prescribed agendas of state and national leaders. There were diverse opinions and independent voices within the group, and some were not willing to join in public condemnations of their church denominations and traditional political associations.

James C. Jackson had few qualms about exposing Christian church negligence and complicity. His experiences were often quite unpleasant. In early April, he asked Charles Weld to set up a speaking engagement in Manlius, his birthplace, but he found when he arrived, his request was denied. The trustees at Trinity Presbyterian Church in Manlius, he said, shut the door against his lecture. He took this as a personal affront, reporting his father "paid as much money as any other person," and the purpose of the church had been for the preaching of the truth. [13]

All was not lost, he reported, as the Methodist Church generously opened their meeting house, and he spoke to a good audience and "was invited to speak the ensuing evening." [14] Still, it was an uphill battle to win the hearts and minds of one's neighbors, a few of whom were sons and daughters of slaveholders.

When the Liberty Party solicited a slate of candidates for local and state officers in 1841, their efforts were ridiculed as wasteful, and pragmatically hopeless. The local Liberty Party nominated Darlin Thompson for a state legislative seat that year. Only 19 voters endorsed the Liberty candidate in the town, while DeWitt tallied 17, and Cicero boasted 48. [15] Certainly there was no band-wagon enthusiasm here, as in the days of the Anti-Masonic excitement ten years earlier, but it was a start.

While the seceding Methodists seemed to be making headway uniting around a strong anti-slavery and temperance creed, the Presbyterian activists in Fayetteville had some cause to be concerned.

The Presbyterian General Assembly left synods, presbyteries, and individual congregations with the task of dealing with disparate voices on the slavery controversy. The balance of the silent and outspoken often shifted with changes in membership, trustees, and pastors. In 1841, Rev. Richard Cleveland replaced Rev. Amos Tuttle in the pastorate in Fayetteville, and the activist phase of clerical and lay leadership tilted toward silence and retreat. Allen Nevins pointed gently to Rev. Cleveland's "conservatism" citing a letter where Cleveland writes in 1847, "I am not much taken with the new-growth reforms of the present day..." [16] Geoffrey Blodgett's assessment is blunt. "Richard Cleveland, he writes, "was a hardline, old school Presbyterian conservative, " not given to engagement in "moral reforms to purge society of its stains, from slavery to saloons...."[17] He represented the style of orthodox Presbyterian clergy who "mistrusted any passionate drive to upset current arrangements or use public coercion to fashion a perfect world." [18]

CHAPTER SEVENTEEN

THE COLORED AMERICAN

> A depressed people cannot be elevated by any other than themselves. Others may remove burdens, plead their cause, afford them facilities, and cheer them with smiles and encouragement. But more than this they cannot do. [1]
>
> Rev. Samuel R. Ward, in
> *Samuel Ringgold Ward, Christian Abolitionist*

In April 1843, Nathan Chapman wrote to his lawyer son, N. R. Chapman in Fayetteville, sharing, as he often did, the family, neighborhood and political news from nearby Madison County. The elder Chapman, co-founder of the Lenox Anti-Slavery Society and Free Church in Canastota, often reported anti-slavery events.[2] He said a slave had spoken at their anti-slavery meeting the previous Sabbath. "A smart man," he told his son, reporting that the audience "took up a collection to assist him in getting an education." [3]

The man was Lewis Clark, an ex-slave who had an unusually light skin complexion, which surprised many audiences. He explained to them his coloring resulted from his mother and grandmother both being fathered by plantation owners. Lewis, and brother Milton, were escaped slaves from Kentucky.

That September, William P. Barrett, from Fenner, urged

local residents to come to the local schoolhouse and Baptist Church to hear Mr. Clark. "Will the friends of humanity come to these meetings," he pleaded, "with hearts that can feel as well as eyes that can weep for the matchless wrongs which we, as a people, have heaped upon the slaves of our common country." [4]

Clark's experience was compelling.

> My mistress had a little slave-girl about seven years old, that used to get terribly abused. She beat her head up against the chimney till it was in a dreadful state and kicked her about as if a dog. The poor child died of bad treatment. Mistress did her best to kill me, but I lived through it...[5]

Years later, Theodore D. Weld wrote to Gerrit Smith saying "intelligent colored men" in the "lecturing field" would "do more in three months to kill prejudice...then all our operations up to now." [6]

Prejudice continued, but Weld was correct in recognizing the power of true witness and testimony. Patrick C. Kennicott called Clark one of the "black persuaders." "Garrison and his white colleagues," he said "could speak with passion about the cruelties inflicted upon innocent slaves by sadistic slave masters, but Lewis Clark *had been there*." [7]

Years later, Lewis Clark recounted he probably spoke at five hundred meetings, and met "a great many warm friends" in New York. Still, he gave a mixed assessment of clergymen. He said most clergymen claimed to be abolitionists, but "are more zealous to apologize for the slaveholders," than they are to do any work of emancipation. [8]

When the anti-slavery movement formally organized in

Central New York in 1835, there were few channels of communication between white and black activists, so first-hand accounts of slavery were rare. This changed after 1838 when anti-slavery societies, the Liberty Party, and men like Gerrit Smith, who aided fugitive slaves, increasingly encouraged ex-slaves to attend and speak at assemblies.

Ex-slaves, black ministers, orators and writers like Frederick Douglass, Samuel R. Ward, Jermain Loguen, Charles L. Remond, H. H. Garnet, and Milton and Lewis Clark, had a powerful impact on audiences, as they traveled the length and breadth of upstate New York. They were telling their own stories, and people flocked to hear them.

Information about, and by, black activists, especially those who lived in New York City, began reaching white abolitionists upstate through the weekly newspaper, *The Colored American*. The paper circulated amongst free people of color in several east coast communities [9] It was originally a regional channel of news, culture, and commentary on such issues as colonization and peaceful emancipation.

In 1838, Charles B. Ray, a black Congregational clergyman and abolitionist, published *The Colored American*. Ray wrote against the colonization scheme, and urged suffrage rights for black Americans. He came to Utica and made an appeal for support at the New York State Anti-Slavery Society meeting. [10] Ray's presence and speech likely impressed Rev. Amos C. Tuttle and Horace Robbins of Fayetteville, and William Eager of DeWitt, who attended the convention. There were few opportunities for Fayetteville and DeWitt residents to hear articulate colored men plead their cause before a primarily white audience at that time, so this occasion offered them such an experience.

In his March 21, 1840 issue, Ray criticized the dissension going on within the movement, believing it was counterproductive. The goal, he reminded colleagues, was to do all we could for the slave, and not "to keep up a war of words" which was "disreputable to our otherwise holy cause."[11]

While it is not clear how many people in upstate New York read *The Colored American*, a few subscribers are known. Rev. S. R. Ward, abolitionist, orator, and ex-slave, who later became a newspaper publisher himself, supported the publication. So too, did William Eager, Rev. John Chester, Alfred Wilkinson, Rev. John. H. Lathrop, and Stephen Smith of Syracuse.[12] Rev. Chester was the pastor of the African Methodist Zion congregation. Lathrop was a deacon at the abolitionist Congregational church. Stephen Smith was a Quaker businessman, who sold property to former Manlius slave, Isaac Wales.

Gerrit Smith, who read and supported the newspaper, carried on frequent correspondence with many black abolitionists. When Benjamin Quarles examined the Gerrit Smith Collection at Syracuse University, he found forty-five letters written to Smith from black leaders prior to 1840.[13]

Like so many reform newspapers whose readership appealed primarily to special interest customers, the weekly struggled to survive. It was fortuitous for the Syracuse black community, that Rev. Jermain Loguen was named a traveling agent for its distribution. Loguen, an ex-slave from Tennessee, completed his ministry education at Oneida Institute, but was enticed to move to Syracuse in 1841. Though the newspaper barely made it through that year, Loguen focused efforts on encouraging educational programs and working with the African

Methodist Zion congregation to develop a cohesive spiritual community. He was the bridge between Syracuse's free colored community and political activists of downstate and Western New York.

Though *The Colored American* ceased publication that year, eliminating a channel of news about events and actions leaders were planning, the promotion of state-wide colored conventions brought activists from smaller communities like Troy, Albany, Utica and Syracuse where efforts among blacks for political rights were developing, in contact with the New York City spokesmen and clergy.

The first such invitation to "colored inhabitants" to discuss "their political disabilities" resulted in a convention in Albany in August 1840. Over forty from twenty-three towns and cities attended the three day meeting.[14] They were small in number, but those who came from New York City, Poughkeepsie, Troy, Albany, Whitesboro, and Syracuse found the experience exhilarating. They discussed issues, strategies, organizing structures, and communications. Like all social groups honoring free speech, they discovered that diversity of thought and means existed within assemblies, whether large or small.

Since the agenda centered on legislative and political strategies to remove restrictions barring most colored men from voting, the new Liberty Party, with its strong anti-slavery platform, was enthusiastically discussed. The assembly chose not to officially endorse the Liberty Party, fearing an alliance would be counter-productive. They were, after all, appealing to representatives of the New York State legislature to eliminate barriers to political rights based upon "complexion," so they chose not to offend incumbent Democrats and Whig lawmakers.

Still, it was obvious the majority supported James Birney, the Liberty Party candidate. Their primary focus was aimed at county organizing to get signatures on petitions urging expanded voting rights for black citizens. That year, Rev. John Chester and Ambrose Dunbar attended the convention and came back home to rally support in Syracuse. [15]

Loguen, Chester, and Dunbar discussed these plans and strategies with free people of color in Syracuse. When the New York State Legislature began their session, Henry Highland Garnet, reported in the February 13, 1841 issue of *The Colored American,* that their petitions were presented in person to the chairmen of the committee. According to Garnet's report, Syracuse sent 70, Rochester 107, Poughkeepsie 101, Utica 84, Troy 80, and New York City 1300. [16]

A few years later, Rev. Loguen spoke at churches on the subject of slavery, but in 1838 only Rev. Charles L. Remond was engaged on a lecture tour, and that was primarily in Massachusetts. Most state and national societies did not hire part-time or full-time black speakers until after 1840, when Samuel Ringgold Ward, Jermain Loguen, Charles L. Remond, Frederick Douglass, and Henry Highland Garnet, were launched on to the speaker's podium in Central New York as anti-slavery society agents, or as speakers for the Liberty Party. In November 1843, the New York State Anti-Slavery Society listed Rev. Samuel Ward, Rev. H. H. Garnet, Milton and Lewis Clark among their agents. [17]

These black anti-slavery spokesmen, according to Charles Wesley, came to be "ardent supporters" of the Liberty Party, though Frederick Douglass, reluctant to part ways with William L. Garrison, did not do so for several years. [18]   Black voters were encouraged not just by Liberty Party policies, but also because the organization "welcomed all colored people into the party," and increasingly into convention leadership roles. [19]

As the Liberty Party held its conventions throughout the state, in Utica, Auburn, Canastota, Cazenovia, Cortland, Fayetteville, and Syracuse, more people had a chance to hear about the realities of slavery unmediated by white speakers or writers. Rev. Samuel R. Ward, a Congregational minister, joined the Liberty Party in 1840 devoting, he said, the rest of his political life within its driving goals while he lived within the United States. [20]

The fact remains that it was only gradually after 1840 that talented abolitionist speakers born in slavery, and ex-slaves like Lewis and Milton Clark, Ezra C. Smith, and Martin R. Delaney, made their way into Central and Western New York to tell their stories and plead the cause of emancipation and equality. The more frequent such events, the more northerners got to see and hear for themselves, and to question portrayals of the "contented slave" and the institution of slavery as "benevolent" and "civilizing." [21] But such opportunities were few and far between for most Manlius, Fayetteville, and DeWitt residents in the early days of the movements.

CHAPTER EIGHTEEN

CRUSADING UPHILL

If you have courage, listen.
If you are a COWARD, lay this tract down.
I write for brave hearts. [1]

James C. Jackson,
*The Duties & Dignities
of American Freemen*

Alvan Stewart, the Liberty Party candidate for Governor of New York State, sounded like a winner in a *Liberty Press* report, though he lost the election by wide margins in November 1842. Why? Because the party vote had increased dramatically, and cheerleading is exhilarating.

The Liberty Party tallied 2,662 votes in the Governor's election of 1840. Two years later they racked up 7,263 votes. Stewart energized the party faithful like a revivalist preacher. "Courage, brave companions of the ballot-box," he cheered. "How great a change! We have a newspaper, an able editor and industrious publisher at Utica, in Central New York, and an organizing and fiscal agent."[2]

The year 1842 was a virtual whirlwind campaign by Liberty Party enthusiasts, and James C. Jackson, then living in Peterboro, and L. P. Noble of Fayetteville, were in the thick of it. Jackson came into the Liberty Party after leaving the American Anti-Slavery Society, having decided political means did not exclude continuing a moral suasion campaign. William Lloyd Garrison was not pleased. Neither were some of his colleagues.

L. P. Noble, however, had joined the political reformers at the very beginning of their breakaway venture. He chaired the mass meeting in Madison County's Peterboro that January. Some calculated the assembly had over 1000 attendees. The event had its critics. Oliver Johnson, a Garrison supporter, took exception to how Liberty Party men dominated the proceedings. He charged promoters with false advertising, rallying attendance about a mass anti-slavery meeting, but having the whole event managed by Liberty Party members.

Johnson, however, was not without graciousness. He praised the "lively and cheerful" setting, and generous hospitality of the people. [3] When Gerrit Smith declined the group's nomination for Governor, Alvan Stewart became the Liberty Party's nominee. Smith made headlines, however, when in his speech he called on all slaves to do what it takes to escape from their owners. Some called his words inflammatory and reckless, an incitement to insurrection.

Regardless of the critical fallout, L. P. Noble and James C. Jackson channeled their enthusiasm into organizing local Liberty associations. In April, Jackson came to Fayetteville where he spoke to a gathering of anti-slavery supporters, and began organizing a local Liberty chapter. [4] He found a great deal of encouragement among the anti-slavery faithful. While Syracuse and Cazenovia meetings mobilized their foot soldiers, Fayetteville supporters sponsored a series of information programs in June. Wesley Bailey publicized them.

Much history is written about the unusually gifted speakers, journalists, and organizers of social reform movements. Men like Gerrit Smith, Alvan Stewart, James C. Jackson, and Wesley Bailey occupy the center of the stage. Their commitment and courage is praiseworthy. They are, however, only part of the story. The anti-slavery movement in the Fayetteville-Manlius area, is not significant because of its well-documented captains and generals, but because movement enthusiasts were exceptional recruiters, and that ordinary men and women stepped forward to perform some practical service.

In Manlius and Fayetteville, there were "rank and file" men and women who came to see slavery as a moral and civic injustice. Some read and subscribed to anti-slavery newspapers, attended public and church meetings on the subject, donated food, clothing and money to help fugitive slaves, raised funds to support anti-slavery agents, signed petitions, and voted to end the slave trade, or stop its extension into new states.

Howard Zinn, an historian who chronicled stories of ordinary American people, claimed the "essential ingredients" of struggles for justice are "human beings who, if only for a moment, if only while beset with fears, step out of line and do something, however small." [5]

As the Liberty Party got underway in Fayetteville, the names of James C. Jackson, L. P. Noble, N. R. Chapman, and Wesley Bailey. were recognized as local crusaders. They were a second wave of activists, who built a political movement on the shoulders of risk-taking choices made years ago by their townsmen. It was Rev. Stephen S. Smith; Rev. Carlos Smith, Rev. Oren Hyde; Rev. William Hutchinson, B. Hibbard, James Stewart, Philip Flint, John McViccar, James Francis, Randal Palmer, Elijah Payne, and Samuel Edwards who first "stepped out of line" and gave public witness in October 1835. They were maligned in the local newspaper for expressing their views. [6] Yet, they stood their ground.

Still, most participants in the early days of the movement, unknown and unheralded, citizens and churchgoers, were seeking to do what they came to believe was right. That there were more than a few, is heartening.

Among subscribers to abolitionist weeklies were Deacon Sanford. B. Palmer and Seymour Pratt, Curren Elms, Daniel H. Eaton, Horace Robbins, H. Barrett, William Boylston, and Chauncey Parker. So too did Charles H. Weld, (brother of Theodore), Darius Northup, Rev. Washington Kingsley, Deacon Samuel Edwards, Darlin Thompson, Andrew Sherwood, James Pinney, Joseph Fitch, and Orlo D. Blanchard. [7]

Then there were the "Ladies in Fayetteville" who donated $4 to the anti-slavery cause in May 1842, and Adam Harrower and William Eager of DeWitt, who were noted as having subscribed to the abolitionist press that month. [8]

When Wesley Bailey later moved to publish the *Liberty Press* in Utica, Manlius and Fayetteville citizens received issues: Joseph Fitch, Andrew Sherwood, Orlo Blanchard, J. I. DePuy, Zopher Adams, Willis L. Gregory, Emerson Kinne, Elijah Gridley, Mrs. A. E. Gridley, Orris Worden, G. Bogardus, Charles Coates and C. Adams, along with some of the early faithful supporters. [9]

There were those who signed anti-slavery petitions protesting the annexing of Texas territory to the United States. Signers included Rev. Ludovicus Weld, Weld's wife Elizabeth, their daughter Cornelia and his brother Ezra. Also, several members of Salmon Sherwood's family; William. M. Clark; Horatio Chapman; Silas William; Zopher Adams; Hamilton White; Phillis Denison; Emily Gregory; Joel, Laura and L. Philena Huntington; Lauriston and Eliza Fish; William Odell, Elizabeth Palmer; Betsey White and others. [10]

There were those who angered their Democrat and Whig neighbors by running for local offices on the banner of Liberty for all! [11]

Philip Flint	Charles Coats
James J. DePuy*	Samuel Gregory
Lawrence DeLancy	Andrew Sherwood
Isaac Carhart	David Hoag
Darlin Thompson	William Cunningham
Orlow D. Blanchard	Frederick H. Westover
Josiah B. Van Schaack	Lucien B. Williams
William Folts	Charles Nutting
Henry DeLong Jr	Orris Worden
John W. Peck	Willis Gregory
Sanford B. Palmer	Peter Multer**
Miles Graham	William Gilman
Thomas Boyd	Caleb Harrington
Nicholas Mickles	

Others include Samuel Edwards, Horace Robbins, William Eager, and Rev. Amos C. Tuttle who attended state anti-slavery conventions, and Azariah Smith and Elijah Rhoades advanced aspects of the antislavery agendas in their legislative careers. There were risk-takers like Dr. George Loomis of DeWitt, who was an aider and abettor of fleeing fugitive slaves, and Methodist Episcopal minister Rev. Alfred D. Peck, also of DeWitt, who defied the warnings of a bishop to avoid aligning himself with those who denounced slaveholding. Then there was Darius Northrup and other members of the Reformed Methodists of High Bridge, whose discipline had made no compromise with slavery since their formation in 1814. The names of the seceding Baptists will come shortly.

The 1837 *Third Annual Report* of the American Anti-Slavery Society reported 112 members in the town of Manlius antislavery society.

There may be more.

**The following excerpt is from a report submitted by
REV. CHARLES L. REMOND
From London, June 1840**

[Rev. Remond traveled to the World Anti-Slavery Convention in London with other members of the American Anti-Slavery Society. His delegation was late. A major controversy had risen when women delegates were refused seating. In protest, William Lloyd Garrison, Charles L. Remond, Nathaniel P. Rogers sat in the gallery in solidarity with their rejected delegate, Lucretia Mott.]

> "....on my arrival I learned much to my sorrow of the rejection of the female delegation...And in few instances in life have I met with greater disappointment, especially in view of the fact, that I was almost entirely indebted to the kind and generous members of the Bangor Female Anti-Slavery Society, the Portland sewing circle, and the Newport Young Ladies Juvenile Anti-Slavery Society, for the aid in visiting this country.
>
> ...Thanks be to Providence, I have yet to learn, that the emancipation of the American slave, from the sepulcher of American slavery, is not of more importance than the rejection of females from the platform of any Anti Slavery Society, Convention, or Conference....
>
> The Colored American Oct. 3, 1840.

CHAPTER NINETEEN

THE WOMAN QUESTION

> ...She [Abby Kelley] is a Non-Resistant... We still hope that our friends will offer every facility that is necessary to a full and fair presentation of the cause she pleads before the people. Let not an intolerant spirit creep up among us...[1]
>
> *The Abolitionist,*
> July 5 & 12, 1842

When Rev. Charles Denison spoke in Fayetteville in January 1842, the small donation offered, $ 7.51, as reported in the *Emancipator,* likely had little to do with his disapproval of women speaking publicly in mixed gender assemblies, that is, "the vexed woman question," but he himself had a lot to do with the issue. [2] Lewis Tappan, Rev. Amos Phelps, and Denison refused to serve on the business committee of the American Anti-Slavery Society on that fateful day in May 1840, when Abby Kelley had been appointed to join them.

Consequently, all hell broke loose, and a large male entourage seceded with them. Since that schism, whenever, and wherever, women lecturers took the podium with male associates in public meetings dominated by conservative clergy and members of their congregation, it often resulted in a disruptive event.

Public speaking by women in mixed gender meetings, and women holding positions of organizational leadership, were unwelcome innovations in 1840. Women participated in anti-slavery activities, but primarily through bazaars and fairs, that is, "functions to raise funds." [3]

Despite their often back-seat public place, their role in advancing the anti-slavery petition campaign was substantial. When Judith Wellman examined petitions sent to Congress from upstate New York, she found that "over 70 percent" of them between 1837 to 1839, "carried women's names, either alone or in conjunction with the names of men." [4] Women in the town of Manlius were among them.

Unlike his conservative abolitionist colleagues, William Lloyd Garrison encouraged gender equality at the podium, in meetings, at the publication office, and on organizational committees. His belief in, and promotion of, a pacifist utopianism, called nonresistance, may have been just as startling, and objectionable, but his disregard of women's traditionally assigned role got a great deal of reaction, and triggered a schism.

All this drama, usually centered in New England, might have had only tangential connection to Central New York except Abby Kelley was coming to town. She, along with Frederick Douglass, John A. Collins, and later, Garrison, were scheduled for a grand speaking tour throughout Central and Western New York starting in 1842. Garrison worried about successes the Liberty Party was having enrolling abolitionists, and was encouraged by colleagues to make personal appeals and arguments to retake ground from the Liberty Party.

As to the role women played in Liberty meetings in upstate New York, while the constitution encouraged attendance, women were generally active in their own gender associations where they exercised diverse leadership skills, though many did attend the large gatherings. Participation varied from state to state, with some local leaders more encouraging than others.

James Jackson had a more liberal view on the participation of women than many abolitionists. While promoting attendance at the mass state convention scheduled in remote Peterboro in Madison County on January 19, 1842, Jackson announced that he wanted both men and women to attend. This was no 1840 London Conference, he said, where American women delegates were refused seating. That will not be the case in Peterboro, he continued, "for here we recognize woman.' "Our custom is to get as many women into our meetings as possible..." [5]

Jackson, like Garrison, recognized the talent, commitment, and witness of women colleagues in the movement. His reflection on the death of Sarah Hunt in the June 1842 issue of *The Abolitionist*, illuminates the writer, as much as the subject.

"She had a clear discriminating mind, forcible and acute," he wrote, "unflinching in the cause of the TRUE AND RIGHT." Jackson then exposed prevailing gender inequalities, saying Hunt understood the difference between inherent rights, and privileges conveyed by others, that society regarded woman "as living in this country by sufferance, not by right..." and that "the difference between her and the slave of the South was one of condition merely." Her condition in time, of course, had been bettered and made "tolerable," but "her rights as a human being" had, Jackson claimed, "never in any society under heaven, been acknowledged." [6]

That Jackson should make such an unequivocal, personal memorial publicly, adding his commentary, distinguishes him from many other journalists, orators, and abolitionists of the time and place. He did not give the same wholehearted endorsement to Abby Kelley, however.

Abby Kelley, like Sarah McClintock Hunt, and the Grimke sisters, was a fearless Quaker abolitionist, but she had other radical views, and in 1842, she was single. She had come in advance of the American Anti-Slavery Society team, and was visiting friends in Utica. [7]

She spoke during the Mass Anti-Slavery Convention in Cazenovia held on July 6 and 7. Her participation was, by local standards, improper, and certainly made many there uncomfortable. Liberty Party leaders and members were out in force. The convention may have numbered as many as 2,000, and when the Methodist chapel could no longer hold such a crowd, the whole contingent paraded over to a spacious country grove to continue.

Jackson praised the civility of participants in his convention report published on July 12. "The spirit of tolerance shown," he wrote, was a model for other assemblies, despite the fact that "nine-tenths of the convention" thought it improper for a woman to speak publicly, thinking it "indecorous" of her to do so. Jackson, claimed that "not a lisp was heard against Abby Kelley." [8] Still, he warned Kelley that if the American Anti-Slavery Society chose to pick a fight with the Liberty wing of abolitionists, they would not back down, otherwise, he chose as editor of *The Abolitionist* to avoid spleen venting.

Judith Wellman believes there was far greater disapproval displayed at the meeting than Jackson acknowledged. When Kelley reportedly called the Liberty Party as dirty a political party, as every other one, and worse, Wellman noted, she "enraged many of the two thousand people in her audience." [9]

For several weeks, critics argued against Kelley's disparaging remark about the Liberty Party. Diplomatically, Jackson continued to plead for fairness and tolerance, urging Kelley to keep her sights on the real foe, the pro-slavery defenders, and remain what he perceived her to be, "noble-souled, tolerant, generous, self-sacrificing." [10]

Abby Kelley Speaks At High Bridge

When Abby Kelley came to Central New York she welcomed opportunities to speak during the month before she moved westward to pre-arranged lecture engagements in the Rochester area. She spoke in Cazenovia on the weekend following the mass anti-slavery convention sponsored by the Liberty Party leaders. According to Rev. Luther Myrick, her second presentation on Saturday was delivered at the Free Church because objections had been raised by trustees at the Methodist meeting house where she had lectured on Friday evening. [11]

Myrick had harsh words for some of her detractors. He challenged those "professed religionists and professed republicans," who criticized Kelley for being out of "her appropriate sphere," while they do nothing and sustain the horrible system of slavery. At one point, he called these critics "dumb dogs, who will not bark." "If professed ministers of Christ and legislators" won't plead for these crushed poor, he said, "then let the women open their mouths." [12]

Undaunted by rejections, Abby Kelley continued to seek speaking venues. She found an opportunity at the High Bridge meeting house soon after her Cazenovia lectures. The July 14 issue of Wesley Bailey's *Methodist Reformer* announced she would speak on Wednesday evening. [13] The notice invited "one and all" to come to hear "the eloquent agent of the American Anti-Slavery Society."

Like most Liberty Party abolitionists, Bailey considered the Garrisonian anti-government, non-resistant agenda that Kelley represented, too radical and abstract. It is likely he was among "the nine-tenths" James C. Jackson reported, that believed her public speaking in Cazenovia was "improper." Still, as uncomfortable as he might be in advancing this controversial female speaker to address a mixed gender public audience, Bailey may have believed Jackson's warning about not falling prey to "an intolerant spirit" was good advice. Such a course of civility showed that he, and the Liberty Party, could not be accused of hypocrisy by their adversaries.

Kelley's presentation was probably delivered on Wednesday, July 20th. The newspaper announcement dated Thursday, July 14, noted the program was scheduled for "Wednesday" evening. The July 21 issue of the *Methodist Reformer* printed an article referencing Kelley, and though not an eye-witness account of what transpired at the meeting house, and how the audience responded to Kelley's lecture, did provide an interesting anecdote and commentary. [14]

Bailey titled this article "Are Christians Hornets?" He selected a story Abby Kelley told. She said she was on her way to speak to an assembly in Connecticut, when she was met by a "deputation" that warned her "against coming." The delegation said her coming would be like "throwing a stone into a hornet's nest." In response she said, "Why, are Christians hornets?" Bailey used this anecdote to liken it to a "pro-slavery church," saying "if you throw the great truths of human liberty and human rights among them," they "immediately exhibit their waspish propensities." It is possible Bailey didn't comment on the meeting because of his printing and distribution deadline, or because he just decided, the less said, the better.

As for Abby Kelley, we know, whatever gracious, civil, or angry reception she stimulated at High Bridge, she continued her westward travels to Seneca Falls and Rochester. She spoke in Waterloo in late July. In Rochester, she aided a foundational meeting of the Western Anti-Slavery Society where Quaker friends Isaac and Amy Post were becoming more active. [15] In late November, she joined William Lloyd Garrison, and other AASS members in giving a series of lectures in Syracuse. [16] Kelley's lecture tour, and speaking programs with Garrison later that fall, stirred up hornets in Cazenovia, Fayetteville, Seneca Falls, Rochester and Syracuse, and in other towns, but not just among public audiences who attended these events. They exposed the fractures the anti-slavery movement contended with within itself. Advocates of non-resistance and moral suasion often fought bitter campaigns against Liberty Party members, while they denounced their pro-slavery opponents.

Abby Kelley's name was mentioned in *The Methodist Reformer* at least on one other occasion that summer, and that was in Rev. Richard Cleveland's presentation to the Society for the Promotion of Moral Reform in August, just weeks after Kelley's lecture at the High Bridge meeting house. The name of this organization, as published, does not specify the gender identity of its members. Was it a female society, or a mixed gender organization?

Female moral reform societies had organized in Central and Western New York since 1835. The New York State Female Moral Reform Society operated out of New York City, where their publication *Advocate of Moral Reform* was printed. Sarah Towne Smith, sister of Rev. Carlos Smith, and Rev. Stephen Smith, was editor of the *Advocate* from 1836 to 1840, and later took over management of the New York Female Reform Society. [17]

A Manlius "F. M. R. S." was recorded in an 1836 issue of *Advocate of Moral Reform*, and Fayetteville was listed an "auxiliary" with "Miss Caroline Collins, secy," and 63 members in 1838. [18] Clearly these women in the village of Manlius and Fayetteville had been actively engaged in reform efforts prior to 1842.

Whether the audience that heard Rev. Cleveland's presentation was a combined association of these local women's groups, or one configured as a mixed audience, is not clear, but I tend to believe the audience consisted of women members of their society and auxiliaries, in association with the state women's organization.

The aims of the woman's moral reform society seemed quite modest and conservative, and some auxiliaries kept a primary focus on cultivating high standards of female purity, especially among those vulnerable to licentiousness, victimization, or prostitution. Others, however, had a broader view, and called attention to the two-way street of prostitution, demanding criminal punishment against male seducers. Many joined the campaign to persuade the New York State legislature to punish such predatory seductions, as the Manlius ladies' petition did in 1839. [19]

What Rev. Cleveland said to the audience in August 1842 was clear, however, since Wesley Bailey published the entire presentation in his October 6 and October 13 editions of the *Methodist Reformer*.

Cleveland situated his reflections within mainstream Presbyterian theology, explaining that "the appropriate station and influence of the female sex," was fixed in the "primeval ordinance of marriage by the direct and immediate care of our Maker." This origin "constituted woman, singly and exclusively, the help meet of her husband." [20] Within this religious moral context, he went on to present "the safe and virtuous education of females." This he noted made it unnecessary to look toward women such as Mary Wollstonecraft, Harriet Livermore, or Abby Kelley as models to admire. [21]

These were the last two issues of the *Methodist Reformer* that Bailey published in Fayetteville. He announced he would begin getting out a newspaper in Cazenovia, or Utica, soon. He had become a public figure in the Liberty Party movement, and within a month, the publisher of their newspaper.

ABBY KELLEY TOURS UPSTATE NEW YORK

"....Abby Kelley addressed the good people of this village last evening [July 27th]. We believe she made a generally favorable impression upon those who heard her – especially upon those who coincide with her sentiment."

July 28, 1842
Seneca Falls Democrat

"Abby Kelley is lecturing on Slavery in western New York. Her efforts are highly spoken of, even by those who think she is 'out of her sphere.'"

Aug 18, 1842
The Courier

"Miss Abby Kelley is delivering lectures in Canandaigua on slavery. Her discourses are represented as being highly colored."

Sept 13, 1842
The Roman Citizen

"...Walnuts, potatoes, and fire crackers flew about the house like hailstones; shouts, screeches, stamping, whistling not surpassed by the rowdies at the Bowery Theater ...characterized the scene..."

Dec 12, 1842, New-York Daily,
Abolition Meeting in Utica

CHAPTER TWENTY

THE BAPTISTS

> It was thought by those who promoted free inquiry that free discussion would dispel ignorance and superstition and would promote harmony; they did not foresee that the result might lead to antagonistic controversy instead. [1]
>
> Douglas M. Strong,
> *Perfectionist Politics*

While Fayetteville's First Baptist Church took a clear position against Freemasonry in 1829, it was reluctant to do so when the anti-slavery controversy arose in the church in the 1840s. The men within the congregation most interested in promoting an immediate end to slavery were L. P. Noble, Nathan R. Chapman, and Samuel Edwards.

Noble was born in Hoosick, New York in 1802. He married Samuel Edward's daughter, Harriet. While he lived many years in Fayetteville, his early business and political activities were in Albany. He owned a commercial Towing Line of vessels from New York City to Oswego.

Noble first became politically active in the Albany Whig Party, but by 1840 he realized the party was not going to adopt a strong emancipation plank, so he joined the political rebel wing of the American Anti-Slavery Society. When these "friends of Independent Anti-Slavery nominations" voted to choose candidates for national office at a May 12, 1841 meeting, they were battling upstream for a consensus on this new tactic. Criticism came from several quarters, including William Lloyd Garrison, who censured the group for taking matters into their own hands. [2]

Noble was right at home in this group of talented breakaways, and in 1842 he chaired the well-attended, enthusiastic Liberty Party convention in Peterboro in January. When host Gerrit Smith declined to run for political office, Alvan Stewart became the party candidate for Governor. It was at this meeting that Smith shocked many, when in a speech to the assembly, he boldly urged slaves to seize opportunities to "run away" and take any "boats" or "horses" they might need to escape. [3]

One observer maintained that L. P. Noble "might have filled high political stations, but his radical views kept him in the minority." [4] It is not surprising that associating with such Liberty Party zealots marked Noble as someone not willing to conform to more popular, less divisive opinions. Given his strong commitment to this cause, Noble was fortunate to have a father-in-law who held similar anti-slavery sentiments.

Noble was a faithful Baptist, and served as a deacon of Fayetteville's First Baptist Church, at times leading Sabbath school programs for the congregation. When the Liberty Party decided to publish a national abolitionist newspaper in Washington, D. C. several years later, he took on the job with Gamaliel Bailey as editor.

If Noble had been a lone voice flailing his radical views to a deaf congregation, he might have ended up as a singular unsuccessful eccentric on the sidelines, but he was not. He was fortunate to have a strong abolitionist colleague in fellow Baptist, Nathan R. Chapman. Chapman, also a devout religious man, believed that what you pledge in your faith you must seek to manifest in your life. He first learned slavery was wrong from his father. The elder Nathan Chapman lived within the stronghold of abolition-minded Peterboro and Canastota in Madison County, and gave constant support to his son's antislavery activities as they arose in Fayetteville.

There are times in life so strikingly opportune that the expression "I was in the right place, at the right time" seems appropriate. Like several other young men who had a disposition toward making the world a better place, Chapman attended Cortland Academy in Homer in the early 1830s. It was the right time, and place, for a budding abolitionist, because Rev. John Keep, pastor of the Congregational Church there, provided witness and leadership. Rev. Keep mentored the educational formation of the school children, and presided over the Board of Trustees. Keep had been inspired by revivalist Charles G. Finney, and believed personal sanctification was not a private comforting piety, but an abiding spiritual strength that actively confronted the foremost social evils of the day, slavery and temperance. He sponsored numerous revivals in the town, and Chapman and some of his classmates, were lastingly influenced by these experiences.

Abel F. Kinney, a cousin of Chapman, was among his schoolmates. In 1836, Kinney was on the school faculty at Homer's Cortland Academy. He wrote to Nathan, telling him what was happening since Chapman had graduated, gone on to Hamilton College, and was teaching in Fayetteville. Kinney described his own exciting teaching experience, temperance activities, and participation in the local anti-slavery movement.

Kinney rejoiced in the "number of thoroughgoing abolitionists" active in the town. "We are now circulating petitions to Congress," he wrote, and his fervent hope was that Congress would be "buried in an accumulated mass of petitions from every part of the non-slave-holding states..." He was optimistic, and believed the day near when the "foul stain" of slavery which "mars the beauty of our beloved country" would "be wiped away forever." [5]

Chapman, like his cousin, began his career in teaching, then became principal at Fayetteville Academy, before opening his law office in Fayetteville in 1841. He found his reform sentiments shared by Noble and Edwards, and a few others at the Fayetteville Baptist Church, and together they pushed the abolitionist agenda into glaring visibility.

Most Baptist ministers, like clergy in Presbyterians and Methodist Episcopal churches in the early 1840s, avoided public involvement in the issue, though there were no hierarchies of bishops, annual conferences, or a General Assembly. However, in September 1841, the Onondaga Baptist Association met in Fayetteville and declared American slavery was not only "a violation of the inalienable rights of man," but it was "a flagrant sin in the sight of God." Therefore, anti-slavery work was an act of "Christian benevolence and effort." [6] This position was a welcome turn of events for Fayetteville's Baptist abolitionists.

In the spring of the following year, they hosted a public debate on slavery at the church. Judge James Watson, adept at managing opposing arguments, presided, and editor Wesley Bailey performed the role of secretary. Noble argued the radical position of seeking peaceful abolition by withholding fellowship and votes from men not committed to abolition. David L. Farnham, a loyal Whig Party member, took the opposing position. [7]

That summer proved to be a nonstop marathon of meetings. One series started in June. Bailey's *Reformer* announced these public discussions hosted around the town. The first was scheduled at the Eagle Village schoolhouse on Friday, June 24. The second was held on Tuesday, June 28 at the schoolhouse near Reuben Butts, and the third at the High Bridge meeting house on Friday, July 1. Seeking to tackle their adversaries head-on, Bailey invited opponents of "immediate abolition" to attend the meeting, pledging "their objections" would be "candidly answered." [8] By this time, Wesley Bailey, L. P. Noble, and Nathan Chapman were solidly in the Liberty Party camp.

The biggest local anti-slavery event of July was the Cazenovia mass anti-slavery meeting, followed by the Abby Kelley lecture at High Bridge. In August, the Fayetteville Baptists invited one of their own to speak. Rev. Elon Galusha, first President of the Baptist Anti-Slavery Committee, was their featured lecturer. Bailey was effusive in complimenting Galusha as "a speaker of the highest order," quoting, and commenting on the talk. Since the speaker, he wrote, demonstrated clearly that American Slavery is the "work of the devil," then, the work of Christians was clear. Their task was "destroying the work of the devil..." [9] This personalized on-site report contrasted with Bailey's remarks that followed Abby Kelley's presentation several weeks earlier.

Chapman, Noble, and Edwards then proceeded to provide an opportunity for their enlightened congregation to step forward with a strong condemnation of slavery. In November, Deacon Hervey Edwards introduced their resolution. Action on the resolution was postponed. On December 12, it "was discussed at length." The heart of the matter was the conviction that American slavery was "contrary to the spirit of the Gospel and Jesus Christ "and consequently sinful." Therefore, the congregation was urged to have "no fellowship with those who traffic in human flesh and hold their fellow man in bondage."[10]

Further action regarding the resolution was postponed until the next meeting. After more discussion, and another meeting, action was again postponed.

It was evident some members did not want a recorded vote. Guilford C. Palmer and Samuel Edwards had enough of these slip-sliding maneuvers, and asked for letters of dismission from the church. Chapman tried to move the resolution forward once again. A vote was taken. The vote was close: 11 to 9. Apparently, it was a disturbing split vote. It was immediately contested, and then rescinded.

Wrangling and resistance continued through the next several months. By May 1843 more than a dozen members of the church had seceded.[11] They included:

Nathan R. Chapman	Harriet Simpson
Sarah E. Chapman	Sanford B. Palmer
Victor M. Kingsley	Polly Palmer
Zerviah Kingsley	Dan H. Eaton
M. L. Simpson	Fidelia D. Eaton
Curran Elms	Abbey J. Travis
Emily Elms	Rev. Washington Kingsley

That summer two prominent abolitionist agents came to Fayetteville. William L. Chapin, who years later was captured in Virginia while trying to help fleeing slaves, spoke to interested residents in early August. Then, on Sunday, August 13, Alvan Stewart, the Liberty Party candidate for Governor, spoke to an audience in the village square. Stewart was well known for engaging an audience. Years later, Henry B. Stanton, testified that Stewart had a unique speaking style, both in the courts as a lawyer and in public. He attributed this to Stewart's "peculiar" way of mixing "argumentation, wit and sarcasm," a style audience found entertaining. [12]

Stewart described his visit to Fayetteville in a letter to Wesley Bailey, who later published it in the *Liberty Press*.

He let his outdoor audience know that his request to speak to them in a religious setting on Sunday was rejected by all four village churches. The Episcopalian, Methodist, Presbyterian and Baptist churches were, he said, all "closed" against his preaching about slavery, as if those 2,700, 000 countrymen "held by the bullet, powder, gun and sword," were inconsequential, and of no spiritual, or moral concern. [13] The propriety of speaking on the Sabbath about slavery was hotly denounced by many clergymen, who knew Gerrit Smith was agitating the controversial question. Most clergy defined the controversy as political, not religious. All four religious leaders denied Stewart's request. So out into the village square he went.

He then contrasted these respectable church buildings of the righteous to those who braved the over 90 degree August temperature to hear him in the square. The "people came from the town and adjoining villages and sat in their wagons, buggies and carriages..." It was clear he knew what was going on in the local Baptist church, since he praised the dissenters. Elder Washington Kingsley, his wife and son, he said "were fighting the great battle of Religion and Liberty." He then named Mr. Edwards, "a gentleman 70 years of age," who was "bold and dauntless" fighting "long and powerfully for the helpless." And lawyer Chapman, he noted, was "pleading the cause of humanity." Friend Noble is still "vigorous" in the cause. Stewart also complimented Charles Wheaton who used his fine singing voice, as he often did on such occasions. At this event Wheaton sang "The Slave Mother's Lament" and three other hymns. [14]

After having gained public notice of their intentions, the Baptist seceders organized themselves under the title Second Baptist Church of Fayetteville. Their numbers expanded when joined by Charles R. Edwards, Jerome Edwards, Cromwell Bullock, Harriet A. Palmiter, Sally Edwards, Electa Edwards, Caroline L. Edwards, L. P. Noble, later Orlow Blanchard, Jonathan C. Worden, Abigail and Helen Worden, Almena Hopkins from Peterboro, Nathan and Hannah Chapman from Lenox, Nathan R. Chapman's father and mother. [15]

In December 1843, they decided to seek recognition as an independent abolitionist Baptist church, and invited fellowship and affirmation from other Baptists leaders and churches to stand with them. These proposed actions did not please Rev. John Smitzer of Fayetteville's Baptist Church. [16]

Rather than just quietly seclude themselves into the general activities of a small local congregation, Second Baptist's leaders made a public display of their actions, identity, and mission, perhaps seeking to inspire others to take similar action. Chapman and Noble issued a region-wide invitation to Baptist congregations and leaders in sympathy with their secession to join them in council. In January 1844, they were publicly recognized by a council of forty-two members from thirteen churches located in Cicero, Onondaga, Syracuse, Marcellus, Lysander, Elbridge, Peterboro, Nelson, Sennett, Lenox, Hannibal and other localities. They included six ministers and several deacons. [17]

Elder Thomas Brown of Marcellus, as moderator, expressed sadness about this separation from the old church, but hoped Second Baptist members, by their kindness, would draw "the old church" to see "the flagrant wrongs of slavery," and encourage them to act "on behalf of the liberty of the Slave." [18]

Second Baptist congregation business and worship activities were most often held in schoolhouse 11 in Fayetteville, though sometimes in homes. Rev. Washington Kingsley was voted their supply pastor, and Rev William Shapscott was chosen to assist when needed.

A candidate for membership knew that his or her religious and moral beliefs directed political choices and actions. When John Calvin Worden, a prospective member, was interviewed as to whether he would ever vote for a pro-slavery candidate, the expected answer was, "No!" And it was. [19]

EXCERPTS FROM A

Letter written by Rev. Washington Kingsley to Nathan R. Chapman

sharing fond memories of their times creating an abolitionist congregation in Fayetteville, 1843-1846.

...I now believe, fully believe- if ever true piety dwelt on earth with mortals it was there with that little circle when weeping over the wrongs of the slave - while praying to god to soften hearts stilled by popularity against feeling for another's woes, Our cause was one of moral sublimity....

Had I power to role back the wheel of time and enjoy again any portion of my life I would elect that as the best – most god-like and consequently the happiest period of my existence. I can see that little circle of friends now all in their places – I see that devotional look – the tear gathers and rolls down the cheek – and I hear the hearty Amen that now and then burst from an overflowing heart. I could give the names of that self-sacrificing circle. But I need not – N. R. Chapman can write them. Dea. Palmer can call over the roll and drop a tear at each precious name. Dea. Noble can tell who had in that heavenly liberty – song " What mean ye bruise and bind my people saith the Lord" Others now alive can speak these names...

I then hoped there was religion enough in the nation to save it from ruin. Was I mistaken?...

[Letter, March 13, 1855, Pittsford, Vermont]

CHAPTER TWENTY-ONE

WHAT HAPPENED ON HIGH BRIDGE HILL?

> ".. in almost every little village, or neighborhood, there is a church controversy going on over these issues. [1]
>
> Douglas Strong,
> quoting William Goodell,
> *Perfectionist Politics*

When Ian Frazier wrote an account of his family's westward migrations, he remarked on the multiplicity of creed and church disputes that led to new meeting houses being erected along every nook and cranny of the landscape. It seemed, he said, the nation "was one big religious argument." [2]

Large numbers, however, did not "come out" from their churches in protest over the issue of slavery, much to the disappointment of abolitionists. Most asked for letters of reference to take with them when they moved on to greener pastures, and likely attached themselves to a worshipping community similar to the one they left. The West was the new land of opportunity. Illinois, Ohio, Michigan and Wisconsin attracted people from Manlius and High Bridge, and elsewhere, to cheap, fertile land, where new jobs opened up, and greater freedom beckoned. [3]

The Reformed Methodist Church at High Bridge was greatly affected when members, entire families, sometimes with neighbors, resettled in the west. In 1839, the little meeting house was cheered at its installation. The revival several months before the structure was completed sparked optimism and harmony. It was a bright witness to the hamlet's diligent efforts to expand manufacturing, commercial attractions, and benefits. That was when hopes ran high that the long economic depression would soon end. But for many, the glimmer of opportunity lay further west, and the congregation seemed to be going through dramatic changes, and shrinking in numbers of worshippers.

The year 1843 was a busy one for social reformers in the town. Anti-slavery discussions and Liberty Party campaigns stimulated a great deal of adversarial activity. Thirteen members of First Baptist Church in Fayetteville took the unusual step of seceding, after their year-long effort failed to convince others in the congregation to publicly exclude slaveholders. In response, they created their own abolitionist church and were joined by similarly committed believers. The temperance movement angered tavern keepers and other beverage venders that year, when advocates focused attention on the licensing boards. So, there was a lot of controversy in the villages, and at High Bridge.

On February 5, 1844, a handful of men, who said they regularly worshipped at the meeting house, met and incorporated a Methodist Episcopal Church under the discipline of the General Conference. They bought a parcel of land less than forty yards east of the existing meeting house to build their church. [4]

HIGH BRIDGE
TOWN OF MANLIUS
Scale 30 Rods to the inch

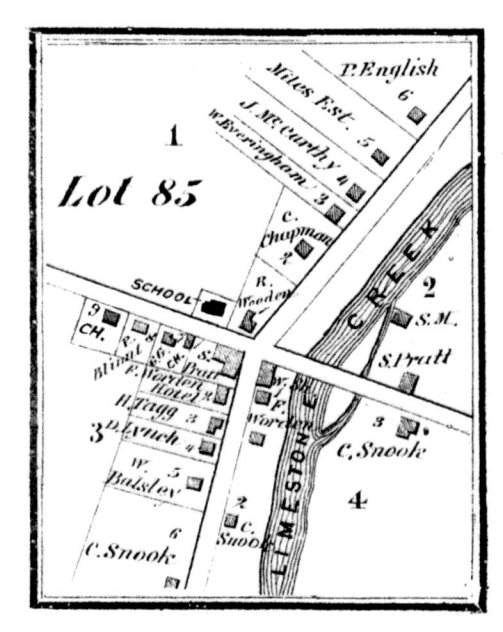

In the 1874 inset map of High Bridge by Homer Sweet, the location of the first church is represented by "9 CH." The second church, incorporated in 1844, is east of this church lot, and is represented by "CH." In Homer Sweet's earlier 1860 map, the uphill church was designated as "W MC." The second meeting house, located almost directly opposite the district school, was referred to then as the "M E Ch."

Why did these men feel compelled to incorporate a second meeting house in a hamlet of less than 50 households? And why downhill, just a stone's throw from the one they used to pray in? Were they seceding over the slavery issue as the Baptists had just done?

Not Necessarily....

A lot had changed in four years. For one thing, some key founding members were no longer there. Rev. Zebina Baker, who was euphoric at the installation of the High Bridge Reformed Methodist meeting house, and who ministered there three years, left to serve a congregation in Sandy Creek.

Rev. Wesley Bailey, needing a more financially secure future, and encouraged by abolitionist colleagues, moved to Utica and began publishing the *Liberty Press*. Death claimed Andrew Balsley, a close friend of Elijah Bailey's family, and the church, in 1842. His son, John A. Balsley, was one of the first trustees of the Reformed Methodist meeting house.[5]

Perhaps leadership changes unsettled the congregation. Unlike Elijah Bailey, and the Reformed Methodist seceders in 1814, founders of the High Bridge Methodist Episcopal Church in 1844 left no statement of beliefs, nor did they publish their motivations.

The Unspoken and Unknown

Generally, people leave an association when they no longer feel comfortable with the policies, or leadership of the organization. Every church had its doctrines and behavioral expectations. New concerns arose, laxity set in, and periodically higher levels of authority, assemblies and conferences met and decided what expectations required restatement, or correction. Most churches disciplined members for immoral and inappropriate activities such as sexual transgressions, drunkenness, dancing, gambling, even card playing. Members who violated these behavioral norms were disciplined, suspended, and at times, excommunicated.

The Reformed Methodists held to similar norms. Few major denominations, however, were as strict about enforcing anti-slavery principles, even when their rules and discipline adopted them years earlier. It was either negligence, or just accommodation to the trend and needs. In contrast, the Reformed Methodists consistently denounced slaveholding, slave buying and selling as did the founders of the seceding Baptist Church in Fayetteville

The Temperance Movement

There were also different attitudes about intoxicating drink. This conflict would likely not have threatened the major stake holders, distillers, tavern owners, and merchants, had not the temperance groups organized to restrict licenses to sellers.

Public testimony and example were one thing, enforcement through law was another. Still, the costs of drunkenness were borne by the town, when tax monies were used to support the homeless, abandoned and orphaned at the county poor house.

The Erie Canal traffic (which enhanced profits for many farmers, manufacturers, storage owners and transporters in and around Fayetteville) had, without intending to do so, increased this problem, and added another more disturbing one. Carol Sheriff claimed at least thirty thousand men, women and children, a quarter of them boys, who were orphans, worked day and night on the canal during the 1840s to keep it in operation. [6] These mobile young, sometimes rootless wage earners, evolved their own detached survivalist lifestyle along the canal banks, and a cluster of serious problems confronted villages.

"From a middle class perspective," she writes, "the canal had become a haven for vice and immorality, the towpaths attracted workers who drank, swore, whored and gambled." [7] The increased flow of intoxicating drinks in and around canals and taverns led to more than just bad examples for young boys who served as drivers along the tow paths. Drunkenness put pressure on local communities to deal with abandoned and impoverished families, in order to pay for their maintenance at the county poor house. So the cost of "bad" behavior was not only harmful to family members, and dangerous for working children, but was a financial cost to employers and taxpayers as well.

As a result churches began to preach more about sobriety, disciplining members, creating mission societies, while concerned citizens rallied to toughen the excise licensing procedures which were authorized by their local town commissioners.

Local Enterprise vs Temperance

These social problems were not remote from High Bridge, nor Limestone Creek, which connected to the Fayetteville feeder and canal traffic. The hamlet had several tavern sites, as Kathy Crowell has documented so well. [9] The earliest appears to have been opened by Jacob Balsley in 1802. He managed it until 1817. Later, a hotel was opened to provide overnight accommodations to travelers. This inn changed hands until Clark Snook came into ownership in June 1844.

When the Reformed Methodist meeting house opened its doors in 1839, members quickly expressed concern about the loose behavior among youth, and declared their intent to rid the neighborhood of "rum-sellers." [10] Since the High Bridge Hotel was then a "regular stage coach stop" between Syracuse and Albany, clearly a conflict of interests existed. [11]

While the Reformed Methodists sought to enforce their strict temperance rule, the Methodist Episcopal Church had done the opposite for several years. It omitted the "sale and use of spirituous liquors section in its discipline." [12] There was, then, a clear distinction between policies and practices of the Methodist Episcopal denomination in 1843, and those of the small Reformed Methodist Society at High Bridge hill.

This erosion in Methodist Episcopal discipline on intoxicating drink only added more fuel to Wesley Bailey's criticisms of the denomination. His temperance views became increasingly evident. In 1841, he chastised Manlius commissioners who granted excise licenses to taverns. The commissioners justified their decisions saying this was "absolutely necessary for the accommodations of travelers." Bailey retorted, how absurd, as only one of them was needed to provide for any travelers into the town. [13]

Two years later, when living in Utica, his *Liberty Press* applauded Manlius citizens for expressing their opinion on the issue. They voted against granting licenses to "dram shops" by "a large vote." Skeptical of conniving politicians, he posed the question to readers: "Now, will the Board defy this public sentiment, or will they withhold licenses from the twelve to fifteen pauper making machines in that town." [14]

All eyes turned to the elected positions of excise license commissioners. It is not surprising that some townsmen were angered when Bailey encouraged temperance crusaders to use electoral politics to advance their moral reforms. It was what the abolitionists were doing. Here the goal was to gain control of excise licensing boards through the ballot box. To use politics to enforce prohibitions, that is, to impose abstinence, necessarily limited the freedom of others. As Altschuler and Saltzgaber observed, there was, "as in other reforms," a distinct difference between those who zealously pursued social reform, and "those accepting individual conversion and example." [15]

Such issues were increasingly fought out at the ballot box, and by departure.

CHAPTER TWENTY-TWO

CONFRONTATION AND THE COSTS OF ZEAL

> I see where the shoe pinches Mr. Speaker. It will pinch more yet ....I'll deal out to the Gentlemen a diet that they'll find it hard to digest! [1]
>
> John Quincy Adams,
> quoted by Joseph Wheelan,
> in *Mr. Adams's Last Crusade*

Wesley Bailey was not standing alone in denouncing the liberal licensing practice in the town of Manlius, since when it came up for a vote, citizens voted licensing down. If his evangelical zeal angered some residents to defend their individual and mercantile rights, its aims of reducing town charity costs, crimes and assaults induced by drunkenness, and perhaps, keep some abandoned women and children out of the poor house, were recognized by many as compelling social goals. The movement gained supporters, increasingly so among employers who wanted sober, productive, reliable workers, and who felt the problem was corrupting, extensive, and costly.

Still, Bailey had once again taken sides. Such polarities strain harmony and civility. When ex-President John Quincy Adams relentlessly introduced citizen anti-slavery petitions in

1842 in defiance of the Congressional gag rule, his actions earned him all manner of slurs and censure. But he persisted in spite of it all.

Wesley Bailey didn't have a lucrative safety net, or the prestige of a former President, but like many prominent evangelical reformers of his day, including Gerrit Smith, he promoted two powerful reform movements, abolition and temperance, simultaneously. His broadening social reform agenda exposed injustice, and disturbed the complacent, but also threatened the livelihoods of some town businessmen.

Understandably, it didn't sell many newspapers, or increase his advertisers. He was almost bankrupt by the summer of 1842. In September, Bailey confessed that during the last few years, he experienced "the most severe trial and anxiety." He was forced to borrow money several times. He believed these circumstances were partly the fault of "being singled out as a special object of hate." [2] This sense of failure, and blame, suggests he may have greatly underestimated resistance and reactions to his own frequent criticisms.

His public argument with Rev. Edward Wadsworth late that summer was a bitter public confrontation. Rev. Wadsworth claimed the local Methodist Episcopal Church had gained members because some had withdrawn from Bailey's High Bridge Reformed Methodist congregation. Bailey's angry reply to Wadsworth on July 28 posed an unpleasant innuendo. He said Wadsworth would "regret" having "broached" the subject, if Bailey disclosed "facts connected to the matter" which he chose "to forbear." [3]

What was this oblique secret all about?

Certainly this dueling reveals as much as it conceals. In

his exploration of moral reformers, Boston Professor, B. P. Bowne, noted righteous reformers at times "alienate the thoughtful and finally get it by the ears themselves." [4] With his back to the wall, Bailey sought to fend off what he saw as a conscious effort by opponents to derail his livelihood. The withdrawal of financial support, subscription, advertising, or donations, was a simple way to show disapproval, whether of a newspaper, or a church.

Whatever the case, he knew he would have to seek opportunities elsewhere. He had a family to support.

The Wesleyan Methodist Connection

Wesley Bailey not only intensified his criticisms of slaveholders, and their apologists, and supported the anti-license campaign, but he changed his church affiliation. Since numerous social behaviors and issues had become public moral and political controversies, one's church affiliation indicated a great deal about one's politics.

In 1843 the Reformed Methodist congregation joined the Wesleyan Methodist Connection, an affiliation of those who seceded from the Methodist Episcopal Church over the years. Bailey encouraged this step. This was not a sudden decision. The RMs collaborated over many years with other independent Methodist sects and churches. In May 1843, however, the number of ex-Methodist Episcopals had increased dramatically, and some of their leaders came together in Utica to forge a cooperative association. [5]

Wesley Bailey, Darius Northrup, Rev. Marcellus Barnum, Adam Harrower and E. J. Ward attended the convention. So did Elder Elijah Bailey, who came as an official delegate from the Reformed Methodist's Massachusetts Conference. [6] Not surprisingly, the assembly rejected episcopacy, restored rights to itinerants and laity, and adopted stronger prohibitions against slavery and intoxicating liquors. [7]

They attained no agreement, however, on the position of whether members of secret societies and lodges should be excluded from their fellowship. The Anti-Masonic furor of fifteen years ago had waned, but some Americans still believed secret lodges were inconsistent with equality rights and republican justice. These republicans saw Freemasonry as destroying a level playing field, "by secretly using its powers to favor the interests of its members..." [8] Those attending the Utica assembly were unable to reach a consensus on this question, so the decision was left to annual conferences and local congregations. [9]

The incorporation document of the High Bridge Methodist Episcopal Church records Asel Wilcox as one of the three trustees selected on February 6, 1844. Wilcox, a High Bridge businessman who invested in plaster mills, among other enterprises, was a former member of Manlius Military Lodge No. 93. His relation to the Freemasons was deeply rooted. Charles Lakin's history of the lodge noted that "Four generations of the Wilcox family appear upon the records of Military lodge." [10] His father, who opened one of the early taverns in the town of Manlius at Lyndon Corners, was also a Freemason. Did this exclusionary attitude become part of the fellowship criteria when the uphill meeting house formally associated with the Wesleyan Methodist Connection in 1843?

No doubt opinions and church rules about slavery, intoxicating drink, and secret societies could polarize a hamlet, or congregation. If this was not enough commotion, what happened when a new political party embraced some of these same principles, and vied for office-holding against the traditional political party slates?

One More Thing to Argue About

The election of 1843 offered plenty to argue about – economic and commercial interests, western territories, the slavery debate, local excise licenses. Three years ago the Liberty Party was scoffed at as a miniscule irritant, but now their national, state, and local membership numbers had increased. They proved themselves capable of being spoilers in a close election.

The town Liberty campaign was energized by strong talented abolitionists. Fayetteville and DeWitt delegates were prominent in the party organization. William Eager presided at the county-wide nominating meeting in Syracuse that summer, and L. P. Noble was nominated for Sheriff. Nathan R. Chapman was chosen to attend the Buffalo convention and the senatorial district meeting, as the county representative. While the Syracuse meeting was in session, attendees took up a collection "to assist a female slave on her way to Canada." [11]

While many staunch abolitionists made efforts to aid fleeing slaves when opportunities arose, some still refused to place their allegiance in a particular party organization. William M. Clark, now in Syracuse, was one of those who continued to defend his independent stance. In a letter written to his cousin in 1843, he agreed that the party might provide a path to freeing the slaves, but he claimed to manifest his abolitionism in his own way, by sympathizing, praying, working and voting for the slaves he said, "but I do not necessarily vote for the Liberty ticket so called..." [12]

On August 30, 1843, the National Liberty Convention in Buffalo added a more explicit local target in their resolutions which was bound to sharpen divisions. They took aim at town level offices.

> Resolved: That we most earnestly recommend that the Liberty Party make efforts to secure the control of the Town power so that every officer shall be a Liberty party man. [13]

This news did not go down well with Democrats and Whigs alike, though the latter had more to lose in a tight race.

It was no secret that many Liberty Party leaders such as Gerrit Smith, Alvan Stewart, L. P. Noble, and Wesley Bailey were activist temperance men. If Liberty Party candidates were nominated, and gained control of local excise boards, they could determine whether licenses were granted, or not. It was happening in other towns. That was a direct challenge to the livelihoods of distillers, merchants, tavern owners, and inn-keepers.

This challenge wasn't taken lightly. Whig Party members rose to the occasion and denounced these zealots. [14] When Whigs included a strong anti-slavery plank in their county convention platform, Bailey saw it as a trick, and blatant contradiction. He mocked the desperation of the Onondaga County Whig convention, naming "old friend" D. L. Farnham, Esq. for putting up an anti-slavery resolution while at the same time supporting Presidential candidate Henry Clay, "the prince of slaveholders." [15]

Clearly, the Reformed Methodist Society on High Bridge hill had changed dramatically. By 1844, they were linked nationally as Wesleyan Methodist Connection associates with a strong reformist orientation, but they had also, with Wesley Bailey's encouragement, identified the Liberty Party wing of the abolitionist movement as best able to express their moral reform goals.

Those who didn't agree with this new direction had many reasons to find another place to worship. The evidence clearly shows that in February a small number did just that, aligned with the Methodist Episcopal Church, and built their own meeting house on the same road.

It is interesting that a similar situation developed in Leon, Cattaraugus County, where Bailey kin had founded a Reformed Methodist congregation in 1822. That church was started under the guidance of Rev. Ezra Amadon, Rev. Elijah Bailey's brother-in-law. Ezra and Elizabeth Bailey Amadon were later joined by John Fairbanks and his wife Experience, another sister of Elijah Bailey, and their families. All were members of the original Vermont seceders.

In 1843, the very same year the controversy erupted in the High Bridge congregation, a dispute divided the Leon membership. According to the county historian, the split arose over the question of whether the church should join the Wesleyans, or continue "adhering to the original organization." As a result, "dissensions ensued, and what with the loss of members by emigration, the interest was so much weakened that the services were discontinued..." [16]

What seemed to Wesley Bailey, and some Reformed Methodists, to be a wise course of action to maintain and defend righteous moral principles and equality rights, didn't appear to others (even to some in his own extended family in

Leon) to be as beneficial, or wise. This new connection seemed to be an abandonment of their original pledge to a simple Bible faith, and an unwelcome politicizing of the movement.

These numerous religious controversies emerged during challenging economic times in the hamlet, town, and nation itself. These were years that coincided with the Erie Canal boom, when a primarily agricultural economy competed with new manufacturing and commercial ventures for advantage. Not everyone shared in prosperous good times, as a result, however.

Asa Eastwood's diary depicted his hardship and struggle during the five years following the panic of 1837. He confessed that he made no gains despite his enterprise and efforts. His circumstance was not an isolated story. While some of the wealthy and well-connected seized the moments and opportunities during the financial crises of 1837 and 1839, many urban workers and cash-stressed farmers suffered considerable losses.

Some men were unable to pay off their debts, and were forced to sell their property, often at a financial loss. James I. DePuy faced such debts. His decided to go west with his family and to start over where land was still cheap. Others in the town with commercial drive and sufficient capital, bought up prime property along the Limestone Creek with a view toward expanding profitable advantages. Several savvy businessmen worked to divert the creek's water power into Fayetteville, and to expand productivity of the mills located along its banks, and in 1845 they succeeded. [17]

Surely religious tensions and controversies over slavery and temperance were troublesome in a small congregation and hamlet, but they cannot be detached from the economic motives, drives and struggles taking place in each family household. There was no equality in attaining economic profit and success. There were winners, losers, and those just managing to meet their financial obligations.

Moral decisions are complex, and often complicated by personal financial concerns.

CHAPTER TWENTY-THREE

THE PRESBYTERIANS & THE LONE SECEDER

....What is the price-current of an
honest man and patriot today?...[1]

Henry David Thoreau,
On the Duty of Civil Disobedience

I have suggested that what motivated a small group of men to come together in February 1844 to incorporate a Methodist Episcopal Church at High Bridge, was a conflict of beliefs that had reached a tipping point. That Wesley Bailey's newspaper tirelessly advanced ever-sharpening arguments about these issues, sometimes stridently, is evident. That this wake-up call provoked thought, heightened conscience and choice, as well as alienation, is common to many hard-fought reform movements.

While it is unclear which one, or ones, of these issues, and their moral, political, or economic implications, was so compelling as to lead to founding a new congregation, it is likely the conflict widened when the Reformed Methodist congregation joined the Wesleyan Methodist Connection in May 1843.

The Presbyterians were able to keep the lid on embarrassing inner dissensions for several years, but they could not stop the protest of a single man. There is no doubt why Monroe Worden withdrew from the Fayetteville Presbyterian Church in April 1844. His secession *was* motivated by slaveholding. In this case, the documents are clear.

After 1840, the Presbyterian General Assembly sought to minimize anti-slavery arguments by scheduling meetings every three years. It was a successful short-term maneuver to delay discomfort, but the June 1843 Assembly confronted the same insistent slavery petitions. Abolitionists still clamored for an answer to the question, whether the church would denounce slavery as a sin, or not, and bring it into the list of grievous behavior that required correction.

Local Presbyterian congregations in Manlius and Fayetteville had members who were anti-slavery activists for several years, but by 1843 some had moved elsewhere. This was true of the Clarks. William M. Clark, had moved to Syracuse, where he was in the thick of helping fugitive slaves get to the safety of Canada. He joined the recently founded abolitionist Congregational Church there.

Rev. Ludovicus and Elizabeth Clark Weld, and daughter Cornelia, left Manlius Presbyterian Church in 1843 and joined their abolitionist son Theodore, and their uncommon daughter-in-law, Angelina, in New Jersey. Cornelia's request for a letter of dismission, "to any evangelical chh where her lot may be cast" seemed to challenge the Manlius Presbyterian Church Session meeting. [2]

The term "any" seemed to imply denominations didn't matter. Evangelical churches preferred good preaching and revivals, rather than emphasis on creed and worship. If the Rev. Charles G. Finney, the great revivalist preacher, was still "persona non grata" among orthodox Presbyterian clergy, he was greatly admired by the Clarks and Welds. Their son Theodore, inspired by Finney, had used his evangelical experience and style to advance the anti-slavery cause. So Session members had some reasons to pause and consider how to deal with Cornelia Weld's request.

The Welds, however, were held in high esteem, whether many in Manlius knew it or not. Theodore had recently aided ex-president John Quincy Adams in Washington, D. C. as Adams prepared his defense against censure charges in the House of Representatives. Congressman Adams had angered many southerners, and their allies, by introducing anti-slavery petitions in defiance of the gag rule. Church members might not have known that Rev. Ludovicus Weld had been a classmate of Adams at Harvard, and that Theodore's grandfather, Rev. Ezra Weld, had baptized the ex-President. [3]

Whatever they knew, Session members must have calculated the pros and cons of prolonging theological questioning of the daughter of retired elder Rev. Ludovicus Weld. So two days later, after a "free discussion," they granted her request. [4]

For six years, John McViccar and Philip Flint had used their roles as members and trustees to foster great sympathy and action on behalf of those enslaved. They had, in the early days, the support of clergymen Rev. Stephen Smith and Rev. Amos Tuttle, and they hosted many abolitionist meetings at the Fayetteville Presbyterian Church. With the appointment of more conservative clergymen after 1841, however, the congregation's anti-slavery members received little encouragement.

This retreat into silence was replicated at the national level. The Presbyterian General Assembly in June 1843 chose to reinforce avoidance, making clear they would make no more statements against slavery because they would only evoke more alienation, and which they said, would not be edifying for the church to do so. The same General Assembly did, however, find it expedient to pass a resolution urging church sessions to discipline members found guilty of engaging in the "fashionable" amusement of "promiscuous dancing." [5]

Anti-slavery newspapers found such contrasting actions shocking, and reacted with disdain. *Signal of Liberty* compared the outrageous inconsistency of disciplining members for dancing, and applying no discipline for slaveholding, to the behavior of Pharisees who "strained at a gnat, and swallowed a camel." [6]

Whether Monroe Worden, who subscribed to the *Liberty Press*, knew details of what transpired at the May 1843 General Assembly, or read Bailey's report rebuking Dr. Wisner for his failing to bring resolutions against slavery to the floor, is not clear. [7] It is difficult to know which event, or moment, was for Worden, the last blatant straw that caused him to this action.

There were certainly many discussions hosted in Fayetteville in the year leading up to his decision. The question of complicity in staying a member of a church that refused to denounce slavery as a sin, was debated publicly in local churches and schools, especially in the summer of 1842. Bailey, of course, repeatedly encouraged abolitionists and Liberty men to "come-out" of their sinful pro-slavery churches. In March he reported a secession from the Vernon Presbyterian Church. It was the action of a single man. William Putnam, he wrote, seceded from the church during a presbytery meeting, declaring "he could not remain in what I considered a pro-slavery church." [8]

Gerrit Smith felt the same way. He was totally disheartened by the Peterboro Presbyterian Church, and General Assembly, which he said, "deliberately" refused "to say that slavery is a sin" [9]

On April 8, 1844, Monroe Worden, then twenty-seven, a son of Jesse and Abiah Worden, made a formal request for a letter of dismission from the Fayetteville Presbyterian Church. His reason - the church maintained fellowship with slaveholders.[10] When the church failed to discipline this grave moral wrong, and required him to be passively complicit, Worden refused.

The Session balked at his request, saying they were not at liberty "to throw a member out of the church into the world," and required Mr. Worden to not only identify a church to which he intended to join, but that they had agreed to receive him. Mr. Worden walked away.

John McViccar was designated by the Session to visit and reason with Worden, a common practice in cases of church discipline, in the hope that some reconciliation to fellowship might occur. Worden did not comply with these entreaties, nor did he attend church session meetings when requested to explain his absence.

Yet the church, though mired and stalled in a series of procedural steps, seemed reluctant to complete the steps required to exclude him. John McViccar must have sympathized with Worden's underlying moral rejection of slavery, and would not have relished his role as emissary to plead with Worden about reconsidering his decision. He failed to persuade him. Three years later, on May 12, 1847, the Session convened and rendered their final decision to suspend him for his "contemptuous" refusal "to obey the voice of the church," and to repent of his "error." [11]

The "error" of individual conscience is most troubling

for those in authority. What consequence might one man's witness have outside his own peace of mind?   It is a question for reflection. Nancy S. Marder argued that the importance of Juror 8 in the 1961 movie *12 Angry Men*, the lone dissenter in a murder trial, was that he "manages to slow down the proceedings so that the jurors must deliberate."   She credited this process of deliberation as a valuable contribution because it led "other jurors to re-examine the evidence, contributing their insights and reach a new understanding." [12]

The "new understanding" reached by a majority, coalesced faster in the Synods of Onondaga, Geneva, and Susquehanna, though it would eventually precipitate a further withdrawal by the few southern synods left within its bounds since the great schism.

It was not until 1857 that "the twenty years battle over the question whether slaveholding was a sin requiring disciplinary action," was ended, noted historian Robert H. Nichols. [13]

Two generations had passed since Monroe Worden chose not to be complicit in slaveholding as a church member, when someone wrote these remembrances into his 1904 obituary memorial:

>   ....
>
> Uprightness in life and thought marked him among men and makes his memory one to be revered. Strong in his convictions, he might stand alone but he would be true to them.
>
> So when "abolitionist" was almost a word of scorn, because he believed "a body with an immortal soul" ought not to be bought and sold, he stood staunch for his principles and rejoiced when victory was with the right. [14]

CHAPTER TWENTY-FOUR

WESTWARD HO!

> ... Father is getting the western fever...he begins to talk of arriving out next summer, but I am inclined to think it will be all moonshine. I hope not. I do not know what is to become of High Bridge when all the folks go west....[1]
>
> Letter to brother, William
> Harriet E. DePuy,
> July 14, 1845

Still, the motives of others are not so clear as those of Monroe Worden. There are complexities in human behavior not so easily explained. No documents yet found define exactly why local residents created the Methodist Episcopal Church at High Bridge. In this instance, differing views on slavery and abolition may have played a part in their decision, but other issues may have held more importance, and we are reminded "We can only work with what we have," which many times, comes down to relying "on the survival of fugitive pieces of paper." [2]

When T. Elmer Bogardus wrote about "Forgotten Villages" in Onondaga County, he recollected the church built down hill at High Bridge "didn't last long." [3] Less than a generation it seems, if the 1865 census record is correct. [4] A surprising number of neighborhood families headed west between 1846 and 1849. More followed a few years later. Whatever the original motives of the founders of High Bridge Methodist Episcopal Church were in February 1844, the "western fever" certainly hastened changes that took place during the years that followed.

Even Rev. Marcellus Barnum, the Reformed Methodist minister who aligned with the Wesleyan Methodist Connection, and who preached a few years to Manlius and Fyler settlement Wesleyans, got the western fever. Urged by his DePuy and Stilwell friends to come west with them and set up a Wesleyan congregation in Wisconsin, he and his family traveled with the DePuys to Metoman in Fond du Lac County. [5] There was nothing new in this group migration of families, neighbors and church members. They followed a pattern chosen by earlier pioneers when families packed up their wagons and ox carts, and left Massachusetts, Connecticut and Vermont and came to the wild frontiers of New York. For some settlers, religious affiliation had a lot to do with fitting in and creating a safe, social, and comfortable community in an unknown environment, so they traveled as families knit together by religious belief and practices.

While exploring his own family migrations, author Ian Frazier observed that while it was true that pioneers held strong doctrinal views and judgments, there seemed to be plenty of room for all kinds of dissenters and sects. If one spot "turned out not to be the Promised land; due to the doctrinal errors of its inhabitants, then maybe that spot there would be." And so they went and recreated what they preferred. [6]

They carried bedrock traditions and values with them, but their eyes, hands, and minds turned anxiously to practical considerations, what must be taken forward, what must be left behind. Harriet DePuy wrote her brother William in Wisconsin to learn more.

> Ma wants I should ask...Have you any fruit of any kind, or whether there are any orchards or nurseries near; whether it is well watered...whether there are any stones for building cisterns, wells, or stone walls or whether it is level of rolling land..
>
> Father wants to know if it is heavy timbered, or light, any fencing timber and what kind of wood there are there?...[7]

The DePuys left in 1847. Evaline Bailey came to High Bridge when she was fifteen years old. She arrived with her father and mother, older brother Alfred, and younger brother Wesley, and sister Philena. She married James I. DePuy, a conscientious, hard-working man of simple faith. Her uncles, aunts and cousins, descendants of the Vermont seceders, were scattered about Central and Western New York.

She was leaving behind the burial place of her mother, Lydia Smith Bailey, who died in 1831, and was buried at High Bridge. The year of westward migration, her brother Wesley was busy publishing the abolitionist *Liberty Press* in Utica, expanding his interests more and more into the temperance movement. He, and Eunice, had left a son buried at High Bridge.

Alfred Bailey remained in Fayetteville, an enterprising grocer. For some time his widowed sister Lydia Conklin, and nephew, lived in his household. Uncle James continued to live out his days as an elder in Lafayette.

Rev. Elijah Bailey, her father, the family patriarch, was then nearing the end of his earthly itinerancy. Harriet wrote to her brother, William, in her final letter before leaving High Bridge, that they had recently received word from Massachusetts and "were expecting every day to hear of Grand pa's death..." [8]

A generation was passing.

James and Evaline DePuy, having tied up grocery and property dealings, packed up their belonging, and headed west with their children to join family, friends, neighbors, and church members who had already done so. [9] No doubt, as they set out, one of Harriet's earlier letters still expressed some of the family's concerns, hopes and dreams.

> Ma wants to know if you have got your gloves...Does it look like High Bridge? Are there good roads, any Indians or bears?...
>
> Lydia wants to know if there are any pretty boys there.... [10]

Sarah Brooks Blair, in her study of the Reformed Methodists, posed a thoughtful question. "Who, then were

The High Bridge Church, incorporated in 1839 by the Reformed Methodist Society, as it looked after renovation, in the early 1900s.

these people with enough conscience to stand up and leave because there were issues on which they could not compromise?" She offered an answer. They were, she continued, those who decided they must "battle the injustices of a church system which did not live up to the republican ideals of the Revolution which was so fresh in their minds." [11]

As they set their faith down in Manlius and Fayetteville, and elsewhere in Central New York, they went a step further. As the debate over slavery intensified, they applied their articles of belief regarding the condemnation of "buying and selling of slaves" adopted twenty years earlier, unflinchingly to the cause of the oppressed slave. They did not tolerate in silence the inequity of their own second-class position as lay members in the Methodist Episcopal Church back in 1814, and they did not tolerate the treatment of black human beings as chattel, and property. They recognized this evil was a moral blot on the Revolutionary ideals of the new nation, and gave witness.

A Page from the Ledger of Registered Slaves in the Town of Scipio (Cayuga County), 1801-1837.

In the first Ledger entry on this page, Jno Fleming certified on December 28th 1808, that a female negro child was born of a negro slave of his on the 15th of September, noting "its name is Esther." This is Esther Wheatley.

ALETHEA A. CONNOLLY

CHAPTER TWENTY-FIVE

AN AFTERWORD

THEY HAD NAMES

But what if we could break down the wall of silence that separates us from the dead and give them voice? We suspect – or want to believe – that they know more than they said in life, more than they had opportunity to say...[1]

Dale Salwak, editor,
AfterWord: Conjuring the Literary Dead

Many families had left the town of Manlius during the first decade of the local anti-slavery movement. DePuys, Barnums, Sherwoods, Balsleys and Russells were part of a grand ever-rippling wave of settlers seeking better opportunities, or joining their children. The elder Welds had gone to New Jersey to be close to their son Theodore's family. The financially-stressed reformer Wesley Bailey, brought his family to urban Utica to gain a wider network of readers and supporters. Abolitionists like the Sedgwicks, Clarks, and Wheatons had moved out of Pompey to Syracuse, where they continued to raise their voices on behalf of those trapped in involuntary servitude.

But there were earlier departures, departures of men and women who were ex-slaves. They too had a backload of anxieties and hopes, as they tried to figure out just what opportunities were open to them. [2] A few slaves were buried somewhere in the town before their time of freedom came.

For freed slaves who found no work locally, or who aspired to marry, or to locate members of their own scattered families, they searched in more promising environments. The 1830 federal census cited 29 free persons of color in the town of Manlius. Ten years later, the census recorded the number of colored residents as 14.

They sought a way to make a living, to provide for their families, to gain some sense of security in a time and place of barriers and limits.

We know, at least two female ex-slaves remained in the town for a very long time. One was a widow who contended with poverty. The other was an unmarried woman who lived as a domestic servant in the household of her former owner's son. One was Peggy Lenison. The other was Esther Wheatley. There may be others.

At first I knew little about these ex-slaves. I found no diaries, journals or letters. Most could not read or write. The imprint of their lives in history was obscure. Still there were fragments.

ISAAC WALES

Some of Isaac Wales' later life caught the attention of historian Timothy Cheney, who wrote about the enterprising Wales in his *Reminiscences of Syracuse*. Isaac, he said, figured out a way to earn money digging along the Erie Canal basin, and with these wages, he paid $80.00 to gain his freedom around 1824, three years before the New York State emancipation law went into effect.[3] Before his self-emancipation, Isaac was a slave in New York State for about twenty years. He was brought by his owner, John Fleming, then of Maryland, first to Scipio, Cayuga County, then to Manlius, Onondaga County.

When "Uncle Ike" died several months after the Civil War ended in 1865, a Syracuse journalist who wrote his obituary added a few details to Cheney's reminiscences. Isaac, he wrote, first borrowed money from Rufus Stanton, Esq. to purchase his freedom, gave the money to Fleming, then worked on the canal to pay off his loan. [4] That is possible.

The obituary praised Wale's "industry, sobriety, and honesty," adding that Isaac had shown unusual compassion, aiding his former master when the latter was inebriated.

This story may or may not be true, but it was quickly disputed. The very next day a letter signed by two former colleagues of John Fleming vigorously rejected this characterization, saying this was a clearly a case of mistaken identity, as there was another man named Fleming, who likely was intended. Their letter was also published by the newspaper. [5] Neither Wales nor Fleming were alive to clarify the story.

In 1996, another Syracuse journalist wrote a column on local black history, and repeated what was published about Isaac Wales in earlier accounts, including the compassion account, which this time headlined the story.[6] The contradicting letter was not included.

It is safe to say, that all his life, Isaac Wales depended on the grip of his hands, bending of his back, strength of his will, and some rugged faith. It is also realistic to say, that freedmen walked no easy street in Syracuse before, or immediately after, the Civil War. Many older freed men, having been barred from an early education, competed at the lower rungs of the employment ladder. A few local citizens offered help. Stephen Smith, a Quaker businessman, helped him get property. Smith sold Isaac and Polly Wales some land in lot 77 in the town of Cicero in 1839. [7] The property, subdivided, mortgaged, and defaulted, never brought a lasting livelihood, but it was a stepping stone forward.

In 1850 Isaac worked and lived in Syracuse. He was in his fifties then. He did manual work, jobs many would not choose, if they had other options. If he dug ditches to gain his freedom, he continued digging, hauling, and tilling to support his large family. In 1852, when being a "cart man" was not enough, Isaac Wales advertised his services to clean people's "vaults." [8] His sons struck out to make their way as best they could.

Less known about Isaac Wales was his involvement with efforts to expand civil rights for colored men. At a three day convention in August, 1841, Wales was appointed to a county committee, along with Rev. Jermain Loguen and Rev. John Chester. The goal was to develop a consciousness within the Syracuse colored community about the importance of "the elective franchise." The immediate effort was getting petitions signed that urged the removal of the $250 property fee required for colored men to vote. These were to be presented to the New York State legislature.[9] It proved a long, tough, uphill struggle, but this was a significant beginning.

Wales was also involved in legal proceedings following the Jerry Rescue in 1851. He was one of sixty-five witnesses subpoenaed to testify at Buffalo in early November, 1851.[10] The federal prosecutors were seeking to indict all participants in the Syracuse rescue of William Henry (Jerry), an alleged fugitive slave. Witnesses were transported to Buffalo and interrogated before Judge Alfred Conklin. Few details of the proceedings were made known. Eight men were indicted. The case dragged on for two years. Rev. Jermain Loguen, Wales' pastor at the African Methodist Episcopal Zion Church, was arrested the following year.[11]

Isaac Wales died in 1865 of dysentery. His funeral services were conducted at African Methodist Episcopal Zion Church. He was buried in an unmarked grave in Potter's Field in Syracuse's Rose Hill Cemetery.

It is believed Isaac Wales and his wife had eight children.[12] The daughters have not yet been traced but some information has been found about two of his sons.

His eldest son, Isaac, became a shoemaker, and joined with other colored citizens in 1867 to form a temperance group titled Mount Olive Lodge.[13] Several years later he moved to Fulton, Oswego County, and bought property there in 1875.[14]

The 1880 federal census for Fulton indicates he was then single.[15] He came back to Syracuse, at least on one memorable occasion. The October 3, 1882 issue of the *Syracuse Morning Standard*, reported, Isaac Wales joined "the elect" commemorating "the once famous Jerry rescue in Syracuse today."[16] Isaac, "the well-known colored shoemaker," as his obituary noted, died of pneumonia, according to the *Fulton Times,* on March 17, 1888.[17]

Another son, Stephen S. Wales, was, as a young man, a laborer living in Marcellus. He later went into religious ministry. In 1869, he presided over a smallAfrican Methodist Episcopal Zion congregation in Schoharie, New York. A few years later he moved to Binghamton where in 1872, he served an AMEZ church of fifty-six colored people.[18] In the mid-1880s, Rev. Stephen Wales was regognized as a presiding elder in Washington, D. C.[19]

In the 1866-67 *Syracuse Directory,* Mrs. Ann Wales, was cited as a "washer-woman." In 1868-69, she is cited as "WALES, Ann, Mrs. widow." The 1871-72 l directory notes her deceased husband. "Wales, Ann. widow Isaac. h. 19 Seward."[20]

According to Christ Church of Manlius burial records a "Robt Wales, a black belonging to John Fleming, d. 29 May 1824 ae 24" died three years short of his emancipation.[21] This may have been Isaac's brother.

PEGGY LENISON

"Aunt Peggy," was the affectionate name local historian Henry C. Van Schaack gave to Peggy Lenison. Van Schaack wrote of Mrs. Lenison's venerable, humble, character, portraying her as a truly biblical suffering servant whose saintly traits drew the community's affection to her in her old age. The eulogy mentions no children. The author seems to indicate her husband purchased her freedom. That is, her husband "served her master faithfully for her freedom; and, in due time, they rejoiced in her deliverance." [22] Her husband was Philip Lenison, and the 1830 census showed them as a household of four "free colored persons." [23]

Philip's name is not found in the 1840 census, and it is likely he died. Mrs. Lension lived for a time in the household of her married daughter, Jane Langley. The Chas. Langley household of "free colored persons" is recorded in Manlius in 1840, and shows one older female being the age Mrs. Lenison might be. [24]

It may be that Jedediah and Rebecca Wood took pity on Mrs. Lenison's plight, for in 1845, they sold a parcel of land to Peggy Lenison for $1 in lot 88 near Eagle Village. [25]

Her daughter Jane seems to have moved, and in the 1855 New York State census she is noted as a widow living in Syracuse. That same year, the census listed a female in Manlius named "Elizabeth Lenison," a black woman, age 77, a widow born in Dutchess County, and having been a resident in Manlius for 49 years. [26] This description fits "Peggy" Lenison. Either Elizabeth was her given name, or an error was made by whoever provided the information to the census taker.

In the 1860 Manlius census, Peggy Lenison is recorded as age 84, B, born in NY, a pauper, who cannot read of write. [27] Amazing what a few jots, a word, or a single letter discloses about a person.

Though Rev. Wesley Bailey denounced the Methodist Episcopal Church as a pro-slavery church, apparently Mrs. Lenison found some comfort at the Manlius Methodist Episcopal Church. She was noted on the 1831 membership list as "Sister Peggy Genson (Tenson) Colored woman." [28]

It is unclear how many children she birthed, but in 1830 she was about 50 years old, and several children might have left the household as adults, married, or been sold into other households. Separation of slave family members was not uncommon. The 1830 federal census showed three children in the household: a young male, a female child under ten, and an older female. There is a David Lenison recorded as living in Syracuse in the 1850s. Thus far, no other Lenisons of African-American descent have been found in the Syracuse area. David led, it seems, a troubled, chaotic life. He was arrested in the 1850s for petit larceny, and later for assault and battery on his wife. [29] In 1860, a David Lenison, headed a household of five living in the 8th ward. Then he is age 58, listed as a day laborer. A wife named Martha, age 40, and four children are listed in the family. [30]

We might know less about the Lenisons were not newspapers of the times eager to publish unusual anecdotal stories in their columns. Such entertaining curiosities were lifted from one newspaper and reprinted in others. The identity of individuals was not as important as the little drama displayed. There was such a story about a "Mrs. Lenison" published in the March 28, 1861 issue of the *Oneida Sachem.*

> At a religious meeting of colored persons in Syracuse, on Sunday, Mrs. Lenison spoke with much feeling, and apparently under great excitement. As she sat down, she shouted, "Blessed Jesus!" and immediately fell into a trance, in which she died about two hours after. She had previously been entirely healthy. [31]

I believe this was Martha, David's wife.

I found Civil War documents for a Philip Lenison, who I believe was Peggy Lenison's grandson. He enrolled in the colored troops during the Civil War. This Philip was working as a porter in Syracuse in 1860, but left the household in the early 60s, and joined the Union Army. After he enrolled in the State of Rhode Island, his family had heard nothing of his service, or whereabouts. Then on March 5, 1891, twenty-six years after the Civil War ended, the *Syracuse Courier*, announced the federal government was looking for kin of a Philip Leniston (or Levison) from Syracuse who was "supposed" to have enlisted in the colored Union troops. [32]

Apparently, the federal government owed him back pay for his service in the Civil War. Mrs. Jane (Lenison) Langley, heard of the inquiry, and notified authorities that Philip was a son of her brother, David Lenison. Mrs. Langley provided other details. When both parents died, she said, she took care of nephews George, Alfred and Phillip. She said Philip was "crestfallen" at his mother's death, went East, later enlisted. She never heard of him again until they learned he had died in a hospital. A nephew Gilbert went to England. The other two boys were placed in an orphanage, later being assigned to families in Homer, one to a farmer, another to a lawyer. [33]

Much of Mrs. Langley's story is verifiable, though information about some of her nephews is fragmentary. Philip Lenison served in Company G, 11th Regiment, United States Colored Heavy Artillery. Documents show he was born in Syracuse and had been a porter. He was garrisoned in defense of New Orleans when he caught diphtheria. He died in a Louisiana camp hospital on February 9, 1864, of putrid decay of the throat, a fact which was recorded on his military death record. [34] His name is inscribed on the African American Civil War Memorial plaque in Washington, D. C. Whether his aunt ever inherited any of his wages is unknown.

Like other members of this family, Jane Langley struggled to find some stability and safety, though the means at hand for poor, widowed, colored women were few. She lived for a time in Syracuse's 8th Ward, with several unidentified females. Two could be daughters, and the younger child, perhaps, a grand daughter. The legibility of the census record itself is problematic. Her employment was listed as tailoress. [35]

Five years later, she lived in Springport, Cayuga County, where she worked as a servant in an educational institution. [36] Though her life was one of toil, it was mitigated by a supportive local Quaker community. When "Aunty Langley" died in 1896, her obituary noted she had been "born in slavery" but obtained her freedom "early in life." She was, it went on to say, a laundress at the Oakwood Seminary, a boarding school sponsored by the Friends (Quakers), until 1880. They kept a room for her when she was unable to work, though in the last seven years of her life, she resided elsewhere, the obituary reported. [37]

ESTHER WHEATLEY

Very little information would have been found about some of the enslaved men and women brought to Manlius had not the *Ledger Record of Slaves in Scipio (1801-1837)* been carefully preserved, and made accessible, through the town of Scipio and researchers of the Underground Railroad in Cayuga County. [38] That such records, required by state law, have not been found for Manlius, is an unfortunate loss. They might have told us the names of slaves owned by Abijah Yerlverton Jr., Charles B. Bristol, Elijah Phillips, Elias Gumaer Jr., Abel Cadwell and other residents of the town. [39]

And had not John Fleming settled in Scipio first, between 1803 and 1814, we might not have known the names and ages of at least these slaves.[40] In Scipio, four slave children were born to his adult female slaves. One of those was Esther Wheatley.

Esther was born on September 15, 1808, which means she was a child when the Flemings moved to Manlius. She stayed in Manlius for the next forty-five years, at least thirty of them in the household of Robert Fleming, John Fleming's son. The 1855 census indicated Mr. Fleming was a tobacco dealer, and Esther a servant who had moved into Manlius from Cayuga County forty years earlier. [41] In 1860, Robert Fleming, then age 64, was listed as a successful farmer with sizeable real and personal estate holdings. The agricultural production census that year for Manlius showed many farmers raising large amounts of tobacco. [42] "Ester" had no occupation listed. She was then age 55, and could not read or write. [43] She lived in Manlius, at least until 1870. Robert Fleming died in August, 1871. [44]

In 1880, according to the census that year, she lived in Ledyard, Cayuga County, with her sister Betsy, and husband Samuel Grover. Esther was single and age 80. [45] When I visited the cemetery behind the old Methodist church in Ledyard, I found the name *Ester Wheatley* on a grave stone. The names of her brother-in-law Samuel Grover, her sister, and his first wife, who predeceased her, were etched on the front section. She likely was buried, and her name carved into the stone, by her nephew, Samuel Grover. [46]

There was a Hiram Wheatley who lived in Moravia, and documents suggest he is Esther's brother. The Scipio ledger of registered slaves shows a child named "Hiram" born on February 14, 1813 belonging to John Fleming. [47] If so, it is not clear whether the Wheatley siblings were separated from their parents, but when John Fleming moved to Manlius, Hiram would have been a young child.

In 1860, he was in Moravia working as a servant in a hotel. In 1870, he was living and working as a farm laborer in Locke. The records show him as not married, and having no children in the household.

It is interesting to observe that John and Chloe Wheatley, and several children, are recorded as free persons of color in Scipio in 1820, seven years before the emancipation date. That some slaves were emancipated early was not unusual. Some were manumitted earlier by owners, who either were morally convinced it was the righteous thing to do, or who did not want the financial burden of supporting them after emancipation. In some cases, slaves were allowed to work off their own purchase price, or were purchased, and released, and given land to till, by Quaker abolitionists, and later by philanthropist abolitionists like Gerrit Smith.

The Wheatley family moved from Scipio to Ledyard by 1830, where they lived for many years, but Esther went with the rest of the Fleming property to Manlius, when she was six years old. [48] She remained in Manlius for almost seventy years. Then, sometime before 1880, she found her way to Ledyard. Was she able to reunite with parents or siblings she had never met, or barely remembered?

The town of Ledyard has a registry book of those who

died in the town starting with the year 1886. The town clerk scrutinized the page listings of deaths for me. She found "Ester Wheatley." Ester died in January 1889, though the day date is blurred. The document shows her father as John Wheatley; her mother as Chloe. The age cited for Ester's death was 90, though it is more likely, 82. [49]

WHITINGTON

In 1815, John Fleming made an agreement with James Higgins, an innkeeper, at a popular tavern in Manlius Village. As Higgins was already in debt to him, Fleming may have believed that this was one way to get back some of the money he was owed, so he contracted out his negro man servant "Whitty," who was in "his possession service and employ," to Higgins from April 1815 to April 1816.

This was all stated in a written agreement by which Higgins was to "victual board and cloth [clothe] the said negro" and also "pay the said plaintiff for the services of said negro seventy dollars at the expiration of the term..." At various points in the penned document, insertions were made, and later crossed-out. For example, immediately following the clause of feeding, boarding and clothing "the said negro," the words "pay him five dollars" was inked out. [50]

The year 1816 became an increasingly bad year for farmers, and just about anyone relying on corn, and other grain crops, in east coast states and Central New York. John Fleming shared in these bad times. Some called it "poverty summer," when a series of frosts doomed crops and livestock, raised prices, leaving many with increasing debt burdens. [51] It proved a bad time to make deals with debtor neighbors. Fleming himself owed money, and he started calling payment from his notes to avoid the same legal proceedings. These were cash poor times.

So John Fleming's Negro man servant, Whitty, performed his full years service, but James Higgins failed to pay Fleming. Fleming went to the Court of Common Pleas to seek fees and damage claims.

The only unusual feature of this debt-related case of "trespass" (as such proceedings were called) was that it involved a labor contract of a "negro man servant." It was the first such document I had seen in Onondaga County records. So I was quite surprised when I came across additional documents. In the midst of my research through microfilmed Minutes of Common Pleas for Onondaga County, I again came across mention of John Fleming and Whitty. This time in the Court of General Session records for the early 1800s, which were microfilmed between segments of the Minutes of Common Pleas, though the microfilm box label made no reference to them.

According to these documents, on September 27, 1816, a case of "The People v. Whitington, A Black man" opened before the Honorable Judge Joshua Foreman, first judge of Common Pleas, and twelve named jurors. Whitington was charged with grand larceny, though no particulars were recorded. James Higgins and John Fleming testified for the People. No one was listed as testifying for the defense. Mr. Edwards presented for defense, Mr. Yelverton for the People (Mr. Yelverton was John Fleming's son-in-law, and also, a slave owner.). Apparently something was wrong. An objection was raised by the defense pleading "a misnomer." The name of the accused was disputed. Counsel for the defense said his name was not Whitington, "but Whitty." [52]

The court adjourned to sort things out. It is curious that defense counsel raised this issue. The jurors returned and soon decided the name of the accused to be "Whitington." The record continues stating that "the Deft. retracted his plea of guilty and plead not guilty." A rather bold move, but one not likely to evoke sympathy, though I imagine that was not the point. The jury then retired. When they returned their foreman announced, "they find the prisoner guilty of grand larceny." Sentencing was put over to the next day, and Whitington was sentenced to "confinement in the State Prison at hard labor for the term of three years & three months," [53] It happened that Auburn State Prison was then under construction.

While John Fleming was trying to collect from James Higgins for the services of "Whitty," another such agreement he made went sour for him. This time, he contracted to hire out his Negro man servant David to Timothy Dimock, for $75 per year. David performed these services with equally poor financial reward to himself, or Fleming. Like Higgins, Dimock failed to pay up when Fleming requested payment. Once again, Fleming went to court. On June 1, 1816, Fleming began legal proceedings in the Court of Common Pleas to obtain judgment. [54]

John Fleming won his case against James Higgins. On January 30, 1817, a final judgment was rendered for plaintiff John Fleming in the amount of $72.82. [55] The Docket of Judgment records showed the judgment was signed and docketed in February, 1817. [56] As to getting payment from Timothy Dimock, he may have been at the head of the line, but things got worse for Dimock. After being sued numerous times in 1817, he finally petitioned for relief as an insolvent debtor in 1820.

As I said, 1816 was a tough year for a lot of people, Whitington, David, John, and Timothy. The so-called "poverty summer" had stretched its icy fingers around the fields and into the barns. Newly planted crops failed, livestock froze and starved, prices rose on grains and flour, and income to buy and pay off debts shrank. Debt proceedings multiplied. Some decided it was a good time to go west. It is doubtful Fleming ever received his money. James Higgins left town some time that year.

This is not the end of Whitington's story, however. He survived these convoluted proceedings and harsh labors. His full name was Whitington Armwood. His prison sentence coincided with the Auburn prison construction, and suggests he may have been used in the prison building project. This could account for him settling in Cayuga County, not far from Auburn, after he completed his sentence. [57]

We do know that from 1830 he lived in Ledyard, Cayuga County not far from many other free persons of color – the Wheatleys, Yates, Carmichaels, Griggs, and Johnsons, until his death on March 16, 1877. Not far from where Jane Langley served at Oakwood Seminary. Not far from where Esther Wheatley rejoined the remnants of her family after leaving Manlius.

The *Auburn Journal* noted in his obituary that Whitington was "born a slave in Maryland, and held a slave in this county until the abolition of slavery in this state." [58] Much of that is true, although some of that bondage was in Manlius. Timothy Armwood, a son of Whittington, owned a small lot at Cooney's Corners in rural Ledyard in the 1850s. [59] Less than a half acre. While life was still one of hard labor for everyone (farm labor for the men and boys; cooking, cleaning, child-raising, servant work for the women), a small community of African Americans, and a supportive population of Friends

(Quakers), often made a harsh life at least more bearable.

In 1914, not long after Sarah Jane Armwood, a daughter of Whitington, died in Ledyard, Coral and Amy Armwood, a nephew and niece, administrators of Sarah's estate, brought a legal action against Jacob Dills, for whom she had worked for forty years, to recover recompense for her services as a domestic.[60]

How did the effort to recover recompense for Sarah Jane Armwood's services resolve? How did these and other descendants find their way into their future? I do not know. I am sure there is more to learn. I invite you....

Wanderings

.....
As I crowded in, they lifted up the bed and
turned it around so that Mama's eyes would face
east....

Her mouth was slightly open, but her breathing took
up so much of her strength that she could not talk.
But she looked at me, or so I felt, to speak for her.
She depended on me for a voice.[63]

Zora Neale Hurston,
*Dust Tracks on a Road,
An Autobiography*

The *Seceders*   185

MORE THANKS

During the course of realizing my debt to earlier historians, authors, publishers, and archivists, I sought permissions to quote and acknowledge their work. Sometimes I was generously told, you don't need my permission, thanks for asking, and while they are cited in my endnotes, they were gracious in encouraging me.

To Sarah D. Brooks Blair, her dissertation on *Reforming Methodism: 1800-1820*; Curtis D. Johnson, author of *Islands of Holiness, Rural Religions in Upstate New York, 1790-1860;* Ted Widmer, author of *Martin Van Buren,* and his interesting article titled "Who Built This City?" Michele Kuykendall for use of the Northwest Nazarene University Wesley Center Online posting of John Wesley's letter to William Wilberforce (1791); Stan Linhorst, Director of Publications, Syracuse Media Group, *The Post-Standard*; Elizabeth Nordbeck, author of "Origins of the Christian Denomination in New England;" Milton C. Sernett, author of *North Star Country, Upstate New York and the Crusade for African American Freedom*; Judith Wellman, author of *The Road to Seneca Falls: Elizabeth Cady Stanton and the First Women's Rights Convention.*

Also, to Smithfield Town Historian Donna Burdick, for access to the publication on *James C. Jackson, Abolitionist*; to Debbie Miller regarding use of the DePuy family Papers at Minnesota Historical Society Library, and Ken Grossi, for letters of Rev. Luther Myrick at the Oberlin College Archives, copied and send to me by Jackie A. Kalinauskas, and last but not least, staff members at the U. S. Copyright Office in Washington, D. C.

For Use of Graphic Images

Though most graphics used were in the public domain, I am grateful to Mike Millner, M. S. L. S. for making the image of Solomon Northrup available to me from the Carolina Digital Library & Archives.

For permission to cite images provided from the original Scipio Town Ledger courtesy of Town of Scipio Historian Sandie Gilliland, a portion of which is in the cover design.

While the image of Manlius Village in the 1840s has been used in many publications, this one was attained from Dwight H. Bruce's *Onondaga's Centennial,* Vol. 1, 782, and artistically displayed on the front cover by Sara Argus.

The image of the inset map of High Bridge from Homer D. Sweet's *New Atlas of Onondaga County, New York*, Walker Brothers & Company, 1874.

I am, once again grateful to Barbara S. Rivette, Town of Manlius Historian, for the photo image of the High Bridge Union Church as it looked when it was restored in the early 1900s.

Additional images came from *Free Dover Pictorial Archive and Clip Art Catalogue*, Books, Reading & Writing Series, selected by Carol Belanger Grafton, 1992.

ENDNOTES

REPOSITORY AND PUBLICATION ABBREVIATIONS:

Cornell University, Ithaca, New York (CU)

Fayetteville Free Library, (Local History), Fayetteville, New York, (FFL-LH)

Fultonhistory.com, (FH)

GenealogyBank, a Division of NewsBank, Inc. Readex, American Newspapers NYSL-AN (GB)

Lemoyne College, Noreen Reale Falcone Library, (LC-NRFL)

Manlius Historical Society, Manlius New York, (MHS)

NewsBank, Inc, (NB)

New York State Library, Microfilm Division, Albany, New York, (NYSL-MD)

Onondaga County Clerk's Office, Syracuse, New York, (OCC)

Onondaga County Surrogate's Office, Syracuse, New York, (OCS)

Onondaga County Clerk's Office, Basement Archives, Syracuse, New York, (OCC-BA)

Onondaga County Public Library, Local History & Archives, Syracuse, New York, (OCPL-LH)

Onondaga Historical Association, Syracuse, New York, (OHA)

Syracuse University Library, Special Collections Research Center, (SUL-SCRC)

Syracuse University Library, Microfilm Division, (SUL-MD)

INTRODUCTION

1. Henry C. Van Schaack, *A History of Manlius Village* (Fayetteville, New York: *Weekly Recorder*, 1873), p. 13.

2. "Good Country Preaching" [my subtitle for this quotation] A light-hearted excerpt from Carl Carmer's *Dark Trees in the Wind, a Cycle of York State Years* (New York: William Sloane Associates, 1949), p. 256.

PROLOGUE

1. *Fayetteville Luminary,* Mar 28, 1839. Microfilm, OCLC 21503571, NY 72 South Cortland 93-31604; 1839:3:14 -1841:9:16. NYSL-MD. Future citations of this source by newspaper only; the same for *South Cortland Luminary*, also on this microfilm, until September 16, 1841.

2. *Fayetteville Luminary,* Aug. 15 & 29, 1839.

CHAPTER ONE: THE SECEDING METHODISTS FROM VERMONT

1. Whitney Cross, *The Burned-Over District, The Social and Intellectual History of Enthusiastic Religion in Western NY, 1800-1850* (Ithaca: Cornell University, 1950), pp. 123-124. LC-NRFL

2. Faxon L. Bowen, "History of the Town of Readsboro,*" History of Bennington County, VT*. Edited by Lewis Cass Aldrich (Syracuse: D. Mason & Co, 1889), pp. 481-489.

3. David Hempton, *Methodism: Empire of the Spirit* (New Haven and London: Yale University Press, 2005), p. 100. See also: Dee E. Andrews, *The Methodists and Revolutionary America, 1760-1800, The Shaping of an Evangelical Culture* (Princeton: Princeton University Press, 2000), p.202.

4. Elizabeth C. Nordbeck, *Origins of the Christian Denomination in New England*, n.p. United Church of Christ: http://www.ucc.org/about-us/hidden-histories-2/origins-of-the-christian.html

5. *Herald of Gospel Liberty,* "The Methodist House Divided Against Itself,*"* (Portsmouth, N. H.: September 16, 1814), VII, no. 3, p. 629.

6. The *Fayetteville Luminary,* published the founding principles of the

Reformed Methodists Society, as presented by Elijah Bailey at the Reformed Methodist Massachusetts Conference in 1839, in the *Luminary's* October 10, 1839 issue. (p. 3-4) The original *Articles* of *The Reformer's Discipline* were published in 1814, in Bennington, Vermont, by Darius Clark.

7. Roy Dodge, "An Open Letter to the Boys of Cardiff," *Tully Independent*, Jan. 4, 1973, p. 16. FH

8. Elijah Bailey was born February 13, 1768 in Bellingham, Norfolk, Massachusetts. Lydia Smith was born abt 1774. They were married in 1791 in Douglas, Worcester, Massachusetts.

9. Wesley Bailey, "History of the Reformed Methodist Church," in *He Pasa Ekklesia, An Original History of the Religious Denominations at Present Existing in the United States,* compiled by I. Daniel Rupp (Philadelphia: J. Y. Humphreys, 1844), p. 475, also pp. 466-475. LC-NRFL

10. *Methodist Reformer* (formerly the *Fayetteville Luminary)*, October 13, 1842. FH

CHAPTER TWO: THE REVIVALS

1. "Enthusiasm," *Autobiography of Elder Jacob Knapp* (Boston: Sheldon & Co, 1868), p. 280. SUL

2. Rev. James H. Hotchkins, *A History of the Purchase and Settlement of Western New York; And of the Rise, Progress and Present State of the Presbyterian Church in that Section* (New York: M. W. Dodd, 1848), p. 172. OCPL-LC

3. Timothy L. Smith, "The Resurgence of Revivalism 1840 – 1857," in *Revivalism and Social Reform, American Protestantism on the Eve of the Civil War* (New York: Abingdon Press, 1957), p. 45. LC-NRFL

4. Robert R. Mathisen, "The Revivalist Years," *Critical Issues in American Religious History* (Waco: Baylor University Press, 2001), p. 211. CU

5. William G. McLoughlin, *Revivals, Awakenings, and Reform, An Essay on Religion and Social Change in America, 1607-1977* (Chicago: University of Chicago Press, 1978), p. 126. LC-NRFL

6. David S. Lovejoy, *Religious Enthusiasm and the Great Awakening* (New Jersey: Prentice-Hall, 1969), p. 17. LC-NRFL

7. Marsena Stone, *A Brief Record of Descendants of Marsena Stone and Rachel Marsh Stone by their grandson, Marsena Stone* (1873); Folder, *Stone,* copy June 1887, pp. 13-14. OHA

8. Rev. James H. Hotchkins, p. 315. The author warns church leaders about "errorists" such as Augustus Littlejohn, David Slie, James Boyle, but especially, Luther Myrick. pp. 171-74. OCPL-LH

9. Ibid

10. In October 1833, the Oneida Presbytery brought charges of heresy against Rev. Luther Myrick. Myrick was considered a serious threat to orthodoxy. He was charged, with being "a perfectionist," among other unapproved deviations. Whitney Cross believed Myrick was not a follower of Charles Finney, but expressed his own unique version of perfectionism. (Cross, p. 278)

11. M. N. N. in the Dutch Reformed church newspaper, *Christian Intelligencer,* October 14, 1837 blamed Finney and Myrick "ultras" for these divisions. Finney supporters, in turn, denigrated their critics as preachers of "endless misery" in their publications, the *New York Christian Messenger,* and *Philadelphia Universalist,* p. 218, vol. 3, "Present State of the New Measures." See at "*books.google.com/books?id=N19GAAAAYAAJ*

12. "An Account of the Trial of Luther Myrick before the Oneida Presbytery, by An Eye Witness," (Syracuse: J. P. Patterson, 1834), p.1-88. This fragile little booklet was located at Colgate University Library. Witnesses for and against Myrick were members of the Manlius Presbyterian Church. The Gregory family spoke for the defense, as did Cornelius Cokely, Mrs. Abigail Gridley, and Rev. John Hale. The prosecution had a longer list. Enos Clark, Hezekiah Barnes, Mrs. Lydia Scofield, Deacon Joseph Hart, the Fosters, Evans, etc. After the trial, Myrick wrote a lengthy lament to Finney sharing details of his trial. Both his grief and anger at this rejection by fellow Presbyterian clergy brothers are evident. He compares his own isolation and disfavor to Finney, and warns him not to accept a pastoral role in New York City. *Letter,* Luther Myrick to Charles G. Finney, Oct. 1, 1834 from the "Finney Papers," at Oberlin College Library, were copied and graciously given to me by Jackie A. Kalinauskas, a direct descendant of Rev. Luther Myrick.

13. Nathan O. Hatch, *The Democratization of American Christianity* (New Haven: Yale University Press, 1989), p. 197. LC-NRFL

14. Prominent among these itinerant perfectionists were Hiram Sheldon, Jarvis Rider, Erasmus Stone, and Martin Sweet.

15. William Hepworth Dixon, Ludwig Wilhelm Sachs's *Spiritual Wives* (London: Hurst and Blackett, 1868), p. 15, See also pp. 239-242. SUL

16. George Wallingford Noyes, *Religious Experiences of John Humphrey Noyes: Founder of the Oneida Community* (New York: Macmillan, 1923), p. 195.

17. *The Witness* names several subscribers of Manlius Centre: John Mabie, Abram S. Huntley, Jos. Cook (2 copies), Cornelius Van Alstine, Henry Wentworth, Marquis L. Worden, Rasivel Bates, and Jas. Huntly. There were a few subscribers in Peterboro, Chittenango, Pompey Hill, Cazenovia and Lafayette. Subscribers listed in the January 22, 1840 issue of *Witness,* Vol. 1, No. Xlll, p. 104. Microfilm. OCPL-LH

18. Marquis de Lafayette Worden (Manlius) made the acquaintance of perfectionists after a conversion experience at a Methodist camp meeting in 1834. He, his brother Leander, and their families, joined the social religious collective, the Oneida Community, in Lenox, Madison County, founded by John Noyes. Their story is interesting. Noyes' utopian community is usually assailed as unorthodox and scandalous, primarily because of its practices of complex marriage and social engineering. These practices were abandoned after 1879, when Noyes fled to Canada to avoid prosecution. Both Worden men, and their wives, left the community before Noyes fled, while most of their children, then adults, remained in the community, married, and were buried there. Letters written by the Worden brothers can be found in the Syracuse University "Oneida Community Collection." SUL-SCRC

19. Wesley Bailey in Rupp, p. 468.

CHAPTER THREE: THE EVIL OF SLAVERY

1. *Republican Monitor,* October 12, 1835. Microfilm, NY 64 Cazenovia 93-31639. One of a series of quotations editor J. J. Fairchild excerpted for the front page of this edition. NYSL-MD

2. *South Cortland Luminary,* September 7, 1837. While the full title of the newspaper was *South Cortland Luminary, and Reformed Methodist Intelligencer,* I will be using the shorter title.

3. John Wesley to William Wilberforce, Volume 8, Letter # 18, 1791, as quoted on Wesley Center Online.

4. *South Cortland Luminary,* July 18, 1837.

5. *South Cortland Luminary,* March 8, 1838.

6. Ibid.

7. *South Cortland Luminary,* April 19, 1838.

8. *South Cortland Luminary,* December 28, 1837 and January 18, 1838.

9. Ibid.

10. *South Cortland Luminary,* November 15, 1838.

11. When Emerson Kinne wrote the Kinne family history, he described his elder sister Eunice with affection. She was, he said, "kind and dutiful" and when their mother Elizabeth died (when Eunice was 13), she took on raising the family, which included eight brothers and two sisters. The children of Prentice and Elizabeth Kinne are: Julius, b. 1802; Emerson, b. 1804; Marvin. 1806; Eunice 1807; Mason Prentice, 1808; Elbridge b. 1810; N. Hildreth b. 1812; Emily b. 1813; Salome b. 1815; Atlas b. 1817; Ansel b. 1820.) Wesley and Eunice Bailey named their second son, Ansel K., who was born November 18, 1835 in Erie County. See: Emerson Kinne, *History and Genealogy of a Branch of the Family Kinne,* Syracuse, 1881), OHA; also KINNE , Surname files, OHA

CHAPTER FOUR: 1835: A GRAND REVOLUTION

1. James Caleb Jackson, quoted by Dr. J. Edward (Ted) Jackson, from *James C. Jackson, Abolitionist* (Peterboro, New York: Smithfield Community Center, 2009), p. 11. Ted Jackson is the great, great, grandson of James Caleb Jackson. His biographical and autobiographical information draw from James C. Jackson's diary and other family documents. See p. 8-13 for his account of Jackson's momentous experience at the 1835 Utica - Peterboro convention and what transpired during those days. The National Abolition Hall of Fame and Museum at Peterboro in 2010 cited this same quote on their website program; *Mobbed in Utica: Welcomed to Peterboro!* http://www.abolitionhof.org/media mobbed.html

2. William Thomas, *The enemies of the Constitution discovered, or, An inquiry into the origin and tendency of popular violence: Containing a complete and circumstantial account of the unlawful proceedings at the city of Utica, October 21st, 1835; the dispersion of the state anti-slavery convention by the agitators, the destruction of a democratic press, and the causes which led thereto. Together with a concise treatise on the practice of the court of his honor Judge Lynch by Defensor* (Utica, New York: Leavitt, Lord & Co., G. Tracy, 1835), p. 95. SUL-SCRC

3. It is certainly likely that young James C. Jackson had personal awareness of the free colored persons, and slaves, in his Manlius neighborhood. William Gardner, Nicholas Randall, and Ralph R. Phelps, lived in the vicinity of the Jackson home, and each owned a slave. (See: 1820 U. S. Census, Manlius, Onondaga, New York, p.185 on Ancestry.com, image 16 of 19 which shows the proximity of these residents. The Christ Church Burial records by Nancy Schiffhauer (1993), document that a slave of R. R. Phelps, named Jenny York, died in June 1820, age 62. MHS

4. Elizabeth M. Simpson, *Mexico, Mother of Towns* (Mexico Independent, NY: 1980), pp. 338-340.

5. Dr. J. Edward (Ted) Jackson, *James C. Jackson, Abolitionist*, p. 8.

6. *Onondaga Standard*, October 7, 1835, Subject Folder, Anti-Slavery, Abolition, (news clipping) OHA

7. Leonard L. Richards, *Gentlemen of Property and Standing, Anti-Abolition Mobs in Jacksonian America (*New York: Oxford University Press, 1970). "Gentlemen of property and standing" was a common reference to prominent members of the influential mercantile and professional class, but when, after October 21, 1835, it was claimed that leaders, who incited mob violence against other American citizens convening that day, were primarily from this class, it was used as a sarcastic denunciation by abolitionists. SUL

8. *Onondaga Standard*, October 28, 1835, p. 2 c. 5. Subject folder, Abolition, Ibid. OHA

9. *The Republican Monitor,* "Mobocracy Triumphant, Utica Disgraced," Oct. 27, 1835, p. 2. NYSL-MD

10. *Cortland Republican*, November 3, 1835 (Cortland, New York: Cortland Free Library; newspaper microfilm), p. 2.

11. *Onondaga Standard,* October 7, 1835, Ibid, OHA

12. William Thomas, pp. 93-95.

13. Dr. J. Edward Jackson, p. 11.

14. Ibid.

CHAPTER FIVE: THE PRESBYTERIANS

1. McKivigan, John R., *The War Against Proslavery Religion, Abolitionism and the Northern Churches, 1830-1865* (Ithaca, New York: Cornell University Press, 1984, reprint 2009), p. 53.

2. See: Molly Oshatz, *Slavery and Sin: The Fight Against Slavery and the Rise of Liberal Protestantism* (New York: Oxford University Press, 2012) The author examines what happened during, and after, the 1818 General Assembly. p. 39. SUL

3. *Proceedings of the New York Anti-Slavery Convention, held at Utica, October 21, and New York Anti-Slavery State Society, held at Peterboro, October 22, 1835,* N. Y. (Utica, New York: Printed at the Standard & Democrat office, 1835) accessed at http://www.archive.org/details/proceedingsofnew00newy.
At Peterboro, Rev. Carlos Smith served on a committee of eight (many of whom were clergy) to select county officers. He was, on recommendation, named Onondaga County representative. The document claims that at least 300 of those members who attended the Utica convention, were in Peterboro the next day to continue their deliberations. See: pp. 44-48, also p. 14. James C. Jackson's personal account says 104 went by canal boat, and then proceeded on foot. p. 11.

4. Ibid, pp. 13-14.

5. *The Trinity Presbyterian Church Trustee Records* (Syracuse, New York) in OHA Collections. James H. Hotchkin's history of Presbyterianism in Western New York State, noted that Rev. Carlos Smith was "officiating as stated supply to the church one or two years." p. 315. But the Manlius Trinity Presbyterian records verify Rev. Carlos Smith's ministry there was

longer. He was hired as stated supply August 1832. After his 1835 contract ended in 1836, he was not hired for the next year.

6. Ibid.

7. Henry Steele Commager, *Theodore Parker: Yankee Crusader* (Little, Brown & Co.:1936, Reprint, 1982), p. 104. SUL

8. *Letter* signed VERITAS, *Onondaga Standard*, October 7, 1835. Subject folder, Anti-Slavery, Abolition, newspaper clipping. OHA

9. Rev. Ethan Smith, *View of the Hebrews*, 1st Edition, 1823, "Oliver's Bookshelf," at http://olivercowdery.com/texts/ethn1823.htm

10. Amy Swerdlow in *The Abolitionist Sisterhood: Women's Political Culture in Antebellum America*, edited by Jean Fagan Yellin and John C. Vanhorne (Ithaca: Cornell University Press, 1994), p. 34.

11. Grace died in 1840. Her sister, Sarah Towne Smith, was then editor of *The Advocate of Moral Reform*. In an obituary published on August 15, 1840, she praised Grace for her moral courage, energy and talents noting that "the cause of the oppressed and downtrodden slave, she early espoused, while her companion, and all her family friends stood aloof from the ranks of abolition." See p. 123. *A* year later, Sarah Towne Smith married her widowed brother-in-law, Rev. Job R. Martyn. See also Amy Aronson, *Taking Liberties: Early American Women's Magazines and Their Readers* (2002), p. 150.

12. Ellen died at the age of 33 in 1846, when the Sedgwick family lived in Syracuse. They had two children. Sedgwick later married Deborah Gannett. His second wife was also a woman from a strong minded anti-slavery family. *Charles Baldwin Sedgwick Papers*. SUSC. For Deborah Gannett see *Appletons'* A*nnual Cyclopedia and Register of Important Events.*, p.467.

13. Luella S. Dunham, "Talks About Pompey Hill," *The Weekly Recorder*, October 9, 1879, submitted by Kathy Crowell.

14. Curtis D. Johnson, *Islands of Holiness, Rural Religion in Upstate New York*, 1790-1860 (Ithaca: Cornell University Press, 1989), p. 122. Johnson states, that while a majority of church members voting supported Rev. John Keep by a margin of 74 to 20, that when 24 members wrote and said they could no longer financially support him, the Cortland Presbytery accepted

Keep's resignation. "The initial victory, "the author notes, "lay with the opponents of change." In addition to N. R. Chapman, Lemuel S. Pomeroy, a classmate who attended Cortland Academy and Hamilton College during Keep's pastorate, followed a similar formation of social conscience that resulted in a religiously-motivated commitment to abolitionism. Pomeroy, like Chapman, seceded from his traditional church affiliation over the slavery issue. Chapman in 1843; Pomeroy in 1846 from the Presbyterian Church in Cortlandville. Both later rejoined their churches. See: Alethea Connolly, *"The Formation of an Anti-Slavery Conscience, Lemuel S. Pomeroy,"* presented at the United Presbyterian Church, Cortland, New York, in May, 2012.

15. Gilbert Barnes, *The Antislavery Impulse, 1830-1844* (The American Historical Association, New York: D. Appleton-Century Co., 1933). For Rev. Keep's role at the Oberlin College board decision., see p.76. SUL

16. Jerry and Shelby Brumbaug, church historians, at First Church Congregational, Painesville, Ohio. E-mail to author, March 30, 2011.

17. *General catalogue of Oberlin College, 1833-1908. Including an account of the principal events in the history of the college, with illustrations of the college buildings.* (Oberlin College, California Digital Library, 1909), p. 173. Google

18. During my research at OHA, I examined a "Family Record," presented by John K. Blenkowski in 1931 to the Onondaga Historical Association in Syracuse, claiming to have been "taken from an old Bible that belonged to Gerrit Smith." Someone, perhaps the OHA archivist, faintly penciled in *"see no Peterboro Smiths in this Bible record."* While, as the notation indicated, the documents were not a family record of Gerrit Smith and his descendants, I believe they are family records of Rev. Carlos and Rev. Stephen Smith, who were prominent in early anti-slavery efforts in Manlius and Fayetteville. Siblings of these brothers, and their parents and descendants, are clearly recorded. Rev. Carlos Smith not only attended the October 22 meeting of the New York State Anti-Slavery Society hosted by Gerrit Smith at Peterboro, but also served on a committee during its proceedings. It is possible that he brought this copy of his family records for the purpose of comparing his family ancestry with Gerrit Smith. It is also possible, that he brought his own Bible, and the family record was enclosed in it, and was left at Gerrit Smith's estate. Still, regardless of speculation, it is a most interesting record that adds to my research findings concerning the local, and significant participation of these "other Smiths" in the early abolition movement in the town of Manlius, Onondaga County. Surname Folder, *Smith*, OHA

19. Milton Sernett, *North Star Country, Upstate New York and the Crusade for African American Freedom* (Syracuse, New York: Syracuse University Press, 2002), p. 36. OCPL

CHAPTER SIX: TAKING SIDES IN FAYETTEVILLE

1. *The Liberator*, October 3, 1835, pp. 2-3. The article titled "To the Friends of Immediate Emancipation in the State of New York," was first printed in the *Oneida Standard & Democrat*. It was reported that on the day of the convention, some individuals in an unruly mob broke into the publishing office and trashed much of the equipment.

2. Ibid.

3. *The Onondaga Chief*, September 2, 9, 16 and 23, 1835. OHA

4. *The Onondaga Chief*, September 30, 1835, p. 2, col. 1 , 2, 5. OHA

5. *Onondaga Standard*, September 30, 1835. Subject folder, Anti-Slavery, Abolition, 1830s. OHA

6. *Onondaga Standard*, October 7, 1835. Ibid.

7. Several anti-abolitionists articles were published alongside the "VERITAS Letter," in the *Onondaga Standard*, October 7, 1835 issue. The author believes efforts of the Fayetteville clergy and laymen cited by this nameless writer, sparked initial public resistance in Onondaga County, and set in motion the development of the county-wide anti-slavery organization which evolved two years later in 1837. Consequently, these Fayetteville activists, played a significant early leadership role. John L. Myers, states that William Goodell lectured in Fayetteville as early as October, 1834 [See: "The Beginning of Anti-Slavery Agencies in New York State, 1833-1836," *New York History*, v. 60, 160]. These efforts were also going on in Peterboro and Smithfield. As discussed, Manlius and Fayetteville men attended the Utica and Peterboro meetings on October 21-22, 1835, and after returning home, helped stimulate local village and town anti-slavery organization activities. The Smith brothers have already been noted, but Fayetteville merchant, John McViccar, also seems to have been one of the very early local supporters of the initial local anti-slavery movement. His name appears as a donor to the American Anti-Slavery Society on the receipt list of the January, 1835 issue of *The Anti-Slavery Record*. Fayetteville donors were listed as " a lady 0.94; A. Goff 1; J. McVickar 3, 4 00." (p. 12)

ENDNOTES 199

McViccar was a trustee of the Fayetteville Presbyterian Church, and in 1836 was named the Onondaga County representative of the New York Anti-Slavery Society at its anniversary meeting. He provided hospitality to organizers at the 1837 meeting in Fayetteville. In the March 1, 1837 issue of *Friend of Man,* William Goodell reported stopping overnight at Fayetteville, after meetings in Madison County, and the next morning proceeding with friends to the Syracuse Baptist church where the group, despite opposition, sought to form a county-wide anti-slavery society. While editor Goodell reported he left prior to the evening session, it seems this is the meeting, that attendees, sensing the evening session might be sabotaged, quietly regrouped at Fayetteville to continue their deliberations. (See: p.146). In the March 22, 1837 issue of *Friend of Man,* Charles Stuart said this Fayetteville meeting was the occasion where the constitution for the Onondaga County Anti-Slavery Society was approved. (See p.158). Members of the early Manlius-Fayetteville anti-slavery movement were therefore instrumental in providing support and momentum for the county-wide organizing efforts in 1837, which they hosted. It is interesting to note the similarity of this 1837 event, with what happened in Utica two years earlier, 1835, when some of an unruly mob broke up an anti-slavery organizing meeting there. Then, delegates went to Peterboro to finish their meeting. Here, organizers left Syracuse because they feared the evening session would be broken up by opponents. In both instances, abrasive vigilante reactions against the abolitionists, seemed, rather than deterring them, to have instead, strengthened their commitment, giving them another "heroic" moment to attract recruits.

8. Lorman Ratner, *Powder Keg, Northern Opposition to the Anti-Slavery Movement, 1831-1840* (New York: Basic Books Inc., 1968), p. 132.

9. Ibid. The 1831 slave insurrection stimulated immediate reprisals against the men and women slaves assumed to be conspirators (one estimate of the number of slaves hung and killed in retaliation was 200). Subsequently, the Virginia State General Assembly passed harsh laws against slaves forbidding them to be taught how to read and write, and requiring that a white minister must be present at their religious gatherings. Other southern states copied such restrictions.

10. *The Onondaga Chief,* October 7, 1835, p. 2. OHA

11. States' rights issues arose over various economic issues. William W. Freehling, in his *Prelude to Civil War, The Nullification Controversy in South*

Carolina 1816-1836 (New York: Oxford University Press, 1992) points out that the tariff was the issue that aroused South Carolina to expound on a states' rights justification for their decision to nullify a federal law. pp. 356 - 58.

12. Donald G. Mathews, ed., Introduction, *Agitation For Freedom* (New York: John Wiley & Sons, 1972), p. 8.

13. Ibid.

14. When New York State held its 1846 election, it placed before eligible white male voters a separate ballot issue. The question was whether the right to vote should be extended to colored men without them having to pay an existing property qualification of $250, and the answer was a resounding No! One-third of voters in the state, however, were willing to extend the franchise. Four counties had majorities that voted to extend suffrage to colored men: Cortland, Oswego, Clinton and Washington. *Onondaga Standard*, November 25, 1846. FH

15. William Lee Miller, in *Arguing About Slavery, The Great Battle in the United States Congress* (New York: Alfred A. Knopf, 1996) mentions several southerners who changed their acceptance of slavery to opposition. He mentions James A. Thome of Kentucky, and William T. Allen of Alabama, who were converted during a series debates on slavery at Lane University in Cincinnati during February 1834, organized by Theodore Weld, a convert of Charles G. Finney. See: 87-89. Most southerners did not own slaves, but were enmeshed in a culture dominated by those that wielded economic, political and social power. Northerners were often complicit, and before 1827, slavery was protected by law in New York State. William T. Allen pointed this out to smug northerners, when he became an anti-slavery agent, and lectured in New York in February and March, 1837. He reported a meeting he attended where a northern deacon preached the justification of slavery. After hearing this "northerner" defend slavery, Allen concluded his report saying, "Well may they cry when we preach to them (Southerners), "Physician, Heal Thyself!" (*Friend of Man*, March 22, 1837, p. 158). Sarah and Angelina Grimke were also anti-slavery lecturers who left their slaveholding South Carolina roots, and moved to Philadelphia. After joining a female anti-slavery society, they inspired vibrant female participation, and controversy, as they lectured and wrote about the plight of the oppressed slave.

CHAPTER SEVEN: AND I WILL BE HEARD

1. *The Liberator*, November 21, 1835. Fair Use Repository, at fair-use.org/the-liberator/

2. *The Liberator*, January 1, 1831. Fair Use Repository, at fair-use.org/the-liberator/

3. Henry Mayer, *All On Fire, William Lloyd Garrison and the Abolition of Slavery* (New York: St. Martin's Press, 1998), p.112. The author clearly admires his subject, noting Garrison was one of the first Americans, after Thomas Paine, to make agitation his professional vocation. It made him a "pariah," to many, but this might also, he noted, be said of Patrick Henry. See: Preface, XVII.

4. Ibid., p. 203.

5. John L. Myers, "The Major Effort of the National Anti-Slavery Agents in New York State, 1836-1837," *New York History* (April 1965), pp. 163, 177, 179. OCPL-LH

6. *Friend of Man*, October 27, 1836. p. 74. The Minutes also note S. S. Smith, and John "McVickar." According to the *Proceedings of the first Annual Meeting of the New-York State Anti-slavery Society, convened at Utica October 19, 1826*, McVickar (McViccar) is named a county Vice-President by the nominating committee. CU

7. *Friend of Man*, March 22, 1837, p. 158. CU

8. First Congregational United Church of Christ, Poughkeepsie, New York. "Antislavery and the Founding of First Congregational Church." This story was located on their website, 2/4/2013. See: http://opentogod.org/Our%20History.htm

CHAPTER EIGHT: THE CENTER CANNOT HOLD

1. *South Cortland Luminary,* August 3, 1837, p. 20.

2. Elizur Wright, ed., "Third Annual Meeting of American Anti-Slavery Society," *Quarterly Anti-Slavery Magazine* (New York: Anti-Slavery Society, MDCCCXXXVI), V. 1, pp. 22, and 94. Googlebooks. Stephen and Carlos Smith might have taken this opportunity to visit their sisters, Grace and Sarah, who lived nearby.

3. Ibid.

4. *Minutes of the General Assembly of the Presbyterian Church in the United States.* Princeton Theological Seminary, Vols. for A. D. 1836-1837 (continuously paged: 233-632; bound together with *Minutes of the General Assembly of the Presbyterian Church in the United States of America* [Old School], with an appendix); 1838-1841. SEE: June 7, 1836; pp. 248, 250, 273, 286. At: archive.org

5. Ibid

6. John McKivigan, p. 45.

7. C. C. Goen, *Broken Churches, Broken Nation* (Macon, Georgia: Mercer Press, 1985), p. 69. SUL

8. Ibid., p. 75.

9. Robert Hastings Nichols, *Presbyterianism In New York State, A History of the Synod and Its Predecessors* (Philadelphia: Westminster Press, 1962), p. 131.

10. Paul K. Conkin, *The Uneasy Center: Reformed Christianity in Antebellum America* (Chapel Hill: University of North Carolina Press, 1996), p. 266. SUL

11. D. W. Lathrop, Ashbel Green, Daniel Whiting, Molton Cropper Rogers, John Bannister Gibson et al,) *The Case of the General Assembly of the Presbyterian Church in the United States of America before the Supreme Court of the Commonwealth of Pennsylvania....*(1839), pp. 45-46. Google

CHAPTER NINE: THE COTTON CONNECTION

1. Victor S. Clark, *History of Manufacturers in the United States, 1607-1860* (Washington, D.C: Carnegie Institution, 1916), 348, 320. Some believed efforts to incorporate Texas as a state fulfilled a vital national economic need. Among benefits, annexation of Texas transferred 1,000,000 pounds of foreign cotton to the domestic crop. SUL

2. John Warner Barber and Henry Howe, *Historical Collections of the State of New York; Containing a General Collection of the Most Interesting Facts, Traditions, Biographical Sketches, Anecdotes, &c.* (New York: S. Tuttle, Chatham Street, 1842), p.386. The authors identified these cotton mills as the Limestone, Manlius, and Cold Spring factories. OHA

3. For details on the Manlius Manufacturing Co., and cotton mills in Manlius Village, see Kathy Crowell and Al Vedder, *Early Businesses in Manlius Village and the Nearby Area*, Seneca Street Industries (November, 1994), pp. 23-26. FFL-LH

4. *William's New York Annual Register, Yr 1835.* (New York, N. Y.: J. Leavitt Pub) See Chart, "Statistical View of the Cotton Manufacturing Establishments in the State of New York, in 1832," p. 150. The number of "persons sustained by said establishments" in Onondaga was 225. The only cotton mills in the county were located in Manlius. Since the chart explanation does not specify that only factory worker were counted as those benefiting, the number may include owners and agents. Labor needs fluctuated with protective tariff levels, and cotton prices. Oneida County, by far, had a greater textile industrial development at his time, with 2,354 persons "sustained" at 20 mills. OHA

5. Kathleen G. Crowell, *Tavern Tales* (Fayetteville: By the author, July 5, 2010), p. 56. FFL-LH

6. U. S. Congress, *Journal: 1st-13th Congress, Repr, 14th Congress*, 1st session, December 22, 1815, p. 82. Googlebooks

7. New York State Census, *Statistics*, 1845 (Albany, New York: Carroll & Cook, 1946), Subject folder, Census. MHS

8. U. S. Census 1850, *Town of Manlius, Onondaga County, New York, Products of Industry*, p. 728. Subject folder, Census. MHS

9. Ibid.

10. Nancy Woloch, "Factory and Mill," *Women and the American Experience* (Boston: McGraw Hill, 2000), p. 141.

11. Woloch, p. 142. An advertisement describing the boarding house buildings included in the sale of the factory property was published in the July 31, 1850 issue of the *New York Tribune*, Subject folder, Town of Manlius, *Miscellaneous, Historical*, (news clipping) OHA

12. For much of this information, I am grateful to Barbara S. Rivette, Town of Manlius Historian, for sending me a copy of a speech she delivered in March, 1982. She described the women factory worker's protest of 1844, and shared with me a news clipping titled "Whig Love For The Laboring

Classes," that appeared in the *Onondaga Standard* on August 14th, 1844.

13. The James O. Rockwell story was first printed by Barber & Howe, in 1842, p. 387. It was used by Henry C. Van Schaack in a series of presentations he gave in 1866, and published in his *A History of Manlius Village*, in 1873), p. 34.

14. Orson Smith, 'We Fought Poverty...Like A Tiger," *The Eagle Bulletin and DeWitt Times*, January 21, 1960, pp. 6-7. Columns in the "Scrapbook of Orson Smith," on microfilm at OHA.

15. Deposition by Franklin May, November 22, 1850 before R. Gilmore, J of Peace. Collection: 2002.151 Box 1, 8-D-2, *Miscellaneous*. OHA. The New York State census for 1855 showed a cotton factory still operating in the town of Manlius; number employed then 25 adults and 23 children. The average monthly wage was $32.00 for males; $12.00 for females.

16. Eugene R. Dattel, "Cotton in a Global Economy: Mississippi, 1800-1860).http://mshistory.k12.ms.us/articles/161/cotton-in-a-global-economy-mississippi-1800-1860

17. See last chapter for more details on slaves that lived in Manlius and what happened to some of them after emancipation.

18. Samuel J. May, *Some Recollections of our Antislavery Conflict* (Boston: Fields, Osgood and Co., 1869), p. 128.

CHAPTER TEN: AN UNCOMMON MARRIAGE

1. *Letter*, J Cross to L Myrick, 1838 (*Union Herald*, May 25, 1838), p. 2. GB

2. Gilbert H. Barnes, *The Antislavery Impulse*, p. 81.

3. Oscar Sherwin, *Prophet of Liberty, The Life and Times of Wendell Phillips* (Westport, CT:Greenwood Press, 1958), pp. 82-84. Benjamin P. Thomas, *Theodore Weld, Crusader for Freedom* (New Brunswick, N. J: Rutgers University Press, 1950), p. 15. Weld's aunt, Sophia Clark, was a social activist in her own right. She founded the Female Charitable Society in Utica, whose incorporation was listed in the 1810 *Utica Almanac*, according to Mary P. Ryan in *Cradle of the Middle Class: The Family in Oneida County, New York, 1790-1865* (Cambridge: Cambridge University Press, 1981) p. 53. Googlebooks

5. Barnes, p. 85.

6. Barnes, p. 105.

7. Judith Wellman, *The Road to Seneca Falls, Elizabeth Cady Stanton and the First Woman's Rights Convention* (Urbana: University of Illinois Press, 2004), p. 50.

8. Wellman, p. 50.

9. Wellman, p. 53.

10. *Letter*, Angelina to Weld from Phila, May 2d, 1838, in Gilbert H. Barnes and Dwight L. Dumond (eds) *Letters of Theodore D. Weld, Angelina Grimke, and Sara Grimke, 1822-1844* (Glouchester, Mass: Peter Smith, American Historical Society, Reprinted Appleton-Century-Crofts, 1933), pp. 652-53.

11. Henry Mayer, p. 246.

12. *Letter*, Sara Grimke to Elizabeth Pease from Manlius. N.Y., May 20?, 1838. Barnes & Dumond, p. 678.

13. Mary P. Ryan, *The Cradle of the Middle Class, The Family in Oneida County, New York* (1983), pp. 123-124. Mary Ryan's examination of women's moral reform activities and goals in Utica in the 1830s shed a great deal of light on my understanding the efforts of Manlius women to pass legislation against seduction in 1839, and directed me to additional resources.

14. "Death of a Pioneer," William Metcalf Clark, Surname folder, *Clark*, (newspaper clipping) OHA. William Clark's surname has been spelled in various records with an "e" ending, and elsewhere without the "e." For consistency I have used the "Clark" spelling.

15. *Letter*, Weld to Angelina, Brookline, April 8, 1838. Barnes & Dumond, p. 128.

16. *Letter*, Sarah Grimke to Elizabeth Pease, May 1838. Barnes & Dumond, p. 78.

17. *Letter*, Angelina G. Weld to Lewis Tappan, Belleville, NJ, 1838, Barnes & Dumond, p. 875.

18. Luther Rawson Marsh, ed., *Writings and Speeches of Alvan Stewart on Slavery* (New York: A. B. Burdick, 1860), Vol 3, p. 88.

CHAPTER ELEVEN: CONFLICT IN FAYETTEVILLE

1. *The Emancipator,* November 1, 1838. V. III, I. 27, p. 108. NewsBank, NYSL-AHN.

2. All quotations used in the text concerning this meeting are taken from J. N. T. Tucker's Minutes, published in the *Union Herald* on February 9, 1839, V. III, no. 40, page 4 col. 1-4. This January 1839 meeting was held in the village of Manlius though the *Union Herald* referred to the location as Manlius Square. Permissions to quote, GB.

3. Selected biographic data on John McViccar from "McViccar Family," gratefully received from Barbara S. Rivette, Fayetteville Village Historian, July 20, 2002, and Kathy Crowell, "Bio—McViccar."

4. McViccar's surname was published as "McVickar" in the *Proceedings of the first annual meeting of the New-York State Anti-Slavery Society, convened at Utica, October 19, 1836..*,p. 6. See: http://archive.org/stream/proceedingsoff00newy#page/6/mode/2up

5. *Friend of Man,* March 22, 1837, p. 158. CU

6. Debate on "modern abolitionism" at the *General Conference of the Methodist Episcopal Church, held in Cincinnati, May, 1836.* Google eBook

7. *Union Herald*, February 9, 1839. Victory Birdseye had already distinguished himself in political service prior to this local election in Onondaga County, and at the state and national level. He had served in the United States Congress 1815-1817, and at the New York Constitutional Convention in 1821. From 1838 to 1840, he was a New York State Assemblyman, and though he lost this election to Congress during the 1838 campaign, he was elected to Congress again in 1841. On numerous occasions he had sought to end slavery, and expand and defend the civil rights of free colored men.

8. Though J. N. T. Tucker served many years prominently in the anti-slavery movement in New York State, either a predisposition to, or sudden onset of, mental instability, led to tragic results many years later. On August, 1854, in his home in Brooklyn, he murdered his three year old son with a razor, and attacked his wife who tried to stop him. At the trial in December, several persons, doctors included, testified according to the December 8, 1854, *New York Herald*, that Tucker as being of "a peculiarly

nervous temperament." In testimony, Tucker's sister described early episodes of his "peculiar behavior," and that he believed people were following him, trying to do him harm. He was declared insane in 1855, and committed to an asylum in Utica. He later escaped to Ohio where, it is said, he "died in a warehouse cellar in Toledo." See accounts in: *Geneva Gazette*, August 11, 1854; *Syracuse Daily Standard,* December 12, 1854; Auburn *Daily American*, May 7, 1855.

9. Donald G. Mathews, *Agitation For Freedom, The Abolition Movement*, (New York: John Wiley & Sons, 1972), p. 11.

10. *Letter of Gerrit Smith to Wm Clark*, Feb. 13, 1839. Clark Family Papers. OHA 3352. See also, *Fifth Annual Report of the Executive Committee of the American Anti-Slavery Society with the Minutes of the Meetings of the Society for Business and Speeches Delivered at the Anniversary Meeting,* May 1, 1838, (New York: William S. Dorr, 1838) accessed in the Digital Collection, Samuel J. May Anti-Slavery Collection, CU. Early members of the anti-slavery societies from Fayetteville, Manlius, and Pompey are named. On page 141, "John M'Vickar" is noted secretary of the Manlius society, dated June 1836, with total membership at 112. On page 142, William M. Clarke under *Onondaga County*, noted as secretary, with *Manlius* following his name, which was his residence at that time. While the alphabetized listing is confusing, it appears that anti-slavery organizations existed this early within the town of Manlius, with a society functioning in Fayetteville. According to an obituary titled "Death of a Pioneer," Clark met his wife Clara Catlin Tyler while in Manlius. They married in 1837, and spent a year in Harford, PA, the home of Clara's father, before coming back to New York. In 1838 they moved to Syracuse, and Clark renewed his abolitionist activities. The *Fifth Annual Report* does not mention Syracuse as having an organized anti-slavery society.

11. J. N. T. Tucker Report, *Friend of Man,* Mar 23, 1839. CU

12. *Republican Monitor* (Cazenovia), November 27, 1838, in the Gerrit Smith Family Papers, Box 151, News Clippings, *The Republican Monitor,* folder 1838, SUSC. See also *Colored American,* "Aspects of Our Cause," March 21, 1840, 2. *Colored American* newspaper collection (Mar 21, 1840-Mar 14, 1841), Microfilm 1390, SUL-MD

13. Article reprinted from *Colored American* was published in Cazenovia's *Republican Monitor* on March 21, 1840. The *Monitor* editor quotes from CA

to challenge those abolitionists who are narrowing the criteria of "true" abolitionists to mean those who only vote for candidates with unequivocal abolitionist commitments. The newspaper *Colored American* advised colleagues: "It appears to me, if as Abolitionists, we will differ in opinion upon minor points, and divide about extraneous things, it were better to adopt the motto of Wesley to Whitefield, when they dissented from each other upon some points,- "agree to disagree," and each go on and do all he can for the slave, than to keep up a war of words, not at all credible to either side, but disreputable to our otherwise holy cause." *Republican Monitor,* Miscellaneous Newspapers-19th Century, p. 2. SUL-SCRC

CHAPTER TWELVE: A CLASH OF TITANS

1. *The National Anti-Slavery Standard,* "Madison Co. A. S. Political Convention," July 2, 1840, p. 1, c 6. NASS reprints Luther Myrick's "third party" comments published in the *Union Herald.* SUL-MD 1389.

2. Henry Mayer, p. 112.

3. August 7, 1839, *Friend of Man,* p. 31. The August 14 issue published Garrison's protest against convention organizers for refusing the "antislavery women of the United States" participation, as well as organizers emphasis on political means to the neglect of those religious means to address "a corrupt church." Garrison advised them to employ their energies within their churches in the same strict manner as they were doing to oblige members to use their right to vote. p. 34. CU

4. *Colored American,* May 23, 1840. The editor described the schism that occurred during the American Anti-Slavery Convention meeting in New York City, May 12-14, 1840. It was precipitated when Abby Kelley, a Quaker woman from Massachusetts, was appointed on the first day of the meeting to the business committee, whereupon a debate ensued. Of the almost 1000 participants attending, the vote appeared split. After calling for "a division of the house," it was found that 557 favored the appointment, and 451 opposed it. Lewis Tappan, A. A. Phelps, and C. W. Dennison, then declined to serve on the committee. The next day a series of resolutions were introduced regarding abolitionist political action and voting for candidates, slavery's impact on the agricultural, commercial, and manufacturing interests of the country and other items. Believing more rancor was to follow, Lewis Tappan, (that year, President of the Society), notified the assembly that a meeting would commence that afternoon in

the basement of the church to form the American and Foreign Anti-Slavery Society. About 300 followed him to attend that meeting. Another 100 were presumed by the newspaper to have gone home. SUL-MD 1390.

5. Dorothy Sterling: *Ahead of Her Time: Abby Kelley and the Politics of Antislavery* (New York: W. W. Norton, 1991), p. 106. The author quotes John G. Whittier's letter, noting Whittier tended to place much blame for the fragmenting of the AASS on Kelley and the women's issue.

6. *Colored American, May 23, 1840*, published a report from *The Emancipator*, on the nomination of delegates to attend the World Anti-Slavery Conference in London which gave interesting details and insights. The American Anti-Slavery Society members, it noted, selected: William Lloyd Garrison, Nathaniel Peabody Rogers, Charles Lennox Remond, and Lucretia Mott. Next, members elected members to the Executive Committee. Nominees chosen were Lucretia Mott of Philadelphia and Lydia Child and Maria M. Chapman of Boston. However, when Charles B. Ray, editor of *Colored American*, moved to add Hester Lane, the motion lost. The article concluded: *"Hester Lane is well known in this city as a woman of good character, and has been a slave, but [the] "principle could not carry her color – eh!"* It seems, Ray added the exclamation *"eh!"* to his observation that the *"principle could not carry her color"* because he questioned their rejection of Hester Lane, a colored woman, when her name was put in nomination. (SUL-MD1390) Another view of this action was suggested by author Shirley J. Yee. In her book on Black women abolitionists, Yee states that Hester Lane's nomination was rejected "because she was known to be a strong supporter of the Tappan faction." (*Black Women Abolitionists: A Study in Activism, 1828-1860* (Knoxville, TN: University of Tennessee Press, 1992), which was quoted in the unpublished manuscripts of Larry Ceplair, *Women Organized Against Slavery, 1688-1870*, (2003), p. 106.

7. John R. McKivigan, p. 75.

8. McKivigan, The author provides a statistical chart showing the percentages of AFASS officer affiliations with various church denominations; 25% were affiliated with the Congregational Church, 22.5% with the New School Presbyterians, 17.5% with the Baptists and 12.5% with the Methodist Episcopal Church. p. 77.

CHAPTER THIRTEEN: SILENCING DEBATE

1. Jermain W. Loguen, *The Rev. J. W. Loguen, as a Slave and as a Freeman. A Narrative of Real Life* (Syracuse: J. K. K. Truair & Co., 1859), p. 357. OHA

2. *Minutes of the General Assembly of the Presbyterian Church in the USA* (New School), (Presbyterian Church of America, 1839), Vol. 9, pp. 20, 22. Googlebooks

3. C. C. Goen, p. 73.

4. "Alumni Memorial, 1897-1898, for Rev. Abishai Scofield," (Schenectady, New York: Union College), p. 15. The Memorial called this friend and co-worker of Gerrit Smith, "enthusiastic and fearless." Scofield went south, and pursued his anti-slavery commitments, administering to the needs of freed men in Camp Nelson, Kentucky, but was driven out by the Ku Klux Klan in 1866. See: Victor B. Howard, *The Evangelical War against Slavery and Caste; the Life and Times of John G. Fee* (Sellinsgrove: Susquehanna University Press, 1996), pp. 158-168. Rev. Scofield died in Spencerport, N.Y. in 1898.

5. *Records of the First Congregational Church of Syracuse, New York*. Item 6682, 10-A-1, MS Box 5, pp. 3-6. OHA

6. Ibid.

7. *Minutes of the Annual Conference of the Methodist Episcopal Church for Years 1839-1845* (New York: T. Mason & G. Lane), Vol. III, p. 86. Also Vol. II, (1838-1839), pp. 562, 652. Googlebooks

8. Ibid.

9. Russell E. Richey, *The Methodist Conference in America, A History* (Nashville: Kingswood Books, Abbington Press, 1996), p. 97.

10. *Oneida Conference Journal, 1829-1863, V.* Ninth Session (Cortlandville, August 30-31, 1837), The Methodist Collection. SUSC-RC

11. Rev. P. Douglass Gorrie, "Rev. Alfred D. Peck," *The Black River Conference Memorial: Containing Sketches of the Life and Character of the M. E. Church* (New York: Carlton & Phillips, 1852), p. 212. OCPL-LH

12. Ibid.

13. I found no information indicating what viewpoint Rev. Benajah Mason held regarding slavery during the years he served in Manlius. Ten years later, however, as a member of Oneida Conference, he is listed in the Methodist Episcopal newspaper as secretary on the Conference committee on slavery. This committee prepared resolutions condemning slavery, and the recently passed fugitive slave law. *Northern Advocate*, August 13, 1851 (Auburn, New York), p. 1.

14. Rev. Lewis Curts, D. D. , *The General Conferences of the Methodist Episcopal Church from 1792 to 1896* (New York: Eaton & Mains, 1900), p. 282.

15. *South Cortland Luminary,* January 4, 11, 18, 1838.

16. *South Cortland Luminary,* April 19, 1838.

17. *South Cortland Luminary,* November 15, 1838.

CHAPTER FOURTEEN: EQUALITY, POLITICS & THE FRATERNITY

1. *Manlius Republican*, November 2, 1830, p. 2. OHA

2. New York State dropped its property requirement for white males when the state legislature revised the Constitution in 1821. It required men of color to own property valued at $250 in order to vote, thus severely limiting the voting right to a small number of colored men.

3. Edward Pessen, *Jacksonian America: Society, Personality, and Politics*. (Homewood, Illinois: The Dorsey Press, 1969), p. 324.

4. Pessen, pp. 98-99.

5. Hal T. Avery, "What Became of Bill Morgan? The Kidnapping That Started a Third Political Party," *Buffalo Evening News*, September 11, 1948, p. 1.

6. Charles McCarthy, *The Antimasonic Party, A Study of Political Antimasonry in the United States, 1827-1840* (1902), p. 375. The Justin Winsor Prize, American Historical Association. At: http://archive.org/stream/antimasonicparty00mccarich/antimasonicparty00mccarich_djvu.txt

7. McCarthy, p. 381. In 1882 Thurlow Weed made this assessment of his anti-masonic involvement. "I now look back through an interval of fifty-six years with a conscious sense of having been governed through the 'anti-masonic' excitement by a sincere desire, first, to vindicate the violated laws of my country, and next, to arrest the great power and dangerous influences of 'secret societies.'" *The Facts Stated. Hon. Thurlow Weed on the Morgan Abduction.* Document for the People (Chicago: National Christian Association, 1882), p. 14. Pamphlet located in Subject folder, Anti-Masonic, OHA.

8. Charles A. Lakin's *History of Military Lodge No. 93, Free and Accepted Masons, Manlius, N. Y.*, published by Eagle Printing House, 1893. MHS. Posted online by Kathy Crowell (1998). See also E. E. Clemons, "The Political State of Manlius in the Early 1830s," edited by H. C. Durston, Historian, Village of Manlius. Durston wrote many articles on local history, including "The Military Lodge" of Manlius, as his 29th Paper. OHA

9. *First Baptist Church, Manlius, Church History*, See: website: http://firstbaptist-manlius.org/1827-1833-charles-morton

10. McCarthy, p. 381.

11. *Onondaga Republican*, August 15, 1830, p. 3. OHA

12. *Onondaga Republican*, September 22, 1830, p. 2. OHA

13. *Onondaga Republican*, October 20, 1830, p. 3. OHA

14. *Onondaga Republican*, October 27, 1830, pp. 2-3. OHA

15. Ibid.

16. Ibid.

17. *Onondaga Republican*, June 1, 1831. The newspaper accuses "the Royal Arch Doctor of the Masonic Repository in his last *weakly* paper," of declining to publish "Mr. Birdseye's report in relation to the Morgan trial." In his June 15th issue, the editor begins with mocking titular labels of "...To that Grand, elect, ineffable, perfect and sublime FREE and ACCEPTED Mason Doctor William Taylor of Manlius, quondam King of the Manlius Chapter...." etc., p. 2. OHA

18. David Jon Volkin, "Manlius; A Study of the Social, Political and Economic Climate of Manlius, New York, 1796 – 1836" (n.d., private printing), p. 42. FFL-LH. The *Cyclopædia of Political Science, Political Economy, and the Political History of the United States*, edited by John J. Lalor (1899) describes the term "Bucktail" as a common nickname used several years for political opponents of the canal system, and therefore those people against DeWitt Clinton in New York State [1.163]. Under Martin Van Buren, the Bucktails gained control, and in 1824 Clinton was ejected from his office of canal commissioner. This action produced a backlash, however, and that same year, Clinton was chosen governor by a popular majority of over 16,000, and again in 1826. After Clinton's death in 1828, the Bucktails became the Democratic party of New York under the control of the Van Buren Albany Regency, which it was often called. See also, Jabez D. Hammond's *Political History of New York, from the ratification of the Federal Constitution, to December 1840* (Phinney & Company, 1844) p. 450+ At: http://archive.org/details/historyofpolitic01hamm

19. Volkin, Ibid.

CHAPTER FIFTEEN: DON'T PANIC!

1. Ted Widmer, *Martin Van Buren* (New York: Times Books, Henry Holt & Co., 2005), p. 16.

2. Revere Thompson, "Panics of Past," *Syracuse Herald*, November 3, 1907, p. 5. FH

3. Robert Gray Gunderson, *The Log Cabin Campaign* (University of Kentucky Press, 1957), p. 13, also p. 19. LC-NRFL

4. Orson Smith, "Philosopher Smith," *Orson Smith Scrapbook*, OHA. Also, for an interesting explanation of the "boom, bust and recovery cycle" phenomenon of Michigan during the 1830s see Willis Frederick Dunbar and George S. May, *Michigan: A History of the Wolverine State,* pp. 224-230. The authors maintain that while there were some advertising scams that glorified empty wastelands as promising boom centers that duped hopeful easterners, the collapse was due to several factors including, the increase in immigrant populations, rapid settlement, an unbounded enthusiasms for internal improvement investments, and unregulated banking institutions that failed to maintain adequate safety net deposits. Red dog money was a nickname given to bank notes that were printed up, but which became almost worthless as they became unredeemable.

5. Carol Sheriff, *The Artificial River: The Erie Canal and the Paradox of Progress*, 1817-1862 (New York: Hill and Wang, 1996), p. 95. OHA

6. In his article on "Industries" Dr. Walter Pendergast, Jr. described the enterprising efforts of John McViccar, Harvey Edwards, and Seymour Pratt to build a mile-long feeder canal from Fayetteville to the Erie Canal waterway, noting unfortunately the village of Manlius was never able to build a connecting canal to the Fayetteville feeder. See: *People and Places, Fayetteville, Manlius, Minoa and Neighbors,* Vol. 1, 1986. p. 84.

7. The *Tribune Almanac and Political Register,* ed. Horace Greeley, et al., puts Seward's 1838 Governor's tally in Onondaga County at 5,684 to Marcy's 5,664, clearly a very close vote. Such close voting experiences intensified campaigns when the Liberty Party put up slates for local, state and national elections, changing the balance of traditional voting patterns. (New York: George Dearborn & Co., 1838), Vol. 4, p.10.

8. These petitions were reported in the *Albany Evening Journal* in 1839 in the following issues: 1-7; 1-14; 1-21; 2-2; 2-4; 2-5; 2-18; 2-19. NYSL-AHN NB

9. *Albany Argus,* March 12, 1839, p. 3. NYSL-AHN NB. Whig Party Assemblyman Azariah Smith, submitted a petition from the "ladies of Manlius" which may be the first such petition sent by women from the town to the New York State legislature. Their petition reflected goals promoted by the women's moral reform society, and its auxiliaries, in New York State. Sophia Clark, Elizabeth Clark Weld's sister-in-law, was very active in this organization in Utica, and it seems likely these goals were shared by the women in Manlius and Fayetteville as they had an active women's moral society. In my text, I noted that Grace Smith Martyn, and Sarah Towne Smith, were leaders in this organization at the time their brothers, the Rev. Stephen and Rev. Carlos, Smith, were ministering in Manlius and Fayetteville in 1834. These sibling and kinship relationships provided a supportive network through which to pursue reform efforts. In addition, the Clark women, as well as some of their Weld kin, were drawn together by their mutual appreciation of their revivalist religious experiences. Ryan's study of female associations and reform movements in Oneida County, provided a valuable context for understanding the motivations of the Manlius women's petition to the state legislature in 1839. (See footnote 11, Chapter 9). Ryan described some of the goals of the women's moral reform society in Utica. She explained the plight of young single women who had no legal protection against predatory male

advances, especially made against them when placed in homes as servants and household workers. Female reformers in Central New York, as in New York City, sought legalized punishment for these predatory offenses, as well as, in come cases, for exposing those males engaged in prostitution.

10. *Petition against annexation of Texas to the Union, Manlius, N.Y., 1837.* Subject folder, Anti-Slavery – *Petitions.* Microfilmed copies. Thanks to Judith Wellman, this information was made available to our historical society. [NARA HR 25-H 1.8 Wellman, Reel 2] OHA.

11. *Petitions,* [James] Bailey, Lafayette, New York, Ibid.

12. Junius P. Rodriques, ed., *Slavery in the United States: A Social, Political and Historical Encyclopedia* (ABC-CLIO, 2007), Vol. 2, pp. 305 and 45. SUL

13. *Fayetteville Luminary,* February 6, 1840. Vote reported on p. 2, c.3-4.

14. *Fayetteville Luminary,* February 6, 1840. Earll lost a bid for re-election and later became Onondaga County Judge.

15. *Republican Monitor,* February, 18, 1840 in Miscellaneous Newspapers - 19th Century. p.1, col. 1-3. SUL-SCRC reprinted the article from the *Albany Evening Journal,* page 3. There were several contested resolutions and votes taken trying to resolve conflicts in dealing with this issue, which were cited in the *Albany Argus.*

16. *Republican Monitor,* April 14, 1840, in Miscellaneous Newspapers-19th Century collection, p. 2, c. 5. SUL-SCRC. In the report of the April 7 vote in the Assembly, Victory Birdseye was one of 56 Yes votes, against 33 men who voted No.

17. "The Diary of Asa Eastwood," *Asa Eastwood Papers,* SULSC-RC MSS 76, Box 2. Sixteen years earlier, Eastwood was an elected delegate to the 1821 New York State Constitutional Convention. There was a contentious debate over extending voting rights to colored men. Eastwood took a moderate position between those who rejected expansion, and those that sought to restrict extension only to colored men who owned property worth $250 or more. Eastwood urged the criteria be lowered to $100. The motion failed. Victory Birdseye, also a delegate, sought to get a more liberal extension of the suffrage, but failed. The final vote ratified the higher eligibility criteria of $250.

18. *Letter,* Francis Baylies of Taunton, to Gen. John E. Wool, Esq. of Troy, N.Y., December 28, 1839. "Letters from a Massachusetts Federalist to a New York Democrat, 1823-1839," *New York History* (July 1967), Vol. XLVIII, no. 3, pp. 272-73. OCPL-LH

CHAPTER SIXTEEN: FRUSTRATION, CIDER & THE LIBERTY PARTY

1. Fred E. Dutcher, *Tippecanoe & Tyler, Too,* in his "Once Upon a Time" column (*Syracuse Post Standard,* September 8, 1930). Subject folder, Politics- Government- Elections, 1840-1845. OHA

2. James Brewer Stuart "Abolitionists, Insurgents, and Third Parties: Sectionalism and Partisan Politics in Northern Whiggery, 1836-1844" in *Crusaders and Compromisers,* ed. Alan M. Kraut (1983), p. 29.

3. Ted Widmer, *Martin Van Buren,* p. 122.

4. Robert G. Gunderson, Ibid., p. 10.

5. *Log Cabin,* December 12, 1840. GB

6. *Fayetteville Luminary,* July 1, 1841, "Utica Convention," Issues of the *Fayetteville Luminary* for 1841 and 1842, were accessed on fultonhistory.com, and have been noted by FH, to distinguish them from early issues on microfilm. Microfilm of later issues are also accessible at the Fayetteville Free Library Local History Room.

7. George Pegler, *The Autobiography of the Life and Times of Rev. George Pegler, Written by Himself* (1875) (Syracuse: Wesleyan Methodist Publishing House, 1879), pp. 404-405.

8. *Fayetteville Luminary,* July 6, 1841. FH

9. *Fayetteville Luminary,* "The Convention," September 16, 1841. FH.

10. *Methodist Reformer,* October 7, 1841. The venture did not prove as successful as hoped, however, as Bailey announced in the November 4th issue that agent Ward had only been able to collect $13.00 of hundreds that were owed by subscribers. FH

11. *Madison & Onondaga Abolitionist,* Jan 11, 1842, p. 67. OHA.

12. Ibid

13. *Madison & Onondaga Abolitionist*, April 19, 1842. p. 122. OHA

14. Ibid.

15. *Madison & Onondaga Abolitionist*, November 16, 1841, p. 35. OHA

16. Allen Nevins, *Grover Cleveland A Study in Courage* (New York: Dodd, Mead, Co., 1933), p. 15. FFL-LH

17. Geoffrey Blodgett, *The Emergence of Grover Cleveland: A Fresh Appraisal*, New York History, V. 73, no. 2 (April 1992), pp.134-35. OCPL-LH. Among the interesting details Town of Manlius Historian, Barbara S. Rivette, shared in her portrait of "Grover Clevelnad: Fayetteville's Hometown Boy," in 1987, is that two of Rev. Richard Cleveland's sons, Richard and Fred, enlisted and served in the Civil War. Son Grover, noted as family supporter, paid the fee to hire a substitute, a common legal practice at that time. See p. 4-5.

18. Ibid. Another factor may also have reinforced Richard Cleveland's reluctance to take sides publicly in the slavery controversy. His wife, Ann Neal, was born and raised in Baltimore, Maryland, a slave state. Many slaves were brought to New York before 1827, and many escaped from Maryland, as it was geographically closer to free states just north. Cleveland also served a couple years as a young clergyman in Virginia before moving north. Ann's father was a book seller, and the family did not own slaves, but they lived in a community of neighbors, some of whom did. Such cultural and personal family experiences and connections influence how one perceives, and acts, regarding controversial issues.

CHAPTER SEVENTEEN: THE COLORED AMERICAN

1. Rev. Samuel Ward quoted by Ronald K. Burke in *Samuel Ringgold Ward, Christian Abolitionist* (New York: Garland Pub, Inc, 1995), p. 82. SUL

2. *Independent Church of Canastota*, Site Presentation Speech, (Madison County Historical Society, Oneida, New York, March 2006), p.1.

3. *Letter*, Nathan Chapman to N. R. Chapman (son), April 26, 1846. Chapman Family Papers, OHA

4. *Liberty Press,* September 26, 1843, p. 183. OHA

5. Lydia Maria Francis Child, "Lewis Clark," *Leaves from a Slave's Journal of Life*, published in *The National Anti-Slavery Standard*, October 20, 27, 1842. pp. 78-79, also 83. SUL-MD 1389

6. *Letter*, Theodore Weld to Gerrit Smith, October 23, 1856, eds. Barnes & Dumond, Vol. II, p. 811.

7. Patrick Kennicott, *Black Persuaders in the Antislavery Movement*," Journal of Black Studies, (1970-1971), p. 20-23. LC-NRFL

8. *Narratives of the Sufferings of Lewis and Milton Clarke, sons of a soldier of the Revolution during a Captivity of More than Twenty Years among the Slaveholders of Kentucky, one of the so-called Christian States of North America,* Dictated by Myself (Boston: B. Marsh, 1846), p. 62.

9. Samuel Cornish, Philip Bell, and Charles Bennett Ray launched *The Weekly Advocate* in 1836. The name was later changed to *The Colored American*. In 1840 Charles B. Ray became the sole owner and editor.

10. "Meeting Fourth Anniversary of New York Anti-Slavery Society, Utica, N. Y. held September 19, 20, 21," in *Friend of Man*, September 26, 1838, p. 266. CU

11. *The Colored American*, "The Aspects of Our Cause," March 21, 1840, V. 1, p. 2. SUL-MD, Microfilm 1390. Some other issues of *Colored American* were examined as part of the collection of "Miscellaneous newspapers -19th Century," at Syracuse University Library Special Collections, and are noted. SUL-SCRC

12. *Colored American* (1840), May 16, July 15, Oct. 10. SUL-MD 1390.

13. Benjamin Quarles, "Letters from Negro Leaders to Gerrit Smith," *Journal of Negro History* (October 1942), Vol 27, no 4, p. 432. Smith exchanged communications with Samuel E. Cornish, a Presbyterian minister, and editor of *Freedom's Journal*, the first black newspaper in the United States. With H. H. Garnet, Cornish organized the effort to overturn property restrictions barring most blacks from voting. Gerrit Smith maintained a frequent correspondence with James McCune Smith. Smith, reported as the first black American medical doctor, was considered one of the foremost intellectuals within the black New York community. LC-NRFL

14. *The Colored American,* "Convention of the Colored Inhabitants of the State of New York, To Consider Their Political Disabilities, Held on August 18th, 19th, and 20th of August, 1840." Abstract of the Proceedings, September 12, 1840. SUL-MD 1390.

15. Ibid.

16. *Colored American,* February 13th 1841. SUL-MD, 1390.

17. *The Liberty Press,* November 7, 1843, p. 207. OHA

18. Charles Wesley, "The Participation of Negroes in Antislavery Political Parties," *The Journal of Negro History,* v. 29, no 1, Jan 1944, 39-40. Frederick Douglass was mentored into the organized abolitionist movement by William L. Garrison's American Anti-Slavery Society. His decision to support the Liberty Party in 1850, caused a painful break with Garrison. LC-NRFL

19. Hanes Walton, Jr., Donald R. Deskins, Jr., Donald Richard Deskins, Jr, Sherman Puckett, *The African American Electorate* (Congressional Quarterly, Inc, 2012). The authors list the following black leaders known to have attended the Liberty Party Convention on August 30, 1843 in Buffalo and who held a convention leadership position: William Wells Brown, H. H. Garnet, J. W. Loguen, Charles B. Ray, Dr. James M. Smith, Samuel R. Ward. p. 181.

20. Charles Wesley, Ibid., p. 39. Wesley quotes from Rev. Samuel R. Ward's *Autobiography of a Fugitive Negro,* written in 1855. Ward attended many Liberty Party and local anti-slavery meetings between 1840 -1850, and went on numerous speaking tours throughout the state. His parents fled from Maryland when he was a child. Ward had the unusual early experiences of pastoring two white congregations in upstate New York. After serving to a hospitable white congregation in South Butler, Wayne County in 1846, he accepted an invitation to serve a small abolitionist congregation in Cortlandville. His *Impartial Citizen* weekly newspaper, though short-lived (1849-1850) detailed his lecture tours and meetings in local towns throughout Central New York. LC-NRFL

21. Robert A. Gibson, *Introduction,* "Slave Narratives: Black Autobiography in Nineteenth-Century America," (Yale-New Haven Teacher's Institute), at: http://www.yale.edu/ynhti/curriculum/units/1985/5/85.05.02.x.html

CHAPTER EIGHTEEN: CRUSADING UPHILL

1. James C. Jackson, *The Duties & Dignities of American Freemen* (Boston: New England Anti-Slavery Tract Assoc, 1843?). Accessed at http://archive.org/details/dutiesdignitieso00jack

2. *Liberty Press,* November 22, 1842. OHA

3. *National Anti-Slavery Standard,* February 10, 1842, *Miscellaneous newspapers-*19th Century, p. 142. SUL-SCRC

4. *The Abolitionist,* April 4, 1842. OHA

5. Howard Zinn, *You Can't Be Neutral on a Moving Train, A Personal History of Our Times* (Boston: Beacon Press, 1994), p. 4. In 1980, Zinn, wrote *A People's History of the United States* which looked at the events and movements of American history from the perspective of "the common people," instead of only publicly acclaimed heroes and heroines.

6. *Veritas,* Ibid., October 7, 1835.

7. *The Madison & Onondaga Abolitionist,* April 19, 1842. OHA

8. *Madison & Onondaga Abolitionist*, May 17, 1842. OHA

9. *The Liberty Press,* November 22, 1842, Vol. 1, no. 2, p.6, col. 5-6. In addition to those who played a leading role at anti-slavery meetings, or had seceded because of this cause from their recent church affiliation, or were early subscribers to the *Madison-Onondaga County Abolitionist,* a number of residents received copies of the *Liberty Press* when Wesley Bailey began publishing it in 1843. Some of the Manlius, DeWitt, and Fayetteville names noted in receipts of *Liberty Press* issues were: L. P. Noble to Jacob Butts and Z. Adams, Mar 7; James C. Jackson for C. W. Weld, Adam Harrower, April 4, 1843; Ansel Kinne, April 11, 1843; S.B. Palmer and Dea S. Edwards, April 18, 1843;E. Gridley, December 7, 1844; George Loomis on March 1, 1845. Loomis was endorsed as the Liberty Party candidate for New York Assembly in the November 5, 1846 issue; Chas Coates, August 9, 1845; Orlo Blanchard, August 13, 1846, was endorsed by the party for the office of county coroner; W. L. Gregory, May 30, 1846; Seymour Pratt, September 10, 1846, G. Bogardus, October 1, 1846; Emerson Kinne,

March 21, 1846. Nathan Chapman, father of N. R. Chapman, rounded up every sympathizer he could find in Clockville! 1844-1846 issues of *Liberty Press*, were accessed at Utica Public Library, Genealogy Room.

10. Petition #38, residents of the Town of Manlius. Subject folder, Anti-Slavery, Petitions, Undated. Legibility of signatures not always clear. OHA

11. Handbill, undated. The source of these names comes from a single, undated sheet of paper that appears to be a copy of a slate of people in the town of Manlius, who were nominated for local offices. The author believes the name James J. DePuy is erroneously spelled, and should be "James I. DePuy." It also seems likely that Peter "Multer" should be Peter "Moulter." Subject folder, *Politics-Government- Elections*, 1840-1845, OHA.

"Letter, Charles Lenox Remond to Charles B. Ray, 30 June 1840," Document 7. Accessed online at http://atlanticslaverydebate.stanford.edu/sites/default/files/shared/ASD/Module1/RemondtoRay1840.pdf *American Slavery Debate, In the Context of Atlantic History, British Anti-Slavery Influence, 1770-1865*, p. 71. Remond's acknowledgment of women's important role in the anti-slavery movement published by C. B. Ray, was not uniformly characteristic of all abolitionists. Like their white colleagues, many black abolitionists expected women to work in their own gender spheres of activities in auxiliary roles. William L. Garrison and Charles L. Remond were two of the earliest abolitionists to publicly disregard these culturally imposed limitations.

CHAPTER NINETEEN: THE WOMAN QUESTION

1. *The Abolitionist*, (1842) July 5, p. 166; July 12, p. 170, and July 19, p. 175. For several weeks, numerous articles were published about the Cazenovia Mass Convention. Abby Kelley was the focus of many published criticisms. Publisher James Jackson tried to avoid being portrayed as inhospitable to anti-slavery colleagues, despite objectional views. Liberty Party men, however, seemed hard-pressed to maintain tolerance when Abby Kelley, one of the Garrison American Anti-Slavery Society team, came into 'their territory" transgressing gender norms and voicing ideological views they saw as distracting and harmful. Still, Jackson sought to call abolitionists to a standard of civility and fair discussion.

2. *Emancipator*, January 20, 1842, Issue 37, p. 183. On May 12, 1840, Rev. Charles W. Denison, a Baptist minister, seceded from the Garrison lead

American Anti-Slavery Society at its meeting in New York City, over the impropriety of including Abby Kelley on the business committee.

3. Milton Sernett, *North Star Country, Upstate New York and the Crusade for African American Freedom* (New York: Syracuse University Press, 2002), p. 62.

4. Judith Wellman, *The Road to Seneca Falls, Elizabeth Cady Stanton and the First Woman's Rights Convention* (Urbana, Illinois: University of Illinois Press, 2004), pp.52-53.

5. *The Madison and Onondaga Abolitionist,* "Madison County Manifesto! Great Mass Meeting! Two Thousand Delegates!" December 21, 1841. OHA

6. *The Abolitionist,* June 28, 1842. OHA

7. Abby Kelley attended the second convention of the American Women's Anti-Slavery Convention in 1838. Sarah Grimke and Angelina Grimke Weld took a very active role in the convention discussions and resolutions. See: *Proceedings of the Anti-Slavery Convention of American Women : held in Philadelphia, May 15th, 16th, 17th and 18th, 1838.* (Philadelphia, Pa, 1838). See: Samuel J. May Anti-Slavery Collection CU.

8. The short list of donors published in the July 12th *Abolitionist,* as attending the Cazenovia meeting, may have resulted from a problem of registration once the meeting was moved outdoors. Perhaps the coming and going into an unenclosed speaking area made such an accounting impossible. Among donors that were listed, however, were. C. A. Wheaton, Darius Northrup, L. P. Noble, "Colored Ladies," and the "Female A. S. Society, of Cazenovia." It is possible other residents from Manlius and Fayetteville attended. (p. 170.) While few newspapers paid compliments to Abby Kelley, author Junius Rodriquez pointed out her contributions to the anti-slavery movement. In his survey of *Slavery in the United States: A Social & Political History,* Vol. 2 (Santa Barbara, CA: ABC-CLIO, 2007) he credits Kelley for the many talents she brought to the anti-slavery movement. Among them, he said, were her organizational skills in planning campaigns, lectures and fund-raising throughout New England, Pennsylvania, New York and the Midwest. It was she, he writes, that inspired other women to travel the anti-slavery lecture circuit, including Lucy Stone, Susan B. Anthony, Sallie Hollie, and Sarah Redmond, Charles Redmond's sister. (pp. 290-291).

9. Judith Wellman, p.112.

10. *The Abolitionist,* July 19, 1842, p. 175. OHA

11. L. M., *The Abolitionist,* Ibid.

12. Ibid.

13. *Methodist Reformer,* July 14, 1842. FH

14. *Methodist Reformer,* July 21, 1842. FH

15. Hugh Barbour, Christopher Densmore et. al. in *Quaker Crosscurrents: Three Hundred Years of Friends in the New York Yearly Meetings* (1995) noted that "in 1842, former Quaker Abby Kelley arrived in Rochester as an agent of the American Anti-Slavery Society, and her visit inspired the formation of the Western New York Anti-Slavery Society," which took place during a meeting at the Bethel Presbyterian Church. Among those attending were Amy Post, and her daughter Mary Hallowell. (p. 173). In 1843, Kelley was again in the Seneca Falls area, and a major disturbance erupted. Authors Glenn C. Altschuler and Jan M. Saltzgaber, identify Abby Kelley's lectures there on abolition and temperance in August 1843, as the occasion for Rhoda Bement's conflict with, and accusations against, her Presbyterian pastor, Rev. Horace P. Bogue. Rhoda Bement believed Rev. Bogue deliberately chose not to honor her request to announce abolition meetings (lectures by Kelley). He denied this accusation. The authors explore the complexity of tensions over Calvinism, Presbyterian concerns for stability, controversies of the slavery and temperance movement, and emerging conflicts over women's role in public, demonstrated by Kelley's speaking in public to mixed gender audiences in the context of Bement's church trial. See: *Revivalism, Social Conscience and Community in the Burned-Over District, The Trial of Rhoda Bement* (Ithaca: Cornell University Press, 1983), pp. 41-42, 50, 57.

16. The November 30, 1842 edition of the *Onondaga Standard* carried remarks by the editor, and commentary by an observer at the lecture series. William Lloyd Garrison and Abby Kelley, and other AASS members spoke. The editor, while not approving the speakers points of view, criticized the disruptive behavior of some of the opponents. The observer praised the openness of the panel of speakers to audience comments. William Lloyd Garrison mentioned this Syracuse lecture series in a letter to his wife, Mrs. Helen E. Garrison. He wrote from Waterloo on Nov. 21, 1842. In his closing remarks, he noted that "Abby Kelley "is tasking her lungs too severely, and ought to be more careful for the future" and that she

"will continue in this part of the country during the winter." This letter was accessed online at: archive.org [*Letter to] My Dear Helen* [manuscript] 1842.

17. Amy Swerdlow, "Abolition's Conservative Sisters: The Ladies' New York City Anti-Slavery Society, 1834-1840" in *"The" Abolitionist Sisterhood: Women's Political Culture in Antebellum America,* edited by Jean Fagan Yellin and John C. Van Horne (Ithaca: Cornell University Press, 1994) p.34. Also, in the August 15, 1840 issue of *Advocate of Moral Reform*, the editor, Sarah Towne Smith, wrote an extensive obituary of her "beloved" sister Grace F. Martyn, who had died on August 1. She praised her sisters many reform efforts and leadership positions. Among others, she cited her role as an early board manager of the N. Y. F. M. R. Society and as president of the N. Y. F. Anti-Slavery Society. It is evident Sarah admired her older sister's courage in actively engaging herself on the side of the oppressed slave, pointing out that others remained passive. She didn't gloss over that circumstance, saying, "the cause of the oppressed and downtrodden slave, she early espoused, while her companion, and all her family friends stood aloof from the ranks of abolition."p.123. According to Steven Mintz, in *Moralists and Modernizers: America's Pre-Civil War Reformers* it was Lydia A. Finney, revivalist Charles G. Finney's wife, that first directed the women's moral reform in 1834 (Baltimore: The John Hopkins University Press, 1995), p. 69. Grace's husband, Rev. J. R. Martyn, took Charles G. Finney's pastoral role in 1836 at the Chatham Street Chapel, where he remained for two years. A year after her sister died, Sarah Towne Smith married her widowed brother-in-law.

18. *Advocate of Moral Reform.* The July 1, 1837 issue notes the F. M. R. S. Manlius, NY, on p. 288, and also a donation from Life Members sent by Mrs. Filenda Nims, from F. M. R. Soc. Manlius, NY on p. 128. The September 15, 1838 issue under "new auxiliaries" notes "one at Fayetteville, NY-63 members, Miss Caroline Collins, secy. The August 1, 1840 issue cites a new auxiliary at Pompey Hill, NY with "Mrs. Dr. Wells, secy" and 15 members. p. 120.

19. See p. 72 for the Albany newspaper item March 9, 1839, citing the petition received in the Senate from Ladies in Manlius.

20. *The Methodist Reformer,* October 6, 1842. After September 23, 1841, the newspaper title *Fayetteville Luminary,* was changed to *Methodist Reformer.*

21. *The Methodist Reformer,* October 13, 1842. Wesley Bailey is listed as publisher of *The Abolitionist* in the Oct 25th issue. On November 15, he published the first issue of *The Liberty Press* in Utica.

22. When Rev. Cleveland concluded his presentation to the woman's moral reform society, he named three women, who, from the manner in which he presented them, told his audience, these women should not be viewed as positive female role models. He mentioned Mary Wollstonecraft, Harriet Livermore, and Abby Kelley. Wollstonecraft an English radical thinker, of the late 18th century, authored *A Vindication of the Rights of Woman* in 1792. Susan B. Anthony and Elizabeth Cady Stanton dedicated their *History of Women's Suffrage* to her in 1881. Harriet Livermore was a preacher. Few churches, or small sects, allowed such evangelizing roles to women in the 1820s and 1830s. The Presbyterian Church had prohibited women exercising such public roles in their churches. See "Female Preaching in Early Nineteenth Century America," by Catherine A. Brekus, at http://www.baylor.edu/content/services/document.php/98759.pdf The third woman mentioned was, Abby Kelley, whose lecture at High Bridge, the month preceding Rev. Cleveland's presentation to the moral reform advocates, had been published in Wesley Bailey's *Methodist Reformer.*

CHAPTER TWENTY: THE BAPTISTS

1. Douglas Strong, *Perfectionist Politics,* p. 20.

2. *Emancipator,* May 20, 1841, p. 11. NYSL-AHN GB

3. *National Anti-Slavery Standard,* February 10, 1842, Miscellaneous newspapers- 19th Century, newspaper collection. SUL-SCRC

4. Lucius Manlius Boltwood, *The History and Genealogy of the Family of Thomas Noble of Westfield, Massachusetts: with genealogical notes of other families by the name of Noble* (1878), p. 642. At http://archive.org/details/historygenealogy00bolt

5. *Letter,* A. F. Kinney to Nathan R. Chapman from Homer, November 22, 1836, Nathan R. Chapman papers, OHA. Also, Cortland documents show Kinney was a tutor in languages at the time of this letter. Chapman was a student at Cortland Academy during 1831 and 1832, according to school catalogues and records titled "order of exercises." These public performances featured student speeches and skills displaying their proficiencies. At the January 11, 1831 exercises, Chapman delivered an

oration on "Improvement of the Mind." See *Cortland Academy* File Box, LV 287, Cortland County Historical Society.

6. *Methodist Reformer*, September 23, 1841. FH

7. *Methodist Reformer*, March 3, 1842. FH

8. *Methodist Reformer*, June 23, 1842. FH

9. *Methodist Reformer*, August 18, 1842. FH

10. *Baptist Church Record Book, 1833-1868* (United Church of Fayetteville: Onondaga County, New York) State American Revolution Bicentennial Commission microfilm program, NYS Archives, A0768-79, MU 1 Reel 75-19-1. See the Nov. 19 and Dec. 12 (1842) meetings. At the November meeting, First Baptist Church Minutes indicate that the "hand of fellowship" had just been withdrawn at this meeting from a female member of the church for the "crime of fornication." At the Dec. 12 meeting, the American slavery resolution was discussed in regard to urging that the church have "no fellowship with those who traffic in human flesh." This resolution occupied a year of argument, and eventually resulted in a secession of a dozen members.

11. Ibid, *Baptist Meeting Minutes*, May 20, 1843.

12. De Alva Stanwood Alexander, *A Political History of the State of New York, 1833-1861* (Port Washington, L. I.: Ira J. Friedman, 1909), Vol. 2, p. 83. Googlebooks

13. *The Liberty Press*, August 22, 1843, p. 163. OHA

14. Ibid

15. *Baptist Church Record Book*, Ibid.

16. *Records of the Second Baptist Church in Fayetteville*, The church was publicly recognized by an ecclesiastical council held on January 10th, 1844. Item 5830, pp.14-15, also 29. OHA

17. Ibid., p. 17.

18. Ibid. pp. 18-19.

19. Ibid., pp. 35-36.

Letter, Rev. Washington Kingsley to Nathan R. Chapman, March 13, 1855, SUSC, Nathan Chapman Collection, Box 2451. A copy of this letter, and other Chapman correspondence, was given to me by Barbara S. Rivette, to whom I am grateful.

CHAPTER TWENTY ONE: WHAT HAPPENED ON HIGH BRIDGE HILL?

1. Douglas Strong, Ibid., quoting William Goodell, p. 114.

2. Ian Frazier, *Family* (New York: Picador, Farrar, Straus and Giroux, 1994), p. 49.

3. *Letter*, Harriet DePuy to William, July 14, 1845, "DePuy Family Papers," (St. Paul, Minnesota: Minnesota Historical Society Library). Harriet's letter to her brother, mentioned the following plans being made: "...Lonson & John Balsley, J. H. Worden and Majors are going to Michigan. Daniel Balsley has concluded to go out to Buffalo and Uncle Ruston goes to Illinois in Sept. Andrew Campbell talks of moving next week, and Dennis Campbell will move into that house. ...I believe Jason Russell has gone to Ohio, and Sam Dixon and Charles are west..."

4. "Incorporation of the Trustees of the High Bridge Methodist Episcopal Society," Recd. Feb 6, 1844. *Miscellaneous Incorporation Records*, Book G, p. 106. The session was presided over by John E. Dow and Andrew B. Campbell, and attended by Azariah Smith and David Gilmor. James Balsley, Jason C. Russell, and Asel Wilcox were elected trustees. Also, David Balsley sold a parcel of land to the trustees of the new church for $50.00 to erect the building. See: Deed Book 85, pp. 133-134. "David Balsley to Trustees of the High Bridge Methodist Episcopal Society on Feb 5, 1844." Recd Feb 6, 1844. OCC

5. "Incorporation of the Reformed Methodist Church and Society," March 15, 1839, *Miscellaneous Incorporation Records*, Book G. p. 27, Recorded March 11, 1841. John A. Balsley and Darius Northrup listed as trustees for 3 years. James I. DePuy and Andrew Sherwood, each 2 years, and Daniel Balsley, 1 year. OCC

6. Carol Sheriff, op. cit., pp. 138-139. The February 11, 1852 issue of the *Northern Christian Advocate* carried an article which estimated the number of boys working on the canal to be between 6,000 and 7,000. The newspaper reported that half of them were orphans.

7. Ibid.

8. Among the mission-oriented moral improvement societies, was the Seaman's Bethel Society, American Seaman's Friend Society, and two auxiliary organizations which, Sheriff explains, established Bethel churches. These hired missionaries to preach to workers and distribute tracts and Bibles. The moral health of society depended on these workers being reintegrated "in the godly community." Whether they liked it or not, the author asserts, members of the middle class could no longer isolate themselves from canal workers....they must join in trying to combat the threat of moral infection. Sheriff, p. 153-155.

9. Kathleen G. Crowell, *Tavern Tales* (New York: Fayetteville Free Library, 2010) p.56-57. All the information about taverns and hotels at High Bridge are from this source. FFL-LH

10. *Fayetteville Luminary*, August 29, 1839. FH

11. Crowell, Ibid.

12. *One Hundred Years of Temperance: A Memorial of the Centennial Temperance Conference....*1886, p. 312. Also Robert Emory, *History of the Discipline of the Methodist Episcopal Church* (1851) p. 86. Googlebooks

13. *Fayetteville Luminary,* April 29, 1841. FH

14. *Liberty Press,* April 18, 1843, p. 9. Bailey remarked: "....any one of these taverns is abundantly sufficient to accommodate all the travelers that pass through this place." OHA The legal meaning of "dram shop" in the United States, though state laws vary, still refers to a bar, tavern, or the like, where alcoholic beverages were sold. Today the law also specifies violations for a host who gives liquor to an intoxicated person. The legal issues involved concern who is liable for injuries and death from such accidents caused by a result of the intoxication impairment.

15. Altschuler and Saltzgaber, p. 53.

CHAPTER TWENTY-TWO: CONFRONTATION & THE COST OF ZEAL

1. Joseph Wheelan, *Mr. Adams's Last Crusade* (New York: Public Affairs, Perseus Books, 2008), p. 191.

2. *Methodist Reformer*, September 22, 1842. FH

3. *Methodist Reformer*, July 28, 1842. FH

4. B. P. Bowne, L. L. D., "Aberrant Moralizers," *The Methodist Review*, William V. Kelley (ed.) LXXXII (New York: Eaton & Maine, 1900), p. 260. Googlebooks. Bowne makes the point that there are "good men on opposite sides of what one called moral questions," a belief, Wesley Bailey may not always have appreciated.

5. *The Albany Patriot*, a Liberty Party newspaper, reported there were 150 preachers and 5,000 to 8,000 seceding Methodist Episcopal members who had seceded before the convention. This report was published in *The Signal of Liberty* (Ann Arbor, MI), June 26, 1843, p. 2. See: http://signalofliberty.aadl.org/signalofliberty/18430821

6. Lucius C. Matlock, *History of American Slavery and Methodism, from 1780 to 1849, and History of the Wesleyan Methodist Connection of America*, (1849), p. 344. (OHA) See also *Cyclopedia of Methodism: Embracing Sketches of its rise, progress and present condition*. Matthew Simpson, ed., p. 923. OHA

7. Matlock, p. 346. The first General Conference of Wesleyan Methodist Churches of the U. S. recognized the following ministers in the New York Conference: L. Lee; P. M. Way; S. Salsbury; W. Bailey; P. R. Sawyer; J. Watson; R. Bennett.

8. William H. Brackney, *The Fruits of a Crusade: Wesleyan Opposition to Secret Societies*, (The General Commission on Archives and History, 1979-07-01), pp. 240-245. See at: *MH-1979-07-Brackney.pdf* Brackney, also observed a class basis to this suspicion. He believed that antimasonry was primarily a movement of "lower classes against the prestige, privilege, and position of the higher strata."

9. The New York Conference was eager to get a unified position settled. It took the lead endorsing a policy excluding any member of a secret society. Wesley Bailey was a delegate to that Conference. In October 1844, The General Conference in Cleveland, Ohio, declared secret society membership "inconsistent with our duties to God and Christianity."

10. Charles A. Lakin, Ibid, p. 100. MHS

11. *Liberty Press*, September 5, 1843, p.172. OHA.

12. W. M. Clark, Syracuse, to Edwin Clark, Oswego. October 6, 1843. Surname folder: Clarke, OHA. Edwin Clarke is a cousin of William M. Clark.

13. *The Liberty Press,* "The National Liberty Convention," Sept 12, 1843, p. 174, c. 4. Apparently local Liberty men took this recommendation seriously because a list of thirty Liberty candidates was selected to run for local positions including town clerk, overseer of the poor, sealer of weights and measures, inspectors of elections etc. A handbill of Liberty Party candidates for the Town of Manlius was found in the OHA Subject folder, *Government, Politics, 1840s* undated. No publication source or date was found, but I estimate this party nominee slate was created for an election between 1843-1847. One of the candidates named was James I. DePuy. DePuy was making plans to move west in 1845, though he did not leave until spring of 1847. Perhaps additional research can identify more precisely the date of this handbill

14. Douglas Strong's *Perfectionist Politics* shows a statistical correlation between abolitionist activist Liberty Party voters, and churches known for having a church reform and abolitionist position. In his Appendix B chart he demonstrates the location of those abolitionist churches and Liberty votes for the election of 1844. He specifically mentions Manlius (High Bridge) with its 67 Liberty votes, and cites WM/U as the abolition church affiliation, suggesting the Wesleyan Methodist/Union congregation there was the compelling impulse for political abolitionist Liberty party support, which it was. Only Cicero and Salina had more Liberty votes in Onondaga County that year, 89 and 81 respectively (See pp. 181-184). Strong sought to demonstrate that some abolitionists also denounced the inequality and hierarchy in their denominational churches, and seceded from these authoritarian structures, promoting "comeouter" movements, and Union congregations. In 1814, the Reformed Methodists of Vermont, had in fact, left their denomination because of the inequality they found in their church structures of authority. As they emigrated west they brought with them their *Articles for Faith and Practice* which condemned slavery. In the late 1830s, and early 1840s, as slavery became a more public controversy, members of the High Bridge Reformed Methodist Society founded in 1839, strengthened their anti-slavery position, and became more visible in the anti-slavery movement in the town of Manlius. However, the numerical strength of the Liberty Party vote in the town, did not, I believe rest solely on the High Bridge Church members, or visible "agitation" of Rev. Wesley Bailey, editor of the *Liberty Press* newspaper in 1843. Support for the

abolitionist movement and Liberty Party, came from several church memberships. The Presbyterians provided early spokesmen and leaders, and First Baptist Church members (and those that founded abolitionist Second Baptist Church) provided strong leadership to Liberty Party efforts in the mid 1840s. Still, the High Bridge Wesleyan "connected" congregation had become a symbol of the strong Liberty abolitionist impulses in the town.

15. "Onondaga," *Liberty Press,* Nov. 7, 1843, p. 207 col. 1. OHA. In the 1844 election, the Liberty Party cast 732 votes in Onondaga County, as reported by the November 22nd issue of the New York *Tribune.* The county vote showed that Democrat James K. Polk defeated Whig Henry Clay, by 382 votes. Whigs denounced the Liberty Parry for causing Clay's defeat. Manlius Liberty men gave James Birney 67 votes that year.

16. Franklin Ellis, N. A. Nash, *History of Cattaraugus County, New York* (Philadelphia: Eerts, Pub., 1879), Vol. II, Part III, Chapter XXXVIII, "Pioneer Settlers," p. 485-490. It was noted that Rev. Ezra Amadon later moved to Wisconsin, and that his son, Ezra, still resided in the town. OCPL-LH

17. I am grateful to Kathy Crowell for reminding me of the importance of these compelling economic forces at play.

CHAPTER TWENTY-THREE: THE LONE SECEDER

1. Henry David Thoreau, *On The Duty of Civil Disobedience,* Project Gutenberg e-book, See: http://www.gutenberg.org/files/71/71-h/71-h.htm

2. Records, *Trinity Presbyterian Society, Manlius, NY,* 7668, Box 1, 3-B-1 (May 11, 21, 1843). OHA

3. Wheelan, op. cit. pp. 194-197. Theodore Weld discovered his family connection to John Q. Adams during several of their late night preparation sessions. It was an extraordinary experience for Weld. When Adams went through this rugged "fiery ordeal" and defeated efforts to bring him to ruin, even his adversaries were amazed at his tenacity, "intellectual and rhetorical gifts." Wheelan records the following remark made by South Carolina Congressman Francis Pickens after Adams had beaten back those seeking to censure him in the House of Representatives: "Well, that is the most extraordinary man on God's footstool." See: p. 201.

4. Records, *Trinity Presbyterian Society, Manlius, NY,* Ibid.

5. Presbyterian Church in the U. S. A. General Assembly, *The Presbyterian Digest of 1907*; at http://www.ebooksread.com/authors-eng/presbyterian-church-in-the-usa-general-assembly/the-presbyterian-digest-of-1907—a-compend-of-the-acts-decisions-and-delivera-ser/page-90-the-presbyterian-digest-of-1907—a-compend-of-the-acts-decisions-and-delivera-ser.shtmlee: 1843, p. 14, N. S. Also, Harriet Beecher Stowe, cited this decision in her extended commentary, *The Key to Uncle Tom's Cabin* (Boston: Jewett, 1854), p. 419. See: http://utc.iath.virginia.edu/uncletom/key/keyt.html

6. "The Presbyterian General Assembly and Slavery," *Signal of Liberty,* June 19, 1843. At: http://signalofliberty.aadl.org/signalofliberty/SL_18430619-p207 The abolitionist newspaper reacted immediately to the contrast of these two policy issues discussed at the 1843 meeting. "In ancient times, the Pharisees strained at a gnat, and swallowed a camel. The General Assembly which could not tell whether it was wrong to enslave a man" passed a resolution urging church discipline against those found guilty by church session discipline proceedings of "promiscuous dancing."

7. *Liberty Press*, "General Assembly Presbyterian Church New School," June 20, 1843. p. 125. Rev. William C. Wisner moderated the 1840 General Assembly. OHA

8. *Liberty Press*, March 28, 1843. OHA

9. Octavius Brooks Frothingham, *Gerrit Smith, A Biography* (New York: Negro Universities Press, 1878, reprinted by G. P. Putnam), p. 54.

10. *Fayetteville Presbyterian Church, Session minutes, May 12, 1847, Trustees minutes 1829-74; Session minutes 1830-71; Ladies' Society record book 1838-5* NYSL Archives, microfilm, 75-19-1. NYSL-MD

11. Ibid.

12. Nancy S. Marder, editor of "Symposium: 50th Anniversary of *12 Angry Men*, published in the Chicago-Kent Law Review in 2007. V. 82, no. 2, p. 887. At: www.cklawreview.com/wp-content/uploads/.../CONTENTS_82-2.pd

13. Robert Hasting Nichols, completed by James Hastings Nichols, *Presbyterianism in New York State, A History of the Synod and Its Predecessors* (Philadelphia: Westminster Press, 1963), pp.157-159.

14. "In Memoriam" WORDEN, Subject folder, news clipping, (undated). OHA. Death date from *Find A Grave* Memorial at http://www.findagrave.com/cgi-bin/fg.cgi?page=gr&GRid=22547787

CHAPTER TWENTY-FOUR: WESTWARD HO!

1. *Letter*, Harriet DePuy to brother William, July 15, 1845 (Minnesota Historical Society). Ibid.

2. Ted Widmer, "Who Built This City?" *New York Times*, September 2, 2012. Kindness of Barbara S. Rivette, for sending me a copy of this article.

3. Bogardus, Ibid.

4. While the High Bridge Methodist Episcopal Church property can be documented extensively through its many years, there is no evidence, yet discovered, that indicates it functioned as a place of worship after the 1860s. The building was adapted for business and commercial purposes, often storage, until the last vestiges of the structure burned down. Over the years, memories of this church occasionally became confused with the "other" Methodist church uphill, which had a much longer lifespan as a center of religious community activity. The "uphill" Reformed Methodist meeting house lasted into the 1930s, though no exact date of its collapse, or removal, has been documented. Kathy Crowell and I uncovered many interesting stories about the residents at High Bridge and Fayetteville who sought to preserve, and continue this meeting house, built first under the auspices of the Reformed Methodists. At one time it was a Sabbath School sponsored by First Baptist Church in Fayetteville, and renamed Elkhorn Union Chapel. Then, Episcopalian leaders promoted the Sabbath school program there. It was directed by a Wesleyan Methodist congregation in the early 1900s with a female presider, and finally in 1923, was incorporated as the High Bridge Union Church. The locations of both church structures, depicted in Homer Sweets early 19th century maps of the hamlet of High Bridge, were confirmed by 1920s and 1950s maps. My conversations with staff members at the Onondaga County Department of Public Transportation and the NYS Department of Transportation in Syracuse, New York proved very beneficial to my research.

5. *Letter*, Harriet DePuy, Ibid.

6. Frazier, pp. 50-51.

7. *Letter*, Harriet DePuy, July 15, 1845.

8. *Letter*, Harriet DePuy, April 19, 1847.

9. *Letter*, Harriet DePuy, April 19, 1847, p. 3. Among the neighbors and friends Harriet's letters mention as heading west were, Lonson Stilwell, Marcellus Barnum, John J. Balsley, Jasper Goodfellow, George and Lamira Blanchard Smith, Daniel Balsley, Andrew Sherwood, Jason C. Russell.

10. Ibid, July 15, 1845.

11. Sarah D. Brooks Blair, *Reforming Methodism: 1800-1820*, Dissertation submitted to the Graduate Division of Religion, in partial fulfillment for a degree, Doctor of Philosophy, (Madison, N.J.: Drew University, May 2008), p. 186.

CHAPTER TWENTY-FIVE: THEY HAD NAMES

1. Dala Salwak, ed., Introduction, *AfterWord: Conjuring the Literary Dead* (Iowa University Press, 2011), p. viii.

2. The 1820 census shows that in addition to thirty free colored persons in the town of Manlius, the following residents owned slaves: John Fleming - 4; Abijah Yelverton, Jr. -2; Elias Gumaer, Jr. – 2; Each of the following are shown to have one slave in 1820: George W. Holbrook, Abel Cadwell, Nicholas Marsh, Nicholas Randall, William Gardner. The Burial Records of Christ Church at the Manlius Historical Society show Jenny York, identified as: "Slave of R. R. Phelps, d. 17 June 1820 ae 62." So, the number of documented slaves in the town in 1820, seems to be fourteen. The records of *Christ Church Burials, Manlius, New York,* were transcribed by Nancy Schiffhauer, 1993. MHS. Ten years previous, the 1810 census records show the number of slaves in the town, to be fifteen, with each of the following owning 1 slave: Sylvanus Tousley, Benjamin Wood, Elijah Phillips Jr., Caleb Hopkinson, Benjamin Booth, Abel Cadwell. Those having more than one that year were: Chas. B. Bristol – 2; Abijah Yelverton, Jr. – 4; Elijah Phillips, Sr. - 3.

3. Timothy C. Cheney, *Reminiscences of Syracuse*, compiled by Parish Johnson (Syracuse: Summers & Brother, 1857), p. 21. OHA

4. "Death of Old Colored Citizen," *Syracuse Daily Standard,* Nov 3, 1865. The obituary says Isaac Wales moved from Scipio, Cayuga County directly to Syracuse. The 1820 federal census records John Fleming in the town of Manlius with four slaves. Property records indicate Fleming bought land in Manlius in 1814. If Wales came directly to Syracuse (then Salina), it was before the 1827 date of emancipation. The obituary goes on to speak of Wales compassion to his former owner, remarking that he used to take care of his former master when the latter was intoxicated. See: FH .1301pdf

5. *Syracuse Daily Standard,* Nov 4, 1865. A letter signed by Samuel L. Edwards and Peter R. Reed, two former colleagues of the deceased John Fleming, vigorously contested the story of John Fleming being an inebriate. See: FH, 1305 pdf

6. John Doherty, "City's first black settler showed his compassion," *Herald – Journal* "Metro" section, February 1, 1996, p. C1. See Subject folder, Wales, (clipping) OHA. Note: The story repeats much information from the 1965 obituary, highlighting the story about Isaac Wales' reported compassion for his elder owner. The letter of Samuel L. Edwards and Peter R. Reed was not mentioned. The Isaac Wales story reappeared in the *Syracuse Post-Standard* on February, 17, 2013, p. A-5, again without mentioning the Edwards and Reed letter, which challenged the story in 1865, when these two friends of Fleming maintained the story of Fleming's alleged inebriation was a case of mistaken identity.

7. S. Smith to Isaac Wales.(1839), *Deed Book* 72, p.268, Lot Cicero #77. OCC

8. See: *Syracuse Daily Standard,* NOTICE submitted by Isaac Wales on Feb. 4, 1852 (accessed on fultonhistory.com, as 0118 pdf) The term "vault" is unclear. While it has been interpreted to refer to cleaning chimneys, I noticed the same term is also used in the 19th and early 20th century literature as being associated with "privy" and "outhouse." See: Holly Bollinger (*Outhouses,* Voyageur Press, 2005, p. 41) where she refers to the Old English term for outhouse as "the necessary vault." When Sue Thomas (*A Second Home: Missouri's Early Schools,* University of Missouri Press, 2006, p. 49) wrote about rural school houses, she mentioned that "usually a 'vault,' or hole, was dug in the ground, and the outhouse was built around it." See: A history of the St. Paul, Minnesota sewer system: http://www.actionsquad.org/Labyrinth/sewerhistory.html. Perhaps someone can do more research on this term.

9. *The Colored American*, "Proceedings of the New York State Convention," September 11, 1841. SUL-MD

10. *Syracuse Standard,* November 11, 12, 15, 19, 24 (1851) carried reports of early Jerry Rescue judicial proceedings in Buffalo. Subject folder, Anti-slavery, Abolition, Jerry Rescue, 1851. OHA

11. *Syracuse Standard*, December 4, 1852. Subject folder, Anti-slavery, Jerry Rescue, 1852. OHA

12. The 1840 U. S. Census, Syracuse, Onondaga, New York records eight children in the Wales household, four males, four females. The 1850 U. S. Census, Onondaga, Syracuse, 2nd ward, p. 194, line 22-29, Family 1320, shows Isaac age 54. It does not show Polly (Polly, presumed his wife, was cited on property transactions in 1839-1840). Also in the household in 1850 were: Matilda, 23; Isaac 20, Maria P. 18, George 15, Harriet 12, Stephen 10, Jane A 7. Isaac Sr. is listed as "cartman," and Isaac Jr., as "shoemaker."

13. Syracuse *Journal*, July 22, 1867. FH

14. According to the *Oswego Daily Times,* April 26, 1875, Margaret Fitzgerald sold a lot in Fulton to Isaac Wales in March, 1875. FH

15. The 1880 U. S. Census, Fulton, Oswego County, shows Isaac Wales is a boarder in the household of Christopher Powell p. 214A, l. 46. He is recorded as "S" (single). The 1860 U. S. Census for Syracuse, Onondaga shows a Helen Wales living with him in Syracuse's 8th Ward. He was 28, she 27, both born in New York. p. 52, Fam 434. Cayuga County research of "African-Americans in the 1865 Census for Cayuga County, NY" shows Jane Langley, a widow, working as a servant in Springport. It also cites Helen Wales, age 37, living and working as a servant in the same establishment as Jane Langley. The record seems to suggest Wales married two times. Census records are not always accurate, though they are classified as primary sources of evidence. Accuracy depends on who gives the information, and who transcribes it. Helen "may" have married Isaac Wales Jr., then separated. See: *"Survey of Sites Relating to the Underground Railroad, Abolitionism, and African American Life in Auburn and Cayuga County, 1820-1870."* The project was coordinated by Judith Wellman for Historical New York Research Associates. At: http://www.rootsweb.ancestry.com/~nycayuga/census/afriamer/1865m_v.html#top

16. *Syracuse Morning Standard*, October 3, 1882, p. 1. Isaac Wales was one of many witnesses called to testify before a Grand Jury in the Jerry Rescue Case which was holding proceedings in Buffalo, N. Y. in the week of November 11-15, 1851. Since there are two "Isaacs" (father and son) it is possible the Isaac who testified in Buffalo, is the son. See also: Syracuse *Daily Standard*, November 13, 1851. FH

17. *Fulton Times,* Obituary, Isaac Wales, (March 20?, 1888). FH

18. "May Festival," *Schoharie Union,* May 6, 1869, Vol. VI, No. 26 at FH .066pdf. For his Binghamton service see *Annals of Binghamton*, Appendix I, African M. E. Church. Online address: http://www.rootsweb.ancestry.com/~nybroome/annals/ap211.htm. The Rev. Stephen S. Wales was pastor of the AME Zion Church in 1872. Church membership then numbered 56.

19. *Washington Bee,* "The Difficulty Settled," Nov. 20, 1886. In the context of a church dispute, Stephen Wales is noted as a local elder who was involved in helping to settle the controversy. See: http://chroniclingamerica.loc.gov/lccn/sn84025891/1886-11-20/ed-1/seq-3/

20. *Syracuse City Directory*, 1866-67, p. 198; 1868-1869, p. 268; *Boyd's City Directory,* 1870-71, p. 321; 1871-72, p. 335. OHA

21. Nancy Schiffhauer transcribed the handwritten records of *Christ Church Burials, Manlius, New York,* 1993. Pages alphabetized by surnames. "Wales" MHS

22. Henry C. Van Schaack, *A History of Manlius Village* (Fayetteville, New York: *Weekly Recorder*, 1873), p. 72.

23. Philip Lenison, 1830 U. S. Census, *Manlius, Onondaga, New York*; p. 375, line 14.

24. Chas Longley, 1840 U. S. Census, *Manlius, Onondaga, New York*; p. 147, line 15.

25. Jedediah Wood to Peggy Lenison, *Deed Book 89*, p. 93, Lot 88, Manlius. OCC

26. Elizabeth Lenison, 1855 New York State Census, *Manlius, Onondaga, New York*, p. 14, line 6, Family 103. OCC-BA

27. Peggy [Lewison], 1860 U. S. Census, *Manlius, Onondaga, New York*, p. 172, line 11, Family 212.

28. *Manlius Methodist Church records* verify Mrs. Lenison was a member, though the spelling of her name, was apparently unclear. She is noted on their spring of 1831 membership list, cited as "Sister Peggy Genson. (Tenson) Colored woman." OHA

29. *Syracuse Standard*, Jan. 24, 1851; May 5, 1851 (assault and battery upon wife Martha); Feb. 23, 1852; May 6, 1853. Index card file, *Lenison*. OHA

30. David [Larison], 1860 U. S. Census, *Syracuse, Ward 8, Onondaga*, p 57, Line 13, Family 478, p. 57.

31. *The Oneida Sachem*, March 28, 1861. FH

32. *Syracuse Weekly Express*, March 26, 1891. FH

33. The 1870 U. S. Census for town of *Scott, Cortland County*, p.4, line 9, Family 29, shows eighteen year old George Lenison, born 1852, listed as "M" (mulatto) in the household of Joseph Kent a farmer. Mr. Kent's race is listed as "B," birth location, Maryland, and his age as 57. His wife, Harriet, also born in Maryland, was noted as age 56, and her race designated as "M." Mr. Kent does not have any personal value recorded, and is a "farm laborer," but his wife has $500 cited in the real estate value column. It may be there is some family relationship between young Lenison and the Kents. Also in the town of Scott is 9 year old Robert Lenison, listed in the household of Milton (Lovinia) Salisbury, a prosperous farmer. Robert is recorded as "B" and born in New York. The Salisburys are recorded as "W." Interesting that he has real estate valued at $3,500, and she as having personal estate value of $6,000. See: p. 28, line 10, Family 259.

34. See 19 page document describing Philip Lenison's service in U. S. Colored Troops, Co. G, 14 Reg't, T. I. Col'd H. Art'y; provided by NARA (National Archives and records Administration) accessed online through Ancestry. com. *U. S. Colored Troops Military Service Records, 1861-1865*. It is noted that while Philip Lenison enlisted under Regiment 14, that the number of the Regiment changed to Regiment 11 of the Colored Troops. From these documents we learn, Philip enlisted at Providence, R. I., on Oct 29, 1863, and that he died at Camp Kenyon, English Turn, Louisiana, from the effects of diphtheria at a hospital there on Feb 19, 1864. An inventory of his belongs consisted in : 1 cap, 1 uniform coat, 1 pair of trousers, 1 pair

flannel drawers, 1 cotton shirt, 1 pair of socks, 1 haversack, 1 knapsack. Philip Lenison is named in the African American Civil War Memorial on plaque B-24: National Park Service. *U.S. Civil War Soldiers, 1861-1865.* Original data: National Park Service, Civil War Soldiers and Sailors System, at <http://www.itd.nps.gov/cwss/>, acquired 2007. Philip Lenison is also mentioned in William H. Chenery's, *The Fourteenth Regiment Rhode Island Heavy Artillery (COLORED) in the War to Preserve the Union, 1861-1865.* (Providence: Snow & Farnham, Printers and Publishers, 1898) online at archive.org.

35. Jane Langley, 1855 New York State Census, 8th Ward, p. 616, Family 219, Onondaga County Archival Records, Bound volume, Basement, Onondaga County Court House, Syracuse, New York.

36. Jane Langley. 1860; U. S. Census, Springport, Cayuga, New York, p. 642, Line 17, Family 333. Also working there as a servant, was Harriet Wales, age 21, line 16.

37. Obituary, *Union Springs Advertiser*, May 7, 1896. FH

38. *Ledger Record of Slaves In Scipio 1801-1837*, p. 2. The transcript reads "Jms. Fleming;" I transcribed the original image as "Jno." See: *co.cayuga.ny.us/history/ugrr/scipiosl.html.* See also, additional information online for identification of ex-slaves and freedom seekers "Freedom Seekers, Abolitionists, and Underground Railroad Helpers, Cayuga County, New York,"compiled by Tanya Warren for the Historical New York Research Associates.

39. Several residents of Manlius owned slaves in Manlius in 1810, before John Fleming moved from Scipio. Abijah Yelverton, Jr., Elijah Phillips and Charles B. Bristol, among them owned nine slaves. Abel Cadwell, Benjamin Booth, Caleb Hopkinson, Elijah Phillips Jr, Sylvanus Tousley and Benjamin Wood, each owned one slave, according to the 1810 census.

40. According to property records in the Onondaga County Clerk's office John Fleming bought land in Manlius in 1814. See: *Property Sales, Town of Manlius, 1800-1819.* Gumaer, Elias Jr. Mary to J. Fleming 1814 (O, 299) lot 95. Submitted by Kathy Crowell.

41. Esther Wheatly, 1855 New York State Census, *Manlius, Onondaga, New York*, (bound) page n.d Fam # 11. Note: The column on the census report for "race" is blank. OCC-BA

42. Robert Fleming, 1860, U. S. Census, *Manlius, Onondaga, New York*; Schedule Type: *Agriculture*, p. *5*; Line 16; Schedule 4.

43. Esther Wheatley in household of Robert Fleming. 1860 U. S. Census, *Manlius, Onondaga, New York*; p. 30, line 39. Family 253. Here Esther's "race" is recorded as "B." See "Ester Wheatly" in 1870 U. S. Census, *Manlius, Onondaga, New York*; p.12, line 29, Family 112. Here she is listed as a *Domestic*. The recorder under race category wrote "w." One again, what is recorded in census records is not necessarily correct. Errors resulted, at times, because the person giving it had incorrect information, chose to give false information, or because the person recording it, did not "hear it," spell it, or transcribe it accurately.

44. *Christ Church Burials,* Nancy Schiffhauer transcribed the handwritten records of *Christ Church Burials, Manlius, New York,* 1993, "Fleming, Robert, d. 13 Aug 1871 ae 74-4-15." MHS

45. Esther Wheatley (sister-in-law) in the household of Samuel Grover, 1880 Census, *Ledyard, Cayuga, New York*; p. 3, line 27, Family 25. All members are records as "B" for race. If the Scipio record of Esther's registered birth is correct, she would have been age 72 at death.

46. Personal visit to old Ledyard cemetery (May 5, 2012), provided the following information on tombstone. Transcribed to the best of my visual ability: *GROVER Samuel Grover. Nov. 11, 1882. In his 70th year. Betsy A. His wife. Died Dec ? 1886. Age 69 yr. Rosalinda. His wife. Nov 15 1851.* On the side section: "Ester Wheatley. Died Jan 15 1889. Age 80 yrs."

47. Hiram Wheatley, 1860 U. S. Census, Moravia, Cayuga, p. 87, line 12, Family 731. And in 1870 U. S. Census, "Heram Wheatey" Locke. Cayuga, New York, p.15, line 17, Family 140. Mr. Wheatley, age 57, a farm laborer, is cited as "M" (mulatto). No real or personal estate.

48. John Wheatley, 1830 U. S. Census, *Ledyard, Cayuga, New York*; p. 276. John Wheatley is recorded in the 1820 Census for the town of Scipio, where his household is numbered seven. 1820 U. S. Census; *Scipio, Cayuga, New York*; p. 120. It seems that John moved his family to Ledyard sometime after 1820, and before 1830.

49. Death, Ester Wheatley. 188, *Vital Records*, Town of Ledyard, Office of Clerk.

50. Onondaga County, *Civil Actions,* "Onon Com Pleas," John Fleming vs James Higgins. Randall & Edwards Atts To File. Filed 18, July, 1816, of the term of May Eighteen hundred & sixteen. OCC-BA

51. William K. Klingaman, Nicholas Klingaman, *The Year Without Summer: 1816 and the Volcano That Darkened the World and Changed History* (St. Martin's Press, 2013); also, see Robert Evans essay, "Blast From the Past," in the *Smithsonian* magazine, July 2002. Accessible online at www.smithsonianmag.com/historyarchaeology/blast.html#ixzz2DqEcSg00.

52. Onondaga County, *Court of General Sessions,* September 27-28, 1816. This set of records is on a microfilm titled *Minutes of Common Pleas,* Books 4-7, located at OCC-BA.

53. Ibid.

54. Onondaga County, *Common Pleas,* John Fleming vs Timothy Dimick, A Yelverton, Jr Atty, Filed 3rd Feby 1817, including sheriff's writ issued September 28, 1816. OCC-BA

55. Onondaga County, *Common Rules,* 1816-1818: January 30, 1817, FHL Film #1010723, Salt Lake City, Salt Lake County, Utah, Film #1010723, John Fleming vs James Higgins. Pltff ordered Judgment final. OCC-BA

56. Onondaga County, *Docket of Judgments,* Book 2, 1817 – (on microfilm; unpaged, must scroll through columns, first column alphabetical by surname as "party against whom judgment is obtained) See: James Higgins, (to John Fleming), OCC-BA.

57. John N. Miskell's *Executions in Auburn Prison, Auburn, New York: 1890 – 1916*© says the construction of Auburn prison started immediately after it was authorized on April 12, 1816. See: www.correctionhistory.org/auburn&osborne/miskell/html/auburnchair_his tory.html

58. *Auburn Journal,* March 28, 1877. Also, the *Auburn News & Democrat* of Thurs, March 29, 1877 wrote: "ARMWOOD – In Ledyard, Friday, March 16, 1877, Whittington Armwood, aged 95 years."

59. "The Friends of Freedom in Auburn and Cayuga County" mention Whitington and son Timothy Armwood on p. 27. See: http://co.cayuga.ny.us/history/ugrr/report/PDF/3.pdf. My research

contributes to what we know about Whittington Armwood's life prior to his residence in Cayuga County, and illuminates some unique aspects of how slave labor was employed in Central New York prior to emancipation.

60. See *Auburn Citizen,* Mar 19, 1913; *Auburn County News,* May 8, 1914, and *Auburn Citizen* May 4, 1914, p. 6.

61. Zora Neale Hurston, "Wanderings," *Dust Tracks on a Road: an Autobiography* (1942) (reprinted New York: Harper Perennial edition, 1991), p. 63. In some ways, Hurston's poignant recount of grief at her mother's death when she was only nine years old, echoes the separations and sorrows of many slaves, like Esther Wheatley, separated early in their lives from their parents. The question of who speaks for them, is still a compelling invitation.

ADDITIONAL BIBLIOGRAPHICAL SOURCES NOT PREVIOUSLY CITED

Aptheker, Herbert. "Militant Abolitionism," *Journal of Negro History*, Vol. 26 (Oct. 1941) 438-484.

Bartlett, Irving H. *The American Mind in the Mid-Nineteenth Century.* New York: Thomas Y. Crowell Company, 1967.

Buckmaster, Henrietta. *Let My People Go: The Story of the Underground Railroad and the Growth of the Abolition Movement.* Columbia: University of South Carolina, 1992.

Barkun, Michael. *Crucible of the Millennium, The Burned-Over District of New York in the 1840s.* Syracuse: Syracuse University Press, 1986.

Cole, Charles C., Jr. "The New Lebanon Convention" in *New York History*, Vol. XXXI (Oct. 1950), 385-397.

Dann, Norman K. *When We Get to Heaven, Runaway Slaves on the Road to Peterboro.* Hamilton: Log Cabin Books, 2008.

Duberman, Martin B., ed. "The Antislavery Vanguard," *New Essays on the Abolitionists*, Vol. 109, New Jersey: Princeton, 1965.

Foner, Eric. "Politics and Prejudice: The Free Soil Party and the Negro, 1849-1853" in the *Journal of Negro History.* Vol. 50 (Oct, 1965) 239-256.

Fox, Dixon Ryan. *The Decline of Aristocracy in the Politics of New York. 1801-1840* edited by Robert V. Remini. New York: Harper Torchbooks, 1965.

Haidt, Jonathan. *The Righteous Mind, Why Good People Are Divided by Politics and Religion.* Pantheon Books, 2012.

Hamm, Thomas D. *God's Government Begun.* Bloomington: Indiana University Press, 1996.

Hammond, John L. *The Politics of Benevolence, Revival Religion and American Voting Behavior.* Norwood, N. J.: Ablex Publishing Corp, 1979.

Hart, Albert Bushnell. *Slavery and Abolition 1831-1841.* New York: J. & J. Harper Editions, 1906.

Jacobs, Harriet A. *Incidents in the Life of a Slave Girl, Written by Herself*, edited by Jean Fagan Yellin. Cambridge: Harvard University Press, 1987.

Johnson, Reinhard O. *The Liberty Party 1840-1848 Anti-Slavery Third Party Politics in the United States.* Baton Rouge: Louisiana University Press, 2009.

Kass, Alvin. *Politics in New York State 1800-1830.* Syracuse: Syracuse University Press, 1965.

Knight, George R. *Millennial Fever, And the End of the World. A Study of Millerite Adventism.* Boise, Idaho: Pacific Press Publishing Association, 1993.

Loucks, Mrs. Esther C. *"The Anti-Slavery Movement in Syracuse From 1839 – 1851"* Thesis for M. A. in History, Syracuse University. 1934 at the Onondaga Historical Association, Syracuse, N.Y.

Mayfield, John. *The New Nation 1800-1845*, edited by David Herbert Donald. New York: Hill and Wang, 1986.

McLoughlin, William G. *Modern Revivalism: Charles Grandison Finney to Billy Graham.* New York: The Ronald Press Company, 1959.

Monroe, Dan. *The Republican Vision of John Tyler.* College Station: Texas A & M University, 2003.

Morone, James A. *Hellfire Nation: The Politics of Sin in American History.* New Haven: Yale University Press, 2003.

Osofsky, Gilbert, ed. *Puttin' On Ole Massa, The Slave Narratives of Henry Bibb, William Wells Brown, and Solomon Northrup.* New York: Harper & Row, 1969.

Palmer, Richard F. The "Old Line Mail" *Stagecoach Days In Upstate New York* Lakemont, N.Y.: North Country Books, 1977.

Perry, Lewis and Fellman, Michael. *Antislavery Reconsidered: New Perspectives on the Abolitionists.* Baton Rouge: Louisiana State University Press, 1979.

Richards, Leonard L. *"Gentlemen of Property and Standing" Anti-Abolition Mobs in Jacksonian America.* New York: Oxford University Press, 1970.

Salerno, Beth A. *Sister Societies, Women's Antislavery Organizations in Antebellum America.* Dekalb, Illinois: Northern Illinois University Press, 2005.

Stewart, Mitchell. *Horatio Seymour of New York.* Cambridge, Mass: Harvard University Press, 1938.

Scott, Donald M. *From Office to Profession: The New England Evangelical Ministry, 1750-1850.* Philadelphia: University of Pennsylvania Press, 1978.

Sorin, Gerald. *The New York Abolitionists: a Case Study of Political Radicalism.* Westport CT: Greenwood Press, 1971.

Spann, Edward K. *Brotherly Tomorrows,Movements for a Cooperative Society in America, 1820-1920.* New York: Columbia University Press, 1989.

Stewart, James Brewer. "Abolitionists, Insurgents, and Third Parties: Sectionalism and Partisan Politics in Northern Whiggery, 1836-1844" in *Crusaders and Compromisers Essays on the Relationship of the Antislavery Struggle to the Antebellum Party System* edited by Alan M. Kraut. Westport, CT: Greenwood Press, 1983.

Stewart, James Brewer, *Holy Warriors: The Abolitionists and American Slavery.* New York: Hill and Wang, 1976.

Thomas, Benjamin. *Theodore Weld: Crusader for Freedom.* New Brunswick, N. J.: Rutgers, 1950.

Weisberger, Bernard. *They Gathered at the River: The Story of the Great Revivalists.* Boston: Little, Brown & Co., 1958.

ABOUT THE AUTHOR

Alethea A. Connolly taught history in New York State high schools, political science in a medium security prison, literacy in southern Louisiana, and wrote for several newspapers in northern New York. For many years, the author was a member of the Sisters of St. Joseph of Carondelet. In 1989, she completed *God Love Ya*, a biography commissioned by the Syracuse Catholic Diocese on the life of Msgr. Charles J. Brady, a beloved Catholic priest who inspired many to work for justice during the Civil Rights Movement of the 1960s and 1970s. From 2007-2013, she was employed as a genealogy coordinator for Project Roots, the history and archive department at CXtec in North Syracuse, established by founder and CEO, William G. Pomeroy.